Reinforcement Learning Algorithms with Python

Learn, understand, and develop smart algorithms for addressing AI challenges

Andrea Lonza

BIRMINGHAM - MUMBAI

Reinforcement Learning Algorithms with Python

Copyright © 2019 Packt Publishing

All rights reserved. No part of this book may be reproduced, stored in a retrieval system, or transmitted in any form or by any means, without the prior written permission of the publisher, except in the case of brief quotations embedded in critical articles or reviews.

Every effort has been made in the preparation of this book to ensure the accuracy of the information presented. However, the information contained in this book is sold without warranty, either express or implied. Neither the author, nor Packt Publishing or its dealers and distributors, will be held liable for any damages caused or alleged to have been caused directly or indirectly by this book.

Packt Publishing has endeavored to provide trademark information about all of the companies and products mentioned in this book by the appropriate use of capitals. However, Packt Publishing cannot guarantee the accuracy of this information.

Commissioning Editor: Pravin Dhandre
Acquisition Editor: Winston Christopher
Content Development Editor: Roshan Kumar
Senior Editor: Jack Cummings
Technical Editor: Joseph Sunil
Copy Editor: Safis Editing
Project Coordinator: Kirti Pisat
Proofreader: Safis Editing
Indexer: Rekha Nair
Production Designer: Nilesh Mohite

First published: October 2019

Production reference: 1181019

Published by Packt Publishing Ltd.
Livery Place
35 Livery Street
Birmingham
B3 2PB, UK.

ISBN 978-1-78913-111-6

www.packt.com

Thanks to you, Mom and Dad, for giving me that light called life and for always being present for me. Fede, you're a furious mad. You've always inspired me to do more. Thanks brother.

Packt.com

Subscribe to our online digital library for full access to over 7,000 books and videos, as well as industry leading tools to help you plan your personal development and advance your career. For more information, please visit our website.

Why subscribe?

- Spend less time learning and more time coding with practical eBooks and Videos from over 4,000 industry professionals

- Improve your learning with Skill Plans built especially for you

- Get a free eBook or video every month

- Fully searchable for easy access to vital information

- Copy and paste, print, and bookmark content

Did you know that Packt offers eBook versions of every book published, with PDF and ePub files available? You can upgrade to the eBook version at www.packt.com and as a print book customer, you are entitled to a discount on the eBook copy. Get in touch with us at customercare@packtpub.com for more details.

At www.packt.com, you can also read a collection of free technical articles, sign up for a range of free newsletters, and receive exclusive discounts and offers on Packt books and eBooks.

Contributors

About the author

Andrea Lonza is a deep learning engineer with a great passion for artificial intelligence and a desire to create machines that act intelligently. He has acquired expert knowledge in reinforcement learning, natural language processing, and computer vision through academic and industrial machine learning projects. He has also participated in several Kaggle competitions, achieving high results. He is always looking for compelling challenges and loves to prove himself.

About the reviewer

Greg Walters has been involved with computers and computer programming since 1972. He is extremely well-versed in Visual Basic, Visual Basic .NET, Python and SQL using MySQL, SQLite, Microsoft SQL Server, Oracle, C++, Delphi, Modula-2, Pascal, C, 80x86 Assembler, COBOL, and Fortran. He is a programming trainer and has trained numerous people on many pieces of computer software, including MySQL, Open Database Connectivity, Quattro Pro, Corel Draw!, Paradox, Microsoft Word, Excel, DOS, Windows 3.11, Windows for Workgroups, Windows 95, Windows NT, Windows 2000, Windows XP, and Linux. He is retired and, in his spare time, is a musician and loves to cook, but he is also open to working as a freelancer on various projects.

Packt is searching for authors like you

If you're interested in becoming an author for Packt, please visit `authors.packtpub.com` and apply today. We have worked with thousands of developers and tech professionals, just like you, to help them share their insight with the global tech community. You can make a general application, apply for a specific hot topic that we are recruiting an author for, or submit your own idea.

Table of Contents

Preface — 1

Section 1: Algorithms and Environments

Chapter 1: The Landscape of Reinforcement Learning — 9
  An introduction to RL — 10
    Comparing RL and supervised learning — 13
    History of RL — 14
    Deep RL — 16
  Elements of RL — 17
    Policy — 17
    The value function — 19
    Reward — 20
    Model — 21
  Applications of RL — 21
    Games — 22
    Robotics and Industry 4.0 — 23
    Machine learning — 23
    Economics and finance — 24
    Healthcare — 24
    Intelligent transportation systems — 24
    Energy optimization and smart grid — 24
  Summary — 25
  Questions — 25
  Further reading — 25

Chapter 2: Implementing RL Cycle and OpenAI Gym — 27
  Setting up the environment — 28
    Installing OpenAI Gym — 29
    Installing Roboschool — 29
  OpenAI Gym and RL cycles — 30
    Developing an RL cycle — 30
    Getting used to spaces — 34
  Development of ML models using TensorFlow — 35
    Tensor — 37
      Constant — 37
      Placeholder — 38
      Variable — 39
    Creating a graph — 40
    Simple linear regression example — 41

Table of Contents

Introducing TensorBoard	44
Types of RL environments	48
Why different environments?	48
Open source environments	49
Summary	51
Questions	52
Further reading	52
Chapter 3: Solving Problems with Dynamic Programming	53
MDP	54
Policy	55
Return	56
Value functions	57
Bellman equation	58
Categorizing RL algorithms	59
Model-free algorithms	60
Value-based algorithms	61
Policy gradient algorithms	61
Actor-Critic algorithms	62
Hybrid algorithms	62
Model-based RL	62
Algorithm diversity	63
Dynamic programming	63
Policy evaluation and policy improvement	64
Policy iteration	66
Policy iteration applied to FrozenLake	67
Value iteration	70
Value iteration applied to FrozenLake	70
Summary	73
Questions	74
Further reading	74

Section 2: Model-Free RL Algorithms

Chapter 4: Q-Learning and SARSA Applications	77
Learning without a model	78
User experience	79
Policy evaluation	80
The exploration problem	80
Why explore?	81
How to explore	81
TD learning	82
TD update	83
Policy improvement	84
Comparing Monte Carlo and TD	84
SARSA	84

The algorithm	85
Applying SARSA to Taxi-v2	86
Q-learning	93
Theory	93
The algorithm	94
Applying Q-learning to Taxi-v2	95
Comparing SARSA and Q-learning	98
Summary	99
Questions	100
Chapter 5: Deep Q-Network	101
Deep neural networks and Q-learning	102
Function approximation	102
Q-learning with neural networks	103
Deep Q-learning instabilities	105
DQN	106
The solution	106
Replay memory	107
The target network	107
The DQN algorithm	107
The loss function	108
Pseudocode	109
Model architecture	111
DQN applied to Pong	112
Atari games	112
Preprocessing	113
DQN implementation	116
DNNs	117
The experienced buffer	118
The computational graph and training loop	119
Results	124
DQN variations	127
Double DQN	128
DDQN implementation	129
Results	130
Dueling DQN	131
Dueling DQN implementation	132
Results	132
N-step DQN	133
Implementation	134
Results	134
Summary	135
Questions	136
Further reading	137
Chapter 6: Learning Stochastic and PG Optimization	139
Policy gradient methods	140

The gradient of the policy	141
Policy gradient theorem	142
Computing the gradient	143
The policy	144
On-policy PG	146
Understanding the REINFORCE algorithm	**147**
Implementing REINFORCE	149
Landing a spacecraft using REINFORCE	152
Analyzing the results	154
REINFORCE with baseline	**155**
Implementing REINFORCE with baseline	157
Learning the AC algorithm	**159**
Using a critic to help an actor to learn	159
The n-step AC model	160
The AC implementation	161
Landing a spacecraft using AC	164
Advanced AC, and tips and tricks	166
Summary	**166**
Questions	**167**
Further reading	**167**
Chapter 7: TRPO and PPO Implementation	**169**
Roboschool	**170**
Control a continuous system	171
Natural policy gradient	**174**
Intuition behind NPG	176
A bit of math	177
FIM and KL divergence	178
Natural gradient complications	179
Trust region policy optimization	**180**
The TRPO algorithm	180
Implementation of the TRPO algorithm	184
Application of TRPO	189
Proximal Policy Optimization	**192**
A quick overview	192
The PPO algorithm	193
Implementation of PPO	193
PPO application	197
Summary	**198**
Questions	**199**
Further reading	**199**
Chapter 8: DDPG and TD3 Applications	**201**
Combining policy gradient optimization with Q-learning	**202**
Deterministic policy gradient	203

Deep deterministic policy gradient — 206
- The DDPG algorithm — 207
- DDPG implementation — 209
- Appling DDPG to BipedalWalker-v2 — 214

Twin delayed deep deterministic policy gradient (TD3) — 216
- Addressing overestimation bias — 216
  - Implementation of TD3 — 217
- Addressing variance reduction — 219
  - Delayed policy updates — 219
  - Target regularization — 219
- Applying TD3 to BipedalWalker — 221

Summary — 224
Questions — 225
Further reading — 225

Section 3: Beyond Model-Free Algorithms and Improvements

Chapter 9: Model-Based RL — 229
Model-based methods — 230
- A broad perspective on model-based learning — 231
  - A known model — 231
  - Unknown model — 233
- Advantages and disadvantages — 235

Combining model-based with model-free learning — 236
- A useful combination — 236
- Building a model from images — 239

ME-TRPO applied to an inverted pendulum — 240
- Understanding ME-TRPO — 240
- Implementing ME-TRPO — 241
- Experimenting with RoboSchool — 246
  - Results on RoboSchoolInvertedPendulum — 247

Summary — 249
Questions — 250
Further reading — 250

Chapter 10: Imitation Learning with the DAgger Algorithm — 251
Technical requirements — 252
- Installation of Flappy Bird — 252

The imitation approach — 253
- The driving assistant example — 254
- Comparing IL and RL — 254
- The role of the expert in imitation learning — 256
- The IL structure — 256
  - Comparing active with passive imitation — 258

Playing Flappy Bird — 258

How to use the environment 259
Understanding the dataset aggregation algorithm 261
    The DAgger algorithm 262
    Implementation of DAgger 262
        Loading the expert inference model 263
        Creating the learner's computational graph 264
        Creating a DAgger loop 265
    Analyzing the results on Flappy Bird 267
IRL 268
Summary 269
Questions 270
Further reading 270

Chapter 11: Understanding Black-Box Optimization Algorithms   271
Beyond RL 272
    A brief recap of RL 272
    The alternative 273
        EAs 273
The core of EAs 274
    Genetic algorithms 277
    Evolution strategies 278
        CMA-ES 278
        ES versus RL 279
Scalable evolution strategies 280
    The core 280
        Parallelizing ES 281
        Other tricks 281
        Pseudocode 282
    Scalable implementation 282
        The main function 284
        Workers 286
Applying scalable ES to LunarLander 289
Summary 290
Questions 291
Further reading 292

Chapter 12: Developing the ESBAS Algorithm   293
Exploration versus exploitation 294
    Multi-armed bandit 295
Approaches to exploration 297
    The □-greedy strategy 297
    The UCB algorithm 298
        UCB1 299
    Exploration complexity 300
Epochal stochastic bandit algorithm selection 301
    Unboxing algorithm selection 301

Under the hood of ESBAS	303
Implementation	304
Solving Acrobot	308
Results	309
Summary	**311**
Questions	**312**
Further reading	**312**
Chapter 13: Practical Implementation for Resolving RL Challenges	**313**
Best practices of deep RL	**314**
Choosing the appropriate algorithm	314
From zero to one	316
Challenges in deep RL	**319**
Stability and reproducibility	319
Efficiency	321
Generalization	321
Advanced techniques	**322**
Unsupervised RL	322
Intrinsic reward	323
Transfer learning	324
Types of transfer learning	325
1-task learning	326
Multi-task learning	327
RL in the real world	**327**
Facing real-world challenges	327
Bridging the gap between simulation and the real world	329
Creating your own environment	329
Future of RL and its impact on society	**330**
Summary	**331**
Questions	**331**
Further reading	**332**
Assessments	**333**
Other Books You May Enjoy	**341**
Index	**345**

Preface

Reinforcement learning (**RL**) is a popular and promising branch of artificial intelligence that involves making smarter models and agents that can automatically determine ideal behavior based on changing requirements. *Reinforcement Learning Algorithms with Python* will help you master RL algorithms and understand their implementation as you build self-learning agents.

Starting with an introduction to the tools, libraries, and setup needed to work in the RL environment, this book covers the building blocks of RL and delves into value-based methods such as the application of Q-learning and SARSA algorithms. You'll learn how to use a combination of Q-learning and neural networks to solve complex problems. Furthermore, you'll study policy gradient methods, TRPO, and PPO, to improve performance and stability, before moving on to the DDPG and TD3 deterministic algorithms. This book also covers how imitation learning techniques work and how Dagger can teach an agent to fly. You'll discover evolutionary strategies and black-box optimization techniques. Finally, you'll get to grips with exploration approaches such as UCB and UCB1 and develop a meta-algorithm called ESBAS.

By the end of the book, you'll have worked with key RL algorithms to overcome challenges in real-world applications, and you'll be part of the RL research community.

Who this book is for

If you are an AI researcher, deep learning user, or anyone who wants to learn RL from scratch, this book is for you. You'll also find this RL book useful if you want to learn about the advancements in the field. Working knowledge of Python is necessary.

What this book covers

Chapter 1, *The Landscape of Reinforcement Learning*, gives you an insight into RL. It describes the problems that RL is good at solving and the applications where RL algorithms are already adopted. It also introduces the tools, the libraries, and the setup needed for the completion of the projects in the following chapters.

Preface

Chapter 2, *Implementing RL Cycle and OpenAI Gym*, describes the main cycle of the RL algorithms, the toolkit used to develop the algorithms, and the different types of environments. You will be able to develop a random agent using the OpenAI Gym interface to play CartPole using random actions. You will also learn how to use the OpenAI Gym interface to run other environments.

Chapter 3, *Solving Problems with Dynamic Programming*, introduces to you the core ideas, terminology, and approaches of RL. You will learn about the main blocks of RL and develop a general idea about how RL algorithms can be created to solve a problem. You will also learn the differences between model-based and model-free algorithms and the categorization of reinforcement learning algorithms. Dynamic programming will be used to solve the game FrozenLake.

Chapter 4, *Q-Learning and SARSA Applications*, talks about value-based methods, in particular Q-learning and SARSA, two algorithms that differ from dynamic programming and scale well on large problems. To become confident with these algorithms, you will apply them to the FrozenLake game and study the differences from dynamic programming.

Chapter 5, *Deep Q-Networks*, describes how neural networks and **convolutional neural networks** (**CNNs**) in particular are applied to Q-learning. You'll learn why the combination of Q-learning and neural networks produces incredible results and how its use can open the door to a much larger variety of problems. Furthermore, you'll apply the DQN to an Atari game using the OpenAI Gym interface.

Chapter 6, *Learning Stochastic and PG Optimization*, introduces a new family of model-free algorithms: policy gradient methods. You will learn the differences between policy gradient and value-based methods, and you'll learn about their strengths and weaknesses. Then you will implement the REINFORCE and Actor-Critic algorithms to solve a new game called LunarLander.

Chapter 7, *TRPO and PPO Implementation*, proposes a modification of policy gradient methods using new mechanisms to control the improvement of the policy. These mechanisms are used to improve the stability and convergence of the policy gradient algorithms. In particular you'll learn and implement two main policy gradient methods that use these techniques, namely TRPO and PPO. You will implement them on RoboSchool, an environment with a continuous action space.

Chapter 8, *DDPG and TD3 Applications*, introduces a new category of algorithms called deterministic policy algorithms that combine both policy gradient and Q-learning. You will learn about the underlying concepts and implement DDPG and TD3, two deep deterministic algorithms, on a new environment.

Chapter 9, *Model-Based RL*, illustrates RL algorithms that learn the model of the environment to plan future actions, or, to learn a policy. You will be taught how they work, their strengths, and why they are preferred in many situations. To master them, you will implement a model-based algorithm on Roboschool.

Chapter 10, *Imitation Learning with the DAgger Algorithm*, explains how imitation learning works and how it can be applied and adapted to a problem. You will learn about the most well-known imitation learning algorithm, DAgger. To become confident with it, you will implement it to speed up the learning process of an agent on FlappyBird.

Chapter 11, *Understanding Black-Box Optimization Algorithms*, explores evolutionary algorithms, a class of black-box optimization algorithms that don't rely on backpropagation. These algorithms are gaining interest because of their fast training and easy parallelization across hundreds or thousands of cores. This chapter provides a theoretical and practical background of these algorithms by focusing particularly on the Evolution Strategy algorithm, a type of evolutionary algorithm.

Chapter 12, *Developing ESBAS Algorithm*, introduces the important exploration-exploitation dilemma, which is specific to RL. The dilemma is demonstrated using the multi-armed bandit problem and is solved using approaches such as UCB and UCB1. Then, you will learn about the problem of algorithm selection and develop a meta-algorithm called ESBAS. This algorithm uses UCB1 to select the most appropriate RL algorithm for each situation.

Chapter 13, *Practical Implementations to Resolve RL Challenges*, takes a look at the major challenges in this field and explains some practices and methods to overcome them. You will also learn about some of the challenges of applying RL to real-world problems, future developments of deep RL, and their social impact in the world.

To get the most out of this book

Working knowledge of Python is necessary. Knowledge of RL and the various tools used for it will also be beneficial.

Download the example code files

You can download the example code files for this book from your account at www.packt.com. If you purchased this book elsewhere, you can visit www.packtpub.com/support and register to have the files emailed directly to you.

You can download the code files by following these steps:

1. Log in or register at www.packt.com.
2. Select the **Support** tab.
3. Click on **Code Downloads**.
4. Enter the name of the book in the **Search** box and follow the onscreen instructions.

Once the file is downloaded, please make sure that you unzip or extract the folder using the latest version of:

- WinRAR/7-Zip for Windows
- Zipeg/iZip/UnRarX for Mac
- 7-Zip/PeaZip for Linux

The code bundle for the book is also hosted on GitHub at https://github.com/PacktPublishing/Reinforcement-Learning-Algorithms-with-Python. In case there's an update to the code, it will be updated on the existing GitHub repository.

We also have other code bundles from our rich catalog of books and videos available at https://github.com/PacktPublishing/. Check them out!

Download the color images

We also provide a PDF file that has color images of the screenshots/diagrams used in this book. You can download it here: http://www.packtpub.com/sites/default/files/downloads/9781789131116_ColorImages.pdf.

Conventions used

There are a number of text conventions used throughout this book.

CodeInText: Indicates code words in text, database table names, folder names, filenames, file extensions, pathnames, dummy URLs, user input, and Twitter handles. Here is an example: "In this book, we use Python 3.7, but all versions above 3.5 should work. We also assume that you've already installed numpy and matplotlib."

A block of code is set as follows:

```
import gym

# create the environment
env = gym.make("CartPole-v1")
# reset the environment before starting
env.reset()

# loop 10 times
for i in range(10):
    # take a random action
    env.step(env.action_space.sample())
    # render the game
    env.render()

# close the environment
env.close()
```

Any command-line input or output is written as follows:

```
$ git clone https://github.com/pybox2d/pybox2d
$ cd pybox2d
$ pip install -e .
```

Bold: Indicates a new term, an important word, or words that you see onscreen. For example, words in menus or dialog boxes appear in the text like this. Here is an example: "In **reinforcement learning** (**RL**), the algorithm is called the agent, and it learns from the data provided by an environment."

Warnings or important notes appear like this.

Tips and tricks appear like this.

Get in touch

Feedback from our readers is always welcome.

General feedback: If you have questions about any aspect of this book, mention the book title in the subject of your message and email us at `customercare@packtpub.com`.

Errata: Although we have taken every care to ensure the accuracy of our content, mistakes do happen. If you have found a mistake in this book, we would be grateful if you would report this to us. Please visit `www.packtpub.com/support/errata`, selecting your book, clicking on the Errata Submission Form link, and entering the details.

Piracy: If you come across any illegal copies of our works in any form on the Internet, we would be grateful if you would provide us with the location address or website name. Please contact us at `copyright@packt.com` with a link to the material.

If you are interested in becoming an author: If there is a topic that you have expertise in and you are interested in either writing or contributing to a book, please visit `authors.packtpub.com`.

Reviews

Please leave a review. Once you have read and used this book, why not leave a review on the site that you purchased it from? Potential readers can then see and use your unbiased opinion to make purchase decisions, we at Packt can understand what you think about our products, and our authors can see your feedback on their book. Thank you!

For more information about Packt, please visit `packt.com`.

Section 1: Algorithms and Environments

This section is an introduction to reinforcement learning. It includes building the theoretical foundation and setting up the environment that is needed in the upcoming chapters.

This section includes the following chapters:

- `Chapter 1`, *The Landscape of Reinforcement Learning*
- `Chapter 2`, *Implementing RL Cycle and OpenAI Gym*
- `Chapter 3`, *Solving Problems with Dynamic Programming*

1
The Landscape of Reinforcement Learning

Humans and animals learn through a process of trial and error. This process is based on our reward mechanisms that provide a response to our behaviors. The goal of this process is to, through multiple repetitions, incentivize the repetition of actions which trigger positive responses, and disincentivize the repetition of actions which trigger negative ones. Through the trial and error mechanism, we learn to interact with the people and world around us, and pursue complex, meaningful goals, rather than immediate gratification.

Learning through interaction and experience is essential. Imagine having to learn to play football by only looking at other people playing it. If you took to the field to play a football match based on this learning experience, you would probably perform incredibly poorly.

This was demonstrated throughout the mid-20th century, notably by Richard Held and Alan Hein's 1963 study on two kittens, both of whom were raised on a carousel. One kitten was able to move freely (actively), whilst the other was restrained and moved following the active kitten (passively). Upon both kittens being introduced to light, only the kitten who was able to move actively developed a functioning depth perception and motor skills, whilst the passive kitten did not. This was notably demonstrated by the absence of the passive kitten's blink-reflex towards incoming objects. What this, rather crude experiment demonstrated is that regardless of visual deprivation, physical interaction with the environment is necessary in order for animals to learn.

Inspired by how animals and humans learn, **reinforcement learning** (RL) is built around the idea of trial and error from active interactions with the environment. In particular, with RL, an agent learns incrementally as it interacts with the world. In this way, it's possible to train a computer to learn and behave in a rudimentary, yet similar way to how humans do.

The Landscape of Reinforcement Learning

This book is all about reinforcement learning. The intent of the book is to give you the best possible understanding of this field with a hands-on approach. In the first chapters, you'll start by learning the most fundamental concepts of reinforcement learning. As you grasp these concepts, we'll start developing our first reinforcement learning algorithms. Then, as the book progress, you'll create more powerful and complex algorithms to solve more interesting and compelling problems. You'll see that reinforcement learning is very broad and that there exist many algorithms that tackle a variety of problems in different ways. Nevertheless, we'll do our best to provide you with a simple but complete description of all the ideas, alongside a clear and practical implementation of the algorithms.

To start with, in this chapter, you'll familiarize yourself with the fundamental concepts of RL, the distinctions between different approaches, and the key concepts of policy, value function, reward, and model of the environment. You'll also learn about the history and applications of RL.

The following topics will be covered in this chapter:

- An introduction to RL
- Elements of RL
- Applications of RL

An introduction to RL

RL is an area of machine learning that deals with sequential decision-making, aimed at reaching a desired goal. An RL problem is constituted by a decision-maker called an **Agent** and the physical or virtual world in which the agent interacts, is known as the **Environment**. The agent interacts with the environment in the form of **Action** which results in an effect. As a result, the environment will feedback to the agent a new **State** and **Reward**. These two signals are the consequences of the action taken by the agent. In particular, the reward is a value indicating how good or bad the action was, and the state is the current representation of the agent and the environment. This cycle is shown in the following diagram:

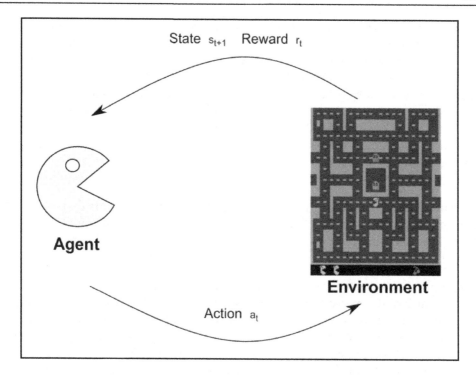

In this diagram the agent is represented by PacMan that based on the current state of the environment, choose which action to take. Its behavior will influence the environment, like its position and that of the enemies, that will be returned by the environment in the form of a new state and the reward. This cycle is repeated until the game ends.

The ultimate goal of the agent is to maximize the total reward accumulated during its lifetime. Let's simplify the notation: if a_t is the action at time t and r_t is the reward at time t, then the agent will take actions $a_0, a_1, \ldots, a_t$, to maximize the sum of all rewards $\sum_{i=0}^{t} r_i$.

To maximize the cumulative reward, the agent has to learn the best behavior in every situation. To do so, the agent has to optimize for a long-term horizon while taking care of every single action. In environments with many discrete or continuous states and actions, learning is difficult because the agent should be accountable for each situation. To make the problem harder, RL can have very sparse and delayed rewards, making the learning process more arduous.

To give an example of an RL problem while explaining the complexity of a sparse reward, consider the well-known story of two siblings, Hansel and Gretel. Their parents led them into the forest to abandon them, but Hansel, who knew of their intentions, had taken a slice of bread with him when they left the house and managed to leave a trail of breadcrumbs that would lead him and his sister home. In the RL framework, the agents are Hansel and Gretel, and the environment is the forest. A reward of +1 is obtained for every crumb of bread reached and a reward of +10 is acquired when they reach home. In this case, the denser the trail of bread, the easier it will be for the siblings to find their way home. This is because to go from one piece of bread to another, they have to explore a smaller area. Unfortunately, sparse rewards are far more common than dense rewards in the real world.

An important characteristic of RL is that it can deal with environments that are dynamic, uncertain, and non-deterministic. These qualities are essential for the adoption of RL in the real world. The following points are examples of how real-world problems can be reframed in RL settings:

- Self-driving cars are a popular, yet difficult, concept to approach with RL. This is because of the many aspects to be taken into consideration while driving on the road (such as pedestrians, other cars, bikes, and traffic lights) and the highly uncertain environment. In this case, the self-driving car is the agent that can act on the steering wheel, accelerator, and brakes. The environment is the world around it. Obviously, the agent cannot be aware of the whole world around it, as it can only capture limited information via its sensors (for example, the camera, radar, and GPS). The goal of the self-driving car is to reach the destination in the minimum amount of time while following the rules of the road and without damaging anything. Consequently, the agent can receive a negative reward if a negative event occurs and a positive reward can be received in proportion to the driving time when the agent reaches its destination.
- In the game of chess, the goal is to checkmate the opponent's piece. In an RL framework, the player is the agent and the environment is the current state of the board. The agent is allowed to move the game pieces according to their own way of moving. As a result of an action, the environment returns a positive or negative reward corresponding to a win or a loss for the agent. In all other situations, the reward is 0 and the next state is the state of the board after the opponent has moved. Unlike the self-driving car example, here, the environment state equals the agent state. In other words, the agent has a perfect view of the environment.

Comparing RL and supervised learning

RL and **supervised learning** are similar, yet different, paradigms to learn from data. Many problems can be tackled with both supervised learning and RL; however, in most cases, they are suited to solve different tasks.

Supervised learning learns to generalize from a fixed dataset with a limited amount of data consisting of examples. Each example is composed of the input and the desired output (or label) that provides immediate learning feedback.

In comparison, RL is more focused on sequential actions that you can take in a particular situation. In this case, the only supervision provided is the reward signal. There's no correct action to take in a circumstance, as in the supervised settings.

RL can be viewed as a more general and complete framework for learning. The major characteristics that are unique to RL are as follows:

- The reward could be dense, sparse, or very delayed. In many cases, the reward is obtained only at the end of the task (for example, in the game of chess).
- The problem is sequential and time-dependent; actions will affect the next actions, which, in turn, influence the possible rewards and states.
- An agent has to take actions with a higher potential to achieve a goal (exploitation), but it should also try different actions to ensure that other parts of the environment are explored (exploration). This problem is called the exploration-exploitation dilemma (or exploration-exploitation trade-off) and it manages the difficult task of balancing between the exploration and exploitation of the environment. This is also very important because, unlike supervised learning, RL can influence the environment since it is free to collect new data as long as it deems it useful.
- The environment is stochastic and nondeterministic, and the agent has to take this into consideration when learning and predicting the next action. In fact, we'll see that many of the RL components can be designed to either output a single deterministic value or a range of values along with their probability.

The third type of learning is **unsupervised learning**, and this is used to identify patterns in data without giving any supervised information. Data compression, clustering, and generative models are examples of unsupervised learning. It can also be adopted in RL settings in order to explore and learn about the environment. The combination of unsupervised learning and RL is called **unsupervised RL**. In this case, no reward is given and the agent could generate an intrinsic motivation to favor new situations where they can explore the environment.

It's worth noting that the problems associated with self-driving cars have also been addressed as a supervised learning problem, but with poor results. The main problem is derived from a different distribution of data that the agent would encounter during its lifetime compared to that used during training.

History of RL

The first mathematical foundation of RL was built during the 1960s and 1970s in the field of optimal control. This solved the problem of minimizing a behavior's measure of a dynamic system over time. The method involved solving a set of equations with the known dynamics of the system. During this time, the key concept of a **Markov decision process (MDP)** was introduced. This provides a general framework for modeling decision-making in stochastic situations. During these years, a solution method for optimal control called **dynamic programming (DP)** was introduced. DP is a method that breaks down a complex problem into a collection of simpler subproblems for solving an MDP.

Note that DP only provides an easier way to solve optimal control for systems with known dynamics; there is no learning involved. It also suffers from the problem of the **curse of dimensionality** because the computational requirements grow exponentially with the number of states.

Even if these methods don't involve learning, as noted by Richard S. Sutton and Andrew G. Barto, we must consider the solution methods of optimal control, such as DP, to also be RL methods.

In the 1980s, the concept of learning by temporally successive predictions—the so-called **temporal difference learning (TD learning)** method—was finally introduced. TD learning introduced a new family of powerful algorithms that will be explained in this book.

The first problems solved with TD learning are small enough to be represented in tables or arrays. These methods are called **tabular methods**, which are often found as an optimal solution but are not scalable. In fact, many RL tasks involve huge state spaces, making tabular methods impossible to adopt. In these problems, function approximations are used to find a good approximate solution with less computational resources.

The adoption of function approximations and, in particular, of artificial neural networks (and deep neural networks) in RL is not trivial; however, as shown on many occasions, they are able to achieve amazing results. The use of deep learning in RL is called **deep reinforcement learning** (**deep RL**) and it has achieved great popularity ever since a deep RL algorithm named **deep q network** (**DQN**) displayed a superhuman ability to play Atari games from raw images in 2015. Another striking achievement of deep RL was with AlphaGo in 2017, which became the first program to beat Lee Sedol, a human professional Go player, and 18-time world champion. These breakthroughs not only showed that machines can perform better than humans in high-dimensional spaces (using the same perception as humans with respect to images), but also that they can behave in interesting ways. An example of this is the creative shortcut found by a deep RL system while playing Breakout, an Atari arcade game in which the player has to destroy all the bricks, as shown in the following image. The agent found that just by creating a tunnel on the left-hand side of the bricks and by putting the ball in that direction, it could destroy much more bricks and thus increase its overall score with just one move.

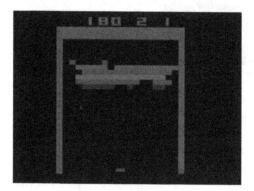

There are many other interesting cases where the agents exhibit superb behavior or strategies that weren't known to humans, like a move performed by AlphaGo while playing Go against Lee Sedol. From a human perspective, that move seemed nonsense but ultimately allowed AlphaGo to win the game (the move is called **move 37**).

Nowadays, when dealing with high-dimensional state or action spaces, the use of deep neural networks as function approximations becomes almost a default choice. Deep RL has been applied to more challenging problems, such as data center energy optimization, self-driving cars, multi-period portfolio optimization, and robotics, just to name a few.

Deep RL

Now you could ask yourself—why can deep learning combined with RL perform so well? Well, the main answer is that deep learning can tackle problems with a high-dimensional state space. Before the advent of deep RL, state spaces had to break down into simpler representations, called **features**. These were difficult to design and, in some cases, only an expert could do it. Now, using deep neural networks such as a **convolutional neural network (CNN)** or a **recurrent neural network (RNN)**, RL can learn different levels of abstraction directly from raw pixels or sequential data (such as natural language). This configuration is shown in the following diagram:

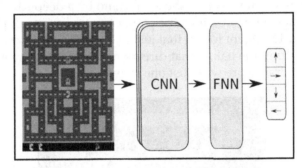

Furthermore, deep RL problems can now be solved completely in an end-to-end fashion. Before the deep learning era, an RL algorithm involved two distinct pipelines: one to deal with the perception of the system and one to be responsible for the decision-making. Now, with deep RL algorithms, these processes are joined and are trained end-to-end, from the raw pixels straight to the action. For example, as shown in the preceding diagram, it's possible to train Pacman end-to-end using a CNN to process the visual component and a **fully connected neural network (FNN)** to translate the output of the CNN into an action.

Nowadays, deep RL is a very hot topic. The principal reason for this is that deep RL is thought to be the type of technology that will enable us to build highly intelligent machines. As proof, two of the more renowned AI companies that are working to solve intelligence problems, namely DeepMind and OpenAI, are heavily researching in RL.

Besides the huge steps achieved with deep RL, there is a long way to go. There are many challenges that still need to be addressed, some of which are listed as follows:

- Deep RL is far too slow to learn compared to humans.
- Transfer learning in RL is still an open problem.
- The reward function is difficult to design and define.
- RL agents struggle to learn in highly complex and dynamic environments such as the physical world.

Nonetheless, the research in this field is growing at a fast rate and companies are starting to adopt RL in their products.

Elements of RL

As we know, an agent interacts with their environment by the means of actions. This will cause the environment to change and to feedback to the agent a reward that is proportional to the quality of the actions and the new state of the agent. Through trial and error, the agent incrementally learns the best action to take in every situation so that, in the long run, it will achieve a bigger cumulative reward. In the RL framework, the choice of the action in a particular state is done by a **policy**, and the cumulative reward that is achievable from that state is called the **value function**. In brief, if an agent wants to behave optimally, then in every situation, the policy has to select the action that will bring it to the next state with the highest value. Now, let's take a deeper look at these fundamental concepts.

Policy

The policy defines how the agent selects an action given a state. The policy chooses the action that maximizes the cumulative reward from that state, not with the bigger immediate reward. It takes care of looking for the long-term goal of the agent. For example, if a car has another 30 km to go before reaching its destination, but only has another 10 km of autonomy left and the next gas stations are 1 km and 60 km away, then the policy will choose to get fuel at the first gas station (1 km away) in order to not run out of gas. This decision is not optimal in the immediate future as it will take some time to refuel, but it will be sure to ultimately accomplish the goal.

The Landscape of Reinforcement Learning

The following diagram shows a simple example where an actor moving in a 4 x 4 grid has to go toward the star while avoiding the spirals. The actions recommended by a policy are indicated by an arrow pointing in the direction of the move. The diagram on the left shows a random initial policy, while the diagram on the right shows the final optimal policy. In a situation with two equally optimal actions, the agent can arbitrarily chooses which action to take:

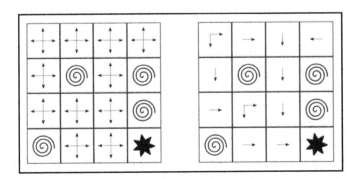

An important distinction is between stochastic policies and deterministic policies. In the deterministic case, the policy provides a single deterministic action to take. On the other hand, in the stochastic case, the policy provides a probability for each action. The concept of the probability of an action is useful because it takes into consideration the dynamicity of the environment and helps its exploration.

One way to classify RL algorithms is based on how policies are improved during learning. The simpler case is when the policy that acts on the environment is similar to the one that improves while learning. Another way to say this is that the policy learns from the same data that it generates. These algorithms are called **on-policy**. **Off-policy** algorithms, in comparison, involve two policies—one that acts on the environment and another that learns but is not actually used. The former is called the **behavior policy**, while the latter is called the **target policy**. The goal of the behavior policy is to interact with and collect information about the environment in order to improve the **passive** target policy. Off-policy algorithms, as we will see in the coming chapters, are more unstable and difficult to design than on-policy algorithms, but they are more sample efficient, meaning that they require less experience to learn.

To better understand these two concepts, we can think of someone who has to learn a new skill. If the person behaves as on-policy algorithms do, then every time they try a sequence of actions, they'll change their belief and behavior in accordance with the reward accumulated. In comparison, if the person behaves as an off-policy algorithm, they (the target policy) can also learn by looking at an old video of themselves (the behavior policy) doing the same skill—that is, they can use old experiences to help them to improve.

The **policy-gradient method** is a family of RL algorithms that learns a parametrized policy (as a deep neural network) directly from the gradient of the performance with respect to the policy. These algorithms have many advantages, including the ability to deal with continuous actions and explore the environment with different levels of granularity. They will be presented in greater detail in Chapter 6, *Learning Stochastic and PG Optimization*, Chapter 7, *TRPO and PPO Implementation*, and Chapter 8, *DDPG and TD3 Applications*.

The value function

The **value function** represents the long-term quality of a state. This is the cumulative reward that is expected in the future if the agent starts from a given state. If the reward measures the immediate performance, the value function measures the performance in the long run. This means that a high reward doesn't imply a high-value function and a low reward doesn't imply a low-value function.

Moreover, the value function can be a function of the state or of the state-action pair. The former case is called a **state-value function**, while the latter is called an **action-value function**:

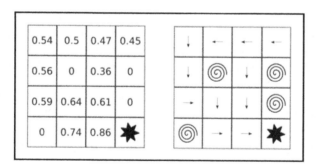

Here, the diagram shows the final state values (on the left side) and the corresponding optimal policy (on the right side).

Using the same gridworld example used to illustrate the concept of policy, we can show the state-value function. First of all, we can assume a reward of 0 in each situation except for when the agent reaches the star, gaining a reward of +1. Moreover, let's assume that a strong wind moves the agent in another direction with a probability of 0.33. In this case, the state values will be similar to those shown in the left-hand side of the preceding diagram. An optimal policy will choose the actions that will bring it to the next state with the highest state value, as shown in the right-hand side of the preceding diagram.

Action-value methods (or value-function methods) are the other big family of RL algorithms. These methods learn an action-value function and use it to choose the actions to take. Starting from `Chapter 3`, *Solving Problems with Dynamic Programming*, you'll learn more about these algorithms. It's worth noting that some policy-gradient methods, in order to combine the advantages of both methods, can also use a value function to learn the appropriate policy. These methods are called **actor-critic methods**. The following diagram shows the three main families of RL algorithms:

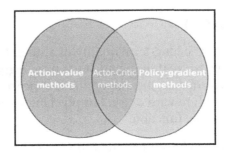

Reward

At each timestep, that is, after each move of the agent, the environment sends back a number that indicates how good that action was to the agent. This is called a **reward**. As we have already mentioned, the end goal of the agent is to maximize the cumulative reward obtained during their interaction with the environment.

In literature, the reward is assumed to be a part of the environment, but that's not strictly true in reality. The reward can come from the agent too, but never from the decision-making part of it. For this reason and to simplify the formulation, the reward is always sent from the environment.

The reward is the only supervision signal injected into the RL cycle and it is essential to design the reward in the correct way in order to obtain an agent with good behavior. If the reward has some flaws, the agent may find them and follow incorrect behavior. For example, *Coast Runners* is a boat-racing game with the goal being to finish ahead of other players. During the route, the boats are rewarded for hitting targets. Some folks at OpenAI trained an agent with RL to play it. They found that, instead of running to the finish line as fast as possible, the trained boat was driving in a circle to capture re-populating targets while crashing and catching fire. In this way, the boat found a way to maximize the total reward without acting as expected. This behavior was due to an incorrect balance between short-term and long-term rewards.

The reward can appear with different frequencies depending on the environment. A frequent reward is called a **dense reward**; however, if it is seen only a few times during a game, or only at its end, it is called a **sparse reward**. In the latter case, it could be very difficult for an agent to catch the reward and find the optimal actions.

Imitation learning and **inverse RL** are two powerful techniques that deal with the absence of a reward in the environment. Imitation learning uses an expert demonstration to map states to actions. On the other hand, inverse RL deduces the reward function from an expert optimal behavior. Imitation learning and inverse RL will be studied in `Chapter 10`, *Imitation Learning with the DAgger Algorithm*.

Model

The model is an optional component of the agent, meaning that it is not required in order to find a policy for the environment. The model details how the environment behaves, predicting the next state and the reward, given a state and an action. If the model is known, planning algorithms can be used to interact with the model and recommend future actions. For example, in environments with discrete actions, potential trajectories can be simulated using look ahead searches (for instance, using the Monte Carlo tree search).

The model of the environment could either be given in advance or learned through interactions with it. If the environment is complex, it's a good idea to approximate it using deep neural networks. RL algorithms that use an already known model of the environment, or learn one, are called **model-based methods**. These solutions are opposed to model-free methods and will be explained in more detail in `Chapter 9`, *Model-Based RL*.

Applications of RL

RL has been applied to a wide variety of fields, including robotics, finance, healthcare, and intelligent transportation systems. In general, they can be grouped into three major areas—automatic machines (such as autonomous vehicles, smart grids, and robotics), optimization processes (for example, planned maintenance, supply chains, and process planning) and control (for example, fault detection and quality control).

The Landscape of Reinforcement Learning

In the beginning, RL was only ever applied to simple problems, but deep RL opened the road to different problems, making it possible to deal with more complex tasks. Nowadays, deep RL has been showing some very promising results. Unfortunately, many of these breakthroughs are limited to research applications or games, and, in many situations, it is not easy to bridge the gap between purely research-oriented applications and industry problems. Despite this, more companies are moving toward the adoption of RL in their industries and products.

We will now take a look at the principal fields that are already adopting or will benefit from RL.

Games

Games are a perfect testbed for RL because they are created in order to challenge human capabilities, and, to complete them, skills common to the human brain are required (such as memory, reasoning, and coordination). Consequently, a computer that can play on the same level or better than a human must possess the same qualities. Moreover, games are easy to reproduce and can be easily simulated in computers. Video games proved to be very difficult to solve because of their partial observability (that is, only a fraction of the game is visible) and their huge search space (that is, it's impossible for a computer to simulate all possible configurations).

A breakthrough in games occurred when, in 2015, AlphaGo beat Lee Sedol in the ancient game of Go. This win occurred in spite of the prediction that it wouldn't. At the time, it was thought that no computer would be able to beat an expert in Go for the next 10 years. AlphaGo used both RL and supervised learning to learn from professional human games. A few years after that match, the next version, named AlphaGo Zero, beat AlphaGo 100 games to 0. AlphaGo Zero learned to play Go in only three days through self-play.

 Self-play is a very effective way to train an algorithm because it just plays against itself. Through self-play, useful sub-skills or behaviors could also emerge that otherwise would not have been discovered.

To capture the messiness and continuous nature of the real world, a team of five neural networks named OpenAI Five was trained to play *DOTA 2*, a real-time strategy game with two teams (each with five players) playing against each other. The steep learning curve in playing this game is due to the long time horizons (a game lasts for 45 minutes on average with thousands of actions), the partial observability (each player can only see a small area around themselves), and the high-dimensional continuous action and observation space. In 2018, OpenAI Five played against the top *DOTA 2* players at The International, losing the match but showing innate capabilities in both collaboration and strategy skills. Finally, on April 13, 2019, OpenAI Five officially defeated the world champions in the game, becoming the first AI to beat professional teams in an esports game.

Robotics and Industry 4.0

RL in industrial robotics is a very active area of research as it is a natural adoption of this paradigm in the real world. The potential and benefit of industrial intelligent robots are huge and extensive. RL enables Industry 4.0 (referred to as the fourth industrial revolution) with intelligent devices, systems, and robots that perform highly complex and rational operations. Systems that predict maintenance, real-time diagnoses, and management of manufacturing activities can be integrated for better control and productivity.

Machine learning

Thanks to the flexibility of RL, it can be employed not only in standalone tasks but also as a sort of fine-tune method in supervised learning algorithms. In many **natural language processing** (NLP) and computer vision tasks, the metric to optimize isn't differentiable, so to address the problem in supervised settings with neural networks, it needs an auxiliary differentiable loss function. However, the discrepancy between the two loss functions will penalize the final performance. One way to deal with this is to first train the system using supervised learning with the auxiliary loss function, and then use RL to fine-tune the network optimizing with respect to the final metric. For instance, this process can be of benefit in subfields such as machine translation and question answering, where the evaluation metrics are complex and not differentiable.

Furthermore, RL can solve NLP problems such as dialogue systems and text generation. Computer vision, localization, motion analysis, visual control, and visual tracking can all be trained with deep RL.

Deep learning proposes to overcome the heavy task of manual feature engineering while requiring the manual design of the neural network architecture. This is tedious work involving many parts that have to be combined in the best possible way. So, why can we not automate it? Well, actually, we can. **Neural architecture design (NAD)** is an approach that uses RL to design the architecture of deep neural networks. This is computationally very expensive, but this technique is able to create DNN architectures that can achieve state-of-the-art results in image classification.

Economics and finance

Business management is another natural application of RL. It has been successfully used for internet advertising with the objective to maximize pay-per-click adverts for product recommendations, customer management, and marketing. Furthermore, finance has benefited from RL for tasks such as option pricing and multi-period optimization.

Healthcare

RL is used in healthcare both for diagnosis and treatment. It can build the baseline for an AI-powered assistant for doctors and nurses. In particular, RL can provide individual progressive treatments for patients—a process known as the dynamic treatment regime. Other examples of RL in healthcare are personalized glycemic control and personalized treatments for sepsis and HIV.

Intelligent transportation systems

Intelligent transportation systems can be empowered with RL to develop and improve all types of transportation systems. Its application can range from smart networks that control congestion (such as traffic signal controls), traffic surveillance, and safety (such as collision predictions), to self-driving cars.

Energy optimization and smart grid

Energy optimization and smart grids are central for intelligent generation, distribution, and consumption of electricity. Decision energy systems and control energy systems can adopt RL techniques to provide a dynamic response to the variability of the environment. RL can also be used to adjust the demand of electricity in response to a dynamic energy pricing or reduce energy usage.

Summary

RL is a goal-oriented approach to decision-making. It differs from other paradigms due to its direct interaction with the environment and for its delayed reward mechanism. The combination of RL and deep learning is very useful in problems with high-dimensional state spaces and in problems with perceptual inputs. The concepts of policy and value functions are key as they give an indication about the action to take and the quality of the states of the environment. In RL, the model of the environment is not required, but it can give additional information and, therefore, improve the quality of the policy.

Now that all the key concepts have been introduced, in the following chapters, the focus will be on actual RL algorithms. But first, in the next chapter, you will be given the grounding to develop RL algorithms using OpenAI and TensorFlow.

Questions

- What is RL?
- What is the end goal of an agent?
- What are the main differences between supervised learning and RL?
- What are the benefits of combining deep learning and RL?
- Where does the term "reinforcement" come from?
- What is the difference between policy and value functions?
- Can the model of an environment be learned through interacting with it?

Further reading

- For an example of a faulty reward function, refer to the following link: `https://blog.openai.com/faulty-reward-functions/`.
- For more information about deep RL, refer to the following link: `http://karpathy.github.io/2016/05/31/rl/`.

Implementing RL Cycle and OpenAI Gym

In every machine learning project, an algorithm learns rules and instructions from a training dataset, with a view to performing a task better. In **reinforcement learning** (RL), the algorithm is called the agent, and it learns from the data provided by an environment. Here, the environment is a continuous source of information that returns data according to the agent's actions. And, because the data returned by an environment could be potentially infinite, there are many conceptual and practical differences among the supervised settings that arise while training. For the purpose of this chapter, however, it is important to highlight the fact that different environments not only provide different tasks to accomplish, but can also have different types of input, output, and reward signals, while also requiring the adaptation of the algorithm in each case. For example, a robot could either sense its state from a visual input, such as an RGB camera, or from discrete internal sensors.

In this chapter, you'll set up the environment required to code RL algorithms and build your first algorithm. Despite being a simple algorithm that plays CartPole, it offers a useful baseline to master the basic RL cycle before moving on to more advanced RL algorithms. Also, because, in the later chapters, you'll code many deep neural networks, here, we'll give you a brief recap about TensorFlow and introduce TensorBoard, a visualization tool.

Almost all the environments used throughout the book are based on the interface open sourced by OpenAI called **Gym**. Therefore, we'll take a look at it and use some of its built-in environments. Then, before moving on to an in-depth examination of RL algorithms in the next chapters, we'll list and explain the strengths and differences of a number of open source environments. In this way, you'll have a broad and practical overview of the problems that can be tackled with RL.

The following topics will be covered in this chapter:

- Setting up the environment
- OpenAI Gym and RL cycles
- TensorFlow
- TensorBoard
- Types of RL environments

Setting up the environment

The following are the three main tools required to create deep RL algorithms:

- **Programming language**: Python is the first choice for the development of machine learning algorithms on account of its simplicity and the third-party libraries that are built around it.
- **Deep learning framework**: In this book, we use TensorFlow because, as we'll see in the *TensorFlow* section, it is scalable, flexible, and very expressive. Despite this, many other frameworks can be used in its place, including PyTorch and Caffe.
- **Environment**: Throughout the book, we'll use many different environments to demonstrate how to deal with different types of problems and to highlight the strengths of RL algorithms.

In this book, we use Python 3.7, but all versions above 3.5 should work. We also assume that you've already installed `numpy` and `matplotlib`.

If you haven't already installed TensorFlow, you can do so through their website or by typing the following in a Terminal window:

```
$ pip install tensorflow
```

Alternatively, you can type the following command, if your machine has GPUs:

```
$ pip install tensorflow-gpu
```

You can find all the installation instructions and the exercises relating to this chapter on the GitHub repository, which can be found here: https://github.com/PacktPublishing/Reinforcement-Learning-Algorithms-with-Python.

Now, let's look at how to install the environments.

Installing OpenAI Gym

OpenAI Gym offers a general interface as well as a broad variety of environments.

To install it, we will use the following commands.

On OSX, we can use the following:

```
$ brew install cmake boost boost-python sdl2 swig wget
```

On Ubuntu 16.04, we will use the following command:

```
$ apt-get install -y python-pyglet python3-opengl zlib1g-dev libjpeg-dev patchelf cmake swig libboost-all-dev libsdl2-dev libosmesa6-dev xvfb ffmpeg
```

On Ubuntu 18.04, we will use the following command:

```
$ sudo apt install -y python3-dev zlib1g-dev libjpeg-dev cmake swig python-pyglet python3-opengl libboost-all-dev libsdl2-dev libosmesa6-dev patchelf ffmpeg xvfb
```

After running the preceding command for your respective OS, the following command is used:

```
$ git clone https://github.com/openai/gym.git
$ cd gym
$ pip install -e '.[all]'
```

Certain Gym environments also require the installation of pybox2d:

```
$ git clone https://github.com/pybox2d/pybox2d
$ cd pybox2d
$ pip install -e .
```

Installing Roboschool

The final environment we are interested in is Roboschool, a simulator for robots. It's easy to install, but if you encounter any errors, take a look at its GitHub repository:

```
$ pip install roboschool
```

OpenAI Gym and RL cycles

Since RL requires an agent and an environment to interact with each other, the first example that may spring to mind is the earth, the physical world we live in. Unfortunately, for now, it is actually used in only a few cases. With the current algorithms, the problems stem from the large number of interactions that an agent has to execute with the environment in order to learn good behaviors. It may require hundreds, thousands, or even millions of actions, requiring way too much time to be feasible. One solution is to use simulated environments to start the learning process and, only at the end, fine-tune it in the real world. This approach is way better than learning just from the world around it, but still requires slow real-world interactions. However, in many cases, the task can be fully simulated. To research and implement RL algorithms, games, video games, and robot simulators are a perfect testbed because, in order to be solved, they require capabilities such as planning, strategy, and long-term memory. Moreover, games have a clear reward system and can be completely simulated in an artificial environment (computers), allowing fast interactions that accelerate the learning process. For these reasons, in this book, we'll use mostly video games and robot simulators to demonstrate the capabilities of RL algorithms.

OpenAI Gym, an open source toolkit for developing and researching RL algorithms, was created to provide a common and shared interface for environments, while making a large and diverse collection of environments available. These include Atari 2600 games, continuous control tasks, classic control theory problems, simulated robotic goal-based tasks, and simple text games. Owing to its generality, many environments created by third parties are using the Gym interface.

Developing an RL cycle

A basic RL cycle is shown in the following code block. This essentially makes the RL model play for 10 moves while rendering the game at each step:

```
import gym

# create the environment
env = gym.make("CartPole-v1")
# reset the environment before starting
env.reset()

# loop 10 times
for i in range(10):
    # take a random action
    env.step(env.action_space.sample())
    # render the game
```

```
    env.render()

# close the environment
env.close()
```

This leads to the following output:

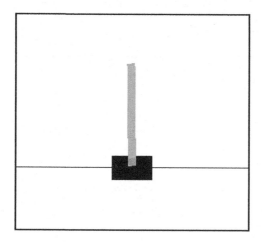

Figure 2.1: Rendering of CartPole

Let's take a closer look at the code. It starts by creating a new environment named `CartPole-v1`, a classic game used in control theory problems. However, before using it, the environment is initialized by calling `reset()`. After doing so, the cycle loops 10 times. In each iteration, `env.action_space.sample()` samples a random action, executes it in the environment with `env.step()`, and displays the result with the `render()` method; that is, the current state of the game, as in the preceding screenshot. In the end, the environment is closed by calling `env.close()`.

 Don't worry if the following code outputs deprecation warnings; they are there to notify you that some functions have been changed. The code will still be functioning correctly.

This cycle is the same for every environment that uses the Gym interface, but for now, the agent can only play random actions without having any feedback, which is essential to any RL problem.

Implementing RL Cycle and OpenAI Gym

 In RL, you may see the terms **state** and **observation** being used almost interchangeably, but they are not the same. We talk about state when all the information pertaining to the environment is encoded in it. We talk about observation when only a part of the actual state of the environment is visible to the agent, such as the perception of a robot. To simplify this, OpenAI Gym always uses the term observation.

The following diagram shows the flow of the cycle:

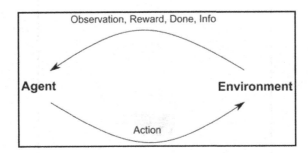

Figure 2.2: Basic RL cycle according to OpenAI Gym. The environment returns the next state, a reward, a done flag, and some additional information

Indeed, the `step()` method returns four variables that provide information about the interaction with the environment. The preceding diagram shows the loop between the agent and environment, as well as the variables exchanged; namely, **Observation**, **Reward**, **Done**, and **Info**. **Observation** is an object that represents the new observation (or state) of the environment. **Reward** is a float number that represents the number of rewards obtained in the last action. **Done** is a Boolean value that is used on tasks that are episodic; that is, tasks that are limited in terms of the number of interactions. Whenever `done` is `True`, this means that the episode has terminated and that the environment should be reset. For example, `done` is `True` when the task has been completed or the agent has died. **Info**, on the other hand, is a dictionary that provides extra information about the environment but that usually isn't used.

If you have never heard of CartPole, it's a game with the goal of balancing a pendulum acting on a horizontal cart. A reward of +1 is provided for every timestep when the pendulum is in the upright position. The episode ends when it is too unbalanced or it manages to balance itself for more than 200 timesteps (collecting a maximum cumulative reward of 200).

We can now create a more complete algorithm that plays 10 games and prints the accumulated reward for each game using the following code:

```
import gym

# create and initialize the environment
env = gym.make("CartPole-v1")
env.reset()

# play 10 games
for i in range(10):
    # initialize the variables
    done = False
    game_rew = 0

    while not done:
        # choose a random action
        action = env.action_space.sample()
        # take a step in the environment
        new_obs, rew, done, info = env.step(action)
        game_rew += rew
        # when is done, print the cumulative reward of the game and reset the environment
        if done:
            print('Episode %d finished, reward:%d' % (i, game_rew))
            env.reset()
```

The output will be similar to the following:

```
Episode:  0, Reward:13
Episode:  1, Reward:16
Episode:  2, Reward:23
Episode:  3, Reward:17
Episode:  4, Reward:30
Episode:  5, Reward:18
Episode:  6, Reward:14
Episode:  7, Reward:28
Episode:  8, Reward:22
Episode:  9, Reward:16
```

The following table shows the output of the step() method over the last four actions of a game:

Observation	Reward	Done	Info
[-0.05356921, -0.38150626, 0.12529277, 0.9449761]	1.0	False	{}
[-0.06119933, -0.57807287, 0.14419229, 1.27425449]	1.0	False	{}
[-0.07276079, -0.38505429, 0.16967738, 1.02997704]	1.0	False	{}
[-0.08046188, -0.58197758, 0.19027692, 1.37076617]	1.0	False	{}
[-0.09210143, -0.3896757, 0.21769224, 1.14312384]	1.0	True	{}

Notice that the environment's observation is encoded in a 1 x 4 array; that the reward, as we expected, is always 1; and that done is True only in the last row when the game is terminated. Also, **Info**, in this case, is empty.

In the upcoming chapters, we'll create agents that play CartPole by taking more intelligent actions depending on the current state of the pole.

Getting used to spaces

In OpenAI Gym, actions and observations are mostly instances of the Discrete or Box class. These two classes represent different spaces. Box represents an n-dimensional array, while Discrete, on the other hand, is a space that allows a fixed range of non-negative numbers. In the preceding table, we have already seen that the observation of CartPole is encoded by four floats, meaning that it's an instance of the Box class. It is possible to check the type and dimension of the observation spaces by printing the env.observation_space variable:

```
import gym

env = gym.make('CartPole-v1')
print(env.observation_space)
```

Indeed, as we expected, the output is as follows:

```
>>   Box(4,)
```

In this book, we mark the output of print() by introducing the printed text with >>.

In the same way, it is possible to check the dimension of the action space:

```
print(env.action_space)
```

This results in the following output:

```
>> Discrete(2)
```

In particular, `Discrete(2)` means that the actions could either have the value 0 or 1. Indeed, if we use the sampling function used in the preceding example, we obtain 0 or 1 (in CartPole, this means left or right):

```
print(env.action_space.sample())
>> 0
print(env.action_space.sample())
>> 1
```

The `low` and `high` instance attributes return the minimum and maximum values allowed by a `Box` space:

```
print(env.observation_space.low)
>> [-4.8000002e+00 -3.4028235e+38 -4.1887903e-01 -3.4028235e+38]
print(env.observation_space.high)
>> [ 4.8000002e+00  3.4028235e+38  4.1887903e-01  3.4028235e+38]
```

Development of ML models using TensorFlow

TensorFlow is a machine learning framework that performs high-performance numerical computations. TensorFlow owes its popularity to its high quality and vast amount of documentation, its ability to easily serve models at scale in production environments, and the friendly interface to GPUs and TPUs.

TensorFlow, to facilitate the development and deployment of ML models, has many high-level APIs, including Keras, Eager Execution, and Estimators. These APIs are very useful in many contexts, but, in order to develop RL algorithms, we'll only use low-level APIs.

Now, let's code immediately using **TensorFlow**. The following lines of code execute the sum of the constants, a and b, created with `tf.constant()`:

```
import tensorflow as tf

# create two constants: a and b
a = tf.constant(4)
b = tf.constant(3)

# perform a computation
c = a + b

# create a session
session = tf.Session()
# run the session. It computes the sum
res = session.run(c)
print(res)
```

A particularity of TensorFlow is the fact that it expresses all computations as a computational graph that has to first be defined and later executed. Only after execution will the results be available. In the following example, after the operation, c = a + b, c doesn't hold the end value. Indeed, if you print c before creating the session, you'll obtain the following:

```
>> Tensor("add:0", shape=(), dtype=int32)
```

This is the class of the c variable, not the result of the addition.

Moreover, execution has to be done inside a session that is instantiated with `tf.Session()`. Then, to perform the computation, the operation has to be passed as input to the run function of the session just created. Thus, to actually compute the graph and consequently sum a and b, we need to create a session and pass c as an input to `session.run`:

```
session = tf.Session()
res = session.run(c)
print(res)

>> 7
```

If you are using Jupyter Notebook, make sure to reset the previous graph by running `tf.reset_default_graph()`.

Tensor

The variables in TensorFlow are represented as tensors that are arrays of any number of dimensions. There are three main types of tensors—`tf.Variable`, `tf.constant`, and `tf.placeholder`. Except for `tf.Variable`, all the other tensors are immutable.

To check the shape of a tensor, we will use the following code:

```
# constant
a = tf.constant(1)
print(a.shape)
>> ()

# array of five elements
b = tf.constant([1,2,3,4,5])
print(b.shape)
>> (5,)
```

The elements of a tensor are easily accessible, and the mechanisms are similar to those employed by Python:

```
a = tf.constant([1,2,3,4,5])
first_three_elem = a[:3]
fourth_elem = a[3]

sess = tf.Session()
print(sess.run(first_three_elem))

>> array([1,2,3])

print(sess.run(fourth_elem))

>> 4
```

Constant

As we have already seen, a constant is an immutable type of tensor that can be easily created using `tf.constant`:

```
a = tf.constant([1.0, 1.1, 2.1, 3.1], dtype=tf.float32, name='a_const')
print(a)

>> Tensor("a_const:0", shape=(4,), dtype=float32)
```

Placeholder

A placeholder is a tensor that is fed at runtime. Usually, placeholders are used as input for models. Every input passed to a computational graph at runtime is fed with `feed_dict`. `feed_dict` is an optional argument that allows the caller to override the value of tensors in the graph. In the following snippet, the a placeholder is overridden by `[[0.1,0.2,0.3]]`:

```
import tensorflow as tf

a = tf.placeholder(shape=(1,3), dtype=tf.float32)
b = tf.constant([[10,10,10]], dtype=tf.float32)

c = a + b

sess = tf.Session()
res = sess.run(c, feed_dict={a:[[0.1,0.2,0.3]]})
print(res)

>> [[10.1 10.2 10.3]]
```

If the size of the first dimension of the input is not known during the creation of the graph, TensorFlow can take care of it. Just set it to `None`:

```
import tensorflow as tf
import numpy as np

# NB: the first dimension is 'None', meaning that it can be of any length
a = tf.placeholder(shape=(None,3), dtype=tf.float32)
b = tf.placeholder(shape=(None,3), dtype=tf.float32)

c = a + b
print(a)

>> Tensor("Placeholder:0", shape=(?, 3), dtype=float32)

sess = tf.Session()
print(sess.run(c, feed_dict={a:[[0.1,0.2,0.3]], b:[[10,10,10]]}))

>> [[10.1 10.2 10.3]]

v_a = np.array([[1,2,3],[4,5,6]])
v_b = np.array([[6,5,4],[3,2,1]])
print(sess.run(c, feed_dict={a:v_a, b:v_b}))

>> [[7. 7. 7.]
    [7. 7. 7.]]
```

This feature is useful when the number of training examples is not known initially.

Variable

A **variable** is a mutable tensor that can be trained using an optimizer. For example, they can be the free variables that constitute the weights and biases of a neural network.

We will now create two variables, one uniformly initialized, and one initialized with constant values:

```
import tensorflow as tf
import numpy as np

# variable initialized randomly
var = tf.get_variable("first_variable", shape=[1,3], dtype=tf.float32)

# variable initialized with constant values
init_val = np.array([4,5])
var2 = tf.get_variable("second_variable", shape=[1,2], dtype=tf.int32,
initializer=tf.constant_initializer(init_val))

# create the session
sess = tf.Session()
# initialize all the variables
sess.run(tf.global_variables_initializer())

print(sess.run(var))

>> [[ 0.93119466 -1.0498083  -0.2198658 ]]

print(sess.run(var2))

>> [[4 5]]
```

The variables aren't initialized until `global_variables_initializer()` is called.

All the variables created in this way are set as `trainable`, meaning that the graph can modify them, for example, after an optimization operation. The variables can be set as non-trainable, as follows:

```
var2 = tf.get_variable("variable", shape=[1,2], trainable=False,
dtype=tf.int32)
```

An easy way to access all the variables is as follows:

```
print(tf.global_variables())

>> [<tf.Variable 'first_variable:0' shape=(1, 3) dtype=float32_ref>,
<tf.Variable 'second_variable:0' shape=(1, 2) dtype=int32_ref>]
```

Creating a graph

A **graph** represents low-level computations in terms of the dependencies between operations. In TensorFlow, you first define a graph, and then create a session that executes the operations in the graph.

The way a graph is built, computed, and optimized in TensorFlow allows a high degree of parallelism, distributed execution, and portability, all very important properties when building machine learning models.

To give you an idea of the structure of a graph produced internally by TensorFlow, the following program produces the computational graph demonstrated in the following diagram:

```
import tensorflow as tf
import numpy as np

const1 = tf.constant(3.0, name='constant1')

var = tf.get_variable("variable1", shape=[1,2], dtype=tf.float32)
var2 = tf.get_variable("variable2", shape=[1,2], trainable=False,
dtype=tf.float32)

op1 = const1 * var
op2 = op1 + var2
op3 = tf.reduce_mean(op2)

sess = tf.Session()
sess.run(tf.global_variables_initializer())
sess.run(op3)
```

This results in the following graph:

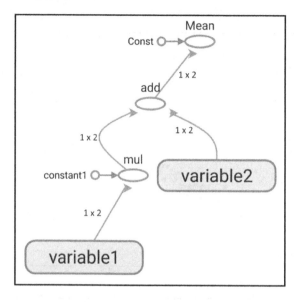

Figure 2.3: Example of a computational graph

Simple linear regression example

To better digest all the concepts, let's now create a simple linear regression model. First, we have to import all the libraries and set a random seed, both for NumPy and TensorFlow (so that we'll all have the same results):

```
import tensorflow as tf
import numpy as np
from datetime import datetime

np.random.seed(10)
tf.set_random_seed(10)
```

Implementing RL Cycle and OpenAI Gym

Then, we can create a synthetic dataset consisting of 100 examples, as shown in the following screenshot:

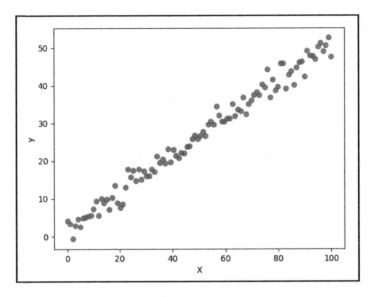

Figure 2.4: Dataset used in the linear regression example

Because this is a linear regression example, $y = W * X + b$, where W and b are arbitrary values. In this example, we set `W = 0.5` and `b = 1.4`. Additionally, we add some normal random noise:

```
W, b = 0.5, 1.4
# create a dataset of 100 examples
X = np.linspace(0,100, num=100)
# add random noise to the y labels
y = np.random.normal(loc=W * X + b, scale=2.0, size=len(X))
```

The next step involves creating the placeholders for the input and the output, and the variables of the weight and bias of the linear model. During training, these two variables will be optimized to be as similar as possible to the weight and bias of the dataset:

```
# create the placeholders
x_ph = tf.placeholder(shape=[None,], dtype=tf.float32)
y_ph = tf.placeholder(shape=[None,], dtype=tf.float32)

# create the variables
v_weight = tf.get_variable("weight", shape=[1], dtype=tf.float32)
v_bias = tf.get_variable("bias", shape=[1], dtype=tf.float32)
```

Then, we build the computational graph defining the linear operation and the **mean squared error** (MSE) loss:

```
# linear computation
out = v_weight * x_ph + v_bias

# compute the mean squared error
loss = tf.reduce_mean((out - y_ph)**2)
```

We can now instantiate the optimizer and call `minimize()` to minimize the MSE loss. `minimize()` first computes the gradients of the variables (`v_weight` and `v_bias`) and then applies the gradient, updating the variables:

```
opt = tf.train.AdamOptimizer(0.4).minimize(loss)
```

Now, let's create a session and initialize all the variables:

```
session = tf.Session()
session.run(tf.global_variables_initializer())
```

The training is done by running the optimizer multiple times while feeding the dataset to the graph. To keep track of the state of the model, the MSE loss and the model variables (weight and bias) are printed every 40 epochs:

```
# loop to train the parameters
for ep in range(210):
    # run the optimizer and get the loss
    train_loss, _ = session.run([loss, opt], feed_dict={x_ph:X, y_ph:y})

    # print epoch number and loss
    if ep % 40 == 0:
        print('Epoch: %3d, MSE: %.4f, W: %.3f, b: %.3f' % (ep, train_loss,
session.run(v_weight), session.run(v_bias)))
```

In the end, we can print the final values of the variables:

```
print('Final weight: %.3f, bias: %.3f' % (session.run(v_weight),
session.run(v_bias)))
```

The output will be similar to the following:

```
>> Epoch:   0, MSE: 4617.4390, weight: 1.295, bias: -0.407
   Epoch:  40, MSE: 5.3334, weight: 0.496, bias: -0.727
   Epoch:  80, MSE: 4.5894, weight: 0.529, bias: -0.012
   Epoch: 120, MSE: 4.1029, weight: 0.512, bias: 0.608
   Epoch: 160, MSE: 3.8552, weight: 0.506, bias: 1.092
   Epoch: 200, MSE: 3.7597, weight: 0.501, bias: 1.418
   Final weight: 0.500, bias: 1.473
```

During the training phase, it's possible to see that the MSE loss would decrease toward a non-zero value (of about 3.71). That's because we added random noise to the dataset that prevents the MSE from reaching a perfect value of 0.

Also, as anticipated, with regard to the weight and bias of the model approach, the values of `0.500` and `1.473` are precisely the values around which the dataset has been built. The blue line visible in the following screenshot is the prediction of the trained linear model, while the points are our training examples:

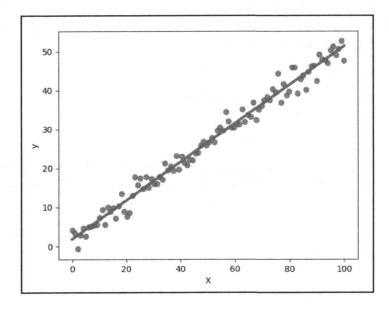

Figure 2.5: Linear regression model predictions

 For all the color references in the chapter, please refer to the color images bundle: `http://www.packtpub.com/sites/default/files/downloads/9781789131116_ColorImages.pdf`.

Introducing TensorBoard

Keeping track of how variables change during the training of a model can be a tedious job. For instance, in the linear regression example, we kept track of the MSE loss and of the parameters of the model by printing them every 40 epochs. As the complexity of the algorithms increases, there is an increase in the number of variables and metrics to be monitored. Fortunately, this is where TensorBoard comes to the rescue.

Chapter 2

TensorBoard is a suite of visualization tools that can be used to plot metrics, visualize TensorFlow graphs, and visualize additional information. A typical TensorBoard screen is similar to the one shown in the following screenshot:

Figure 2.6: Scalar TensorBoard page

The integration of TensorBoard with TensorFlow code is pretty straightforward as it involves only a few tweaks to the code. In particular, to visualize the MSE loss over time and monitor the weight and bias of our linear regression model using TensorBoard, it is first necessary to attach the loss tensor to `tf.summar.scalar()` and the model's parameters to `tf.summary.histogram()`. The following snippet should be added after the call to the optimizer:

```
tf.summary.scalar('MSEloss', loss)
tf.summary.histogram('model_weight', v_weight)
tf.summary.histogram('model_bias', v_bias)
```

Then, to simplify the process and handle them as a single summary, we can merge them:

```
all_summary = tf.summary.merge_all()
```

At this point, we have to instantiate a `FileWriter` instance that will log all the summary information in a file:

```
now = datetime.now()
clock_time = "{}_{}.{}.{}".format(now.day, now.hour, now.minute, now.second)
file_writer = tf.summary.FileWriter('log_dir/'+clock_time, tf.get_default_graph())
```

The first two lines create a unique filename using the current date and time. In the third line, the path of the file and the TensorFlow graph are passed to `FileWriter()`. The second parameter is optional and represents the graph to visualize.

The final change is done in the training loop by replacing the previous line, `train_loss, _ = session.run(..)`, with the following:

```
train_loss, _, train_summary = session.run([loss, opt, all_summary], feed_dict={x_ph:X, y_ph:y})
file_writer.add_summary(train_summary, ep)
```

First, `all_summary` is executed in the current session, and then the result is added to `file_writer` to be saved in the file. This procedure will run the three summaries that were merged previously and log them in the log file. TensorBoard will then read from this file and visualize the scalar, the two histograms, and the computation graph.

Remember to close `file_writer` at the end, as follows:

```
file_writer.close()
```

Finally, we can open TensorBoard by going to the working directory and typing the following in a terminal:

```
$ tensorboard --logdir=log_dir
```

This command creates a web server that listens to port 6006. To start TensorBoard, you have to go to the link that TensorBoard shows you:

Chapter 2

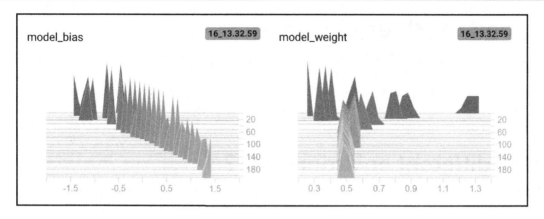

Figure 2.7: Histogram of the linear regression model's parameters

You can now browse TensorBoard by clicking on the tabs at the top of the page to access the plots, the histograms, and the graph. In the preceding—as well as the following—screenshots, you can see some of the results visualized on those pages. The plots and the graphs are interactive, so take some time to explore them in order to improve your understanding of their use. Also check the TensorBoard official documentation (`https://www.tensorflow.org/guide/summaries_and_tensorboard`) to learn more about the additional features included in TensorBoard:

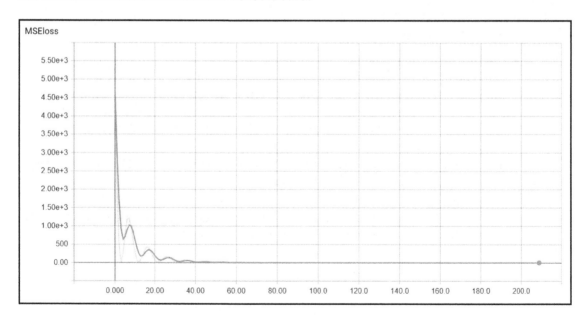

Figure 2.8: Scalar plot of the MSE loss

Types of RL environments

Environments, similar to labeled datasets in supervised learning, are the essential part of RL as they dictate the information that has to be learned and the choice of algorithms. In this section, we'll take a look at the main differences between the types of environments and list some of the most important open source environments.

Why different environments?

While, for real applications, the choice of environment is dictated by the task to be learned, for research applications, usually, the choice is dictated by intrinsic features of the environment. In this latter case, the end goal is not to train the agent on a specific task, but to show some task-related capabilities.

For instance, if the goal is to create a multi-agent RL algorithm, the environment should have at least two agents with a means to communicate with one another, regardless of the end task. Instead, to create a lifelong learner (agents that continuously create and learn more difficult tasks using the knowledge acquired in previous easier tasks), the primary quality that the environment should have is the ability to adapt to new situations and a realistic domain.

Task aside, environments can differ by other characteristics, such as complexity, observation space, action space, and reward function:

- **Complexity**: Environments can spread across a wide spectrum, from the balance of a pole to the manipulation of physical objects with a robot hand. More complex environments can be chosen to show the capability of an algorithm to deal with a large state space that mimics the complexity of the world. On the other hand, simpler ones can be used to show only some specific qualities.
- **Observation space**: As we have already seen, the observation space can range from the full state of the environment to only a partial observation perceived by the perception systems, such as row images.
- **Action space**: Environments with a large continuous action space challenge the agent to deal with real-value vectors, whereas discrete actions are easier to learn as they have only a limited number of actions available.

- **Reward function**: Environments with hard explorations and delayed rewards, such as Montezuma's revenge, are very challenging to solve. Surprisingly, only a few algorithms are able to reach human levels. For this reason, these environments are used as a test bed for algorithms that propose to address the exploration problem.

Open source environments

How can we design an environment that meets our requirements? Fortunately, there are many open source environments that are built to tackle specific or broader problems. By way of an example, CoinRun, shown in the following screenshot, was created to measure the generalization capabilities of an algorithm:

Figure 2.9: The CoinRun environment

We will now list some of the main open source environments available. These are created by different teams and companies, but almost all of them use the OpenAI Gym interface:

Figure 2.10: Roboschool environment

- **Gym Atari** (https://gym.openai.com/envs/#atari): Includes Atari 2600 games with screen images as input. They are useful for measuring the performance of RL algorithms on a wide variety of games with the same observation space.
- **Gym Classic control** (https://gym.openai.com/envs/#classic_control): Classic games that can be used for the easy evaluation and debugging of an algorithm.
- **Gym MuJoCo** (https://gym.openai.com/envs/#mujoco): Includes continuous control tasks (such as Ant, and HalfCheetah) built on top of MuJoCo, a physics engine that requires a paid license (a free license is available for students).
- **MalmoEnv** (https://github.com/Microsoft/malmo): An environment built on top of Minecraft.
- **Pommerman** (https://github.com/MultiAgentLearning/playground): A great environment for training multi-agent algorithms. Pommerman is a variant of the famous Bomberman.
- **Roboschool** (https://github.com/openai/roboschool): A robot simulation environment integrated with OpenAI Gym. It includes an environment replica of MuJoCo, as shown in the preceding screenshot, two interactive environments to improve the robustness of the agent, and one multiplayer environment.

- **Duckietown** (`https://github.com/duckietown/gym-duckietown`): A self-driving car simulator with different maps and obstacles.
- **PLE** (`https://github.com/ntasfi/PyGame-Learning-Environment`): PLE includes many different arcade games, such as Monster Kong, FlappyBird, and Snake.
- **Unity ML-Agents** (`https://github.com/Unity-Technologies/ml-agents`): Environments built on top of Unity with realistic physics. ML-agents allow a great degree of freedom and the possibility to create your own environment using Unity.
- **CoinRun** (`https://github.com/openai/coinrun`): An environment that addresses the problem of overfitting in RL. It generates different environments for training and testing.
- **DeepMind Lab** (`https://github.com/deepmind/lab`): Provides a suite of 3D environments for navigation and puzzle tasks.
- **DeepMind PySC2** (`https://github.com/deepmind/pysc2`): An environment for learning the complex game, StarCraft II.

Summary

Hopefully, in this chapter, you have learned about all the tools and components needed to build RL algorithms. You set up the Python environment required to develop RL algorithms and programmed your first algorithm using an OpenAI Gym environment. As the majority of state-of-the-art RL algorithms involve deep learning, you have been introduced to TensorFlow, a deep learning framework that you'll use throughout the book. The use of TensorFlow speeds up the development of deep RL algorithms as it deals with complex parts of deep neural networks such as backpropagation. Furthermore, TensorFlow is provided with TensorBoard, a visualization tool that is used to monitor and help the algorithm debugging process.

Because we'll be using many environments in the subsequent chapters, it's important to have a clear understanding of their differences and distinctiveness. By now, you should also be able to choose the best environments for your own projects, but bear in mind that despite the fact that we provided you with a comprehensive list, there may be many others that could better suit your problem.

That being said, in the following chapters, you'll finally learn how to develop RL algorithms. Specifically, in the next chapter, you will be presented with algorithms that can be used in simple problems where the environment is completely known. After those, we'll build more sophisticated ones that can deal with more complex cases.

Questions

1. What's the output of the `step()` function in Gym?
2. How can you sample an action using the OpenAI Gym interface?
3. What's the main difference between the `Box` and `Discrete` classses?
4. Why are deep learning frameworks used in RL?
5. What's a tensor?
6. What can be visualized in TensorBoard?
7. To create a self-driving car, which of the environments mentioned in the chapter would you use?

Further reading

- For the TensorFlow official guide, refer to the following link: `https://www.tensorflow.org/guide/low_level_intro`.
- For the TensorBoard official guide, refer to the following link: `https://www.tensorflow.org/guide/summaries_and_tensorboard`.

3
Solving Problems with Dynamic Programming

The purposes of this chapter are manifold. We will introduce many topics that are essential to the understanding of reinforcement problems and the first algorithms that are used to solve them. Whereas, in the previous chapters, we talked about **reinforcement learning** (**RL**) from a broad and non-technical point of view, here, we will formalize this understanding to develop the first algorithms to solve a simple game.

The RL problem can be formulated as a **Markov decision process** (**MDP**), a framework that provides a formalization of the key elements of RL, such as value functions and the expected reward. RL algorithms can then be created using these mathematical components. They differ from each other by how these components are combined and on the assumptions made while designing them.

For this reason, as we'll see in this chapter, RL algorithms can be categorized into three main categories that can overlap each other. This is because some algorithms can unify characteristics from more than one category. Once these pivotal concepts have been explained, we'll present the first type of algorithm, called dynamic programming, which can solve problems when given complete information about the environment.

The following topics will be covered in this chapter:

- MDP
- Categorizing RL algorithms
- Dynamic programming

Solving Problems with Dynamic Programming

MDP

An MDP expresses the problem of sequential decision-making, where actions influence the next states and the results. MDPs are general and flexible enough to provide a formalization of the problem of learning a goal through interactions, the same problem that is addressed with RL. Thus we can express and reason with RL problems in terms of MDPs.

An MDP is four-tuple (S,A,P,R):

- S is the state space, with a finite set of states.
- A is the action space, with a finite set of actions.
- P is a transition function, which defines the probability of reaching a state, s', from s through an action, a. In $P(s', s, a) = p(s'| s, a)$, the transition function is equal to the conditional probability of s' given s and a.
- R is the reward function, which determines the value received for transitioning to state s' after taking action a from state s.

An illustration of an MDP is given in the following diagram. The arrows represent the transitions between two states, with the transition probabilities attached to the tail of the arrows and the rewards on the body of the arrows. For their properties, the transition probabilities of a state must add up to 1. In this example, the final state is represented with a square (state S_5) and for simplicity, we have represented an MDP with a single action:

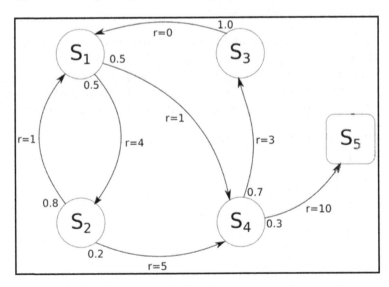

Figure 3.1 Example of an MDP with five states and one action

The MDP is controlled by a sequence of discrete time steps that create a trajectory of states and actions (S_0, A_0, S_1, A_1, ...), where the states follow the dynamics of the MDP, namely the state transition function, $p(s'|s, a)$. In this way, the transition function fully characterizes the environment's dynamics.

By definition, the transition function and the reward function are determined only by the current state, and not from the sequence of the previous states visited. This property is called the **Markov property**, which means that the process is memory-less and the future state depends only on the current one, and not on its history. Thus, a state holds all the information. A system with such a property is called **fully observable**.

In many practical RL cases, the Markov property does not hold up, and for practicality, we can get around the problem by assuming it is an MDP and using a finite number of previous states (a finite history): S_t, S_{t-1}, S_{t-2}, ..., S_{t-k}. In this case, the system is **partially observable** and the states are called **observations**. We'll use this strategy in the Atari games, where we'll use row pixels as the input of the agent. This is because the single frame is static and does not carry information about the speed or direction of the objects. Instead, these values can be retrieved using the previous three or four frames (it is still an approximation).

The final objective of an MDP is to find a policy, π, that maximizes the cumulative reward, $\sum_{t=0}^{\infty} R_\pi(s_t, s_{t+1})$, where R_π is the reward obtained at each step by following the policy, π. A solution of an MDP is found when a policy takes the best possible action in each state of the MDP. This policy is known as the **optimal policy**.

Policy

The policy chooses the actions to be taken in a given situation and can be categorized as deterministic or stochastic.

A deterministic policy is denoted as $a_t = \mu(s_t)$, while a stochastic policy can be denoted as $a_t \sim \pi(.|s_t)$, where the tilde symbol (~) means **has distribution**. Stochastic policies are used when it is better to consider an action distribution; for example, when it is preferable to inject a noisy action into the system.

Generally, stochastic policies can be categorical or Gaussian. The former case is similar to a classification problem and is computed as a softmax function across the categories. In the latter case, the actions are sampled from a Gaussian distribution, described by a mean and a standard deviation (or variance). These parameters can also be functions of states.

Solving Problems with Dynamic Programming

When using parameterized policies, we'll define them with the letter θ. For example, in the case of a deterministic policy, it would be written as $\mu_\theta(s_t)$.

Policy, decision-maker, and agent are three terms that express the same concept, so, in this book, we'll use these terms interchangeably.

Return

When running a policy in an MDP, the sequence of state and action ($S_0, A_0, S_1, A_1, ...$) is called **trajectory** or **rollout**, and is denoted by τ. In each trajectory, a sequence of rewards will be collected as a result of the actions. A function of these rewards is called **return** and in its most simplified version, it is defined as follows:

$$G(\tau) = r_0 + r_1 + r_2 + ... = \sum_{t=0}^{\infty} r_t \qquad (3.1)$$

At this point, the return can be analyzed separately for trajectories with infinite and finite horizons. This distinction is needed because in the case of interactions within an environment that do not terminate, the sum previously presented will always have an infinite value. This situation is dangerous because it doesn't provide any information. Such tasks are called continuing tasks and need another formulation of the reward. The best solution is to give more weight to the short-term rewards while giving less importance to those in the distant future. This is accomplished by using a value between 0 and 1 called the **discount factor** denoted with the symbol λ. Thus, the return G can be reformulated as follows:

$$G(\tau) = r_0 + \lambda r_1 + \lambda^2 r_2 + ... = \sum_{t=0}^{\infty} \lambda^t r_t \qquad (3.2)$$

This formula can be viewed as a way to prefer actions that are closer in time with respect to those that will be encountered in the distant future. Take this example—you win the lottery and you can decide when you would like to collect the prize. You would probably prefer to collect it within a few days rather than in a few years. λ is the value that defines how long you are willing to wait to collect the prize. If $\lambda = 1$, that means that you are not bothered about when you collect the prize. If $\lambda = 0$, that means that you want it immediately.

In cases of trajectories with a finite horizon, meaning trajectories with a natural ending, tasks are called **episodic** (it derives from the term episode, which is another word for trajectory). In episodic tasks, the original formula (1) works, but nevertheless, it is preferred to have a variation of it with the discount factor:

$$G(\tau) = r_0 + \lambda r_1 + \lambda^2 r_2 + \ldots = \sum_{t=0}^{k} \lambda^t r_t \qquad (3.3)$$

With a finite but long horizon, the use of a discount factor increases the stability of algorithms, considering that long future rewards are only partially considered. In practice, discount factor values between 0.9 and 0.999 are used.

A trivial but very useful decomposition of formula (3) is the definition of return in terms of the return at timestep $t + 1$:

$$G_t(\tau) = r_t + \lambda G_{t+1}(\tau) \qquad (3.4)$$

When simplifying the notation, it becomes the following:

$$G_t = r_t + \lambda G_{t+1} \qquad (3.5)$$

Then, using the return notation, we can define the goal of RL to find an optimal policy, π, that maximizes the expected return as $argmax_\pi E_\pi[G(\tau)]$, where $E_\pi[\cdot]$ is the expected value of a random variable.

Value functions

The return $G(\tau)$ provides a good insight into the trajectory's value, but still, it doesn't give any indication of the quality of the single states visited. This quality indicator is important because it can be used by the policy to choose the next best action. The policy has to just choose the action that will result in the next state with the highest quality. The **value function** does exactly this: it estimates the **quality** in terms of the expected return from a state following a policy. Formally, the value function is defined as follows:

$$V_\pi(s) = E_\pi[G|s_0 = s] = E_\pi[\sum_{t=0}^{k} \lambda^t r_t | s_0 = s]$$

Solving Problems with Dynamic Programming

The **action-value function**, similar to the value function, is the expected return from a state but is also conditioned on the first action. It is defined as follows:

$$Q_\pi(s, a) = E_\pi[G|s_0 = s, a_0 = a] = E_\pi[\sum_{t=0}^{k} \lambda^t r_t | s_0 = s, a_0 = a]$$

The value function and action-value function are also called the **V-function** and **Q-function** respectively, and are strictly correlated with each other since the value function can also be defined in terms of the action-value function:

$$V_\pi(s) = E_\pi[Q_\pi(s, a)]$$

Knowing the optimal Q^*, the optimal value function is as follows:

$$V^*(s) = max_a Q^*(s, a)$$

That's because the optimal action is $a^*(s) = argmax_a Q^*(s, a)$.

Bellman equation

V and **Q** can be estimated by running trajectories that follow the policy, π, and then averaging the values obtained. This technique is effective and is used in many contexts, but is very expensive considering that the return requires the rewards from the full trajectory.

Luckily, the Bellman equation defines the action-value function and the value function recursively, enabling their estimations from subsequent states. The Bellman equation does that by using the reward obtained in the present state and the value of its successor state. We already saw the recursive formulation of the return (in formula (5)) and we can apply it to the state value:

$$V_\pi(s) = E_\pi[G_t|s_0 = s] = E_\pi[r_t + \gamma G_{t+1}|s_0 = s]$$
$$= E_\pi[r_t + \gamma V_\pi(s_{t+1})]|s_t = s, a_t \sim \pi(s_t)] \qquad (3.6)$$

Similarly, we can adapt the Bellman equation for the action-value function:

$$\begin{aligned} Q_\pi(s,a) &= E_\pi[G_t | s_t = s, a_t = a] \\ &= E_\pi[r_t + \gamma G_{t+1} | s_t = s, a_t = a] \\ &= E_\pi[r_t + \gamma Q_\pi(s_{t+1}, a_{t+1}) | s_t = s, a_t = a] \end{aligned} \quad (3.7)$$

Now, with (6) and (7), V_π and Q_π are updated only with the values of the successive states, without the need to unroll the trajectory to the end, as required in the old definition.

Categorizing RL algorithms

Before deep diving into the first RL algorithm that solves the optimal Bellman equation, we want to give a broad but detailed overview of RL algorithms. We need to do this because their distinctions can be quite confusing. There are many parts involved in the design of algorithms, and many characteristics have to be considered before deciding which algorithm best fits the actual needs of the user. The scope of this overview presents the big picture of RL so that in the next chapters, where we'll give a comprehensive theoretical and practical view of these algorithms, you will already see the general objective and have a clear idea of their location in the map of RL algorithms.

The first distinction is between model-based and model-free algorithms. As the name suggests, the first requires a model of the environment, while the second is free from this condition. The model of the environment is highly valuable because it carries precious information that can be used to find the desired policies; however, in most cases, the model is almost impossible to obtain. For example, it can be quite easy to model the game tic-tac-toe, while it can be difficult to model the waves of the sea. To this end, model-free algorithms can learn information without any assumptions about the environment. A representation of the categories of RL algorithms is visible in figure 3.2.

Solving Problems with Dynamic Programming

Here the distinction is shown between model-based and model-free, and two widely known model-free approaches, namely policy gradient and value-based. Also, as we'll see in later chapters, a combination of those is possible:

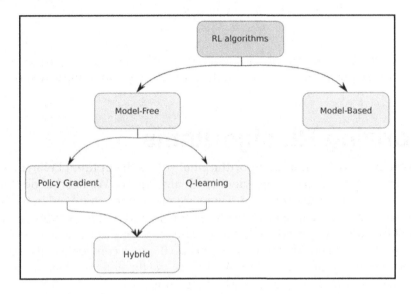

Figure 3.2. Categorization of RL algorithms

The first distinction is between model-free and model-based. Model-free RL algorithms can be further decomposed in policy gradient and value-based algorithms. Hybrids are methods that combine important characteristics of both methods.

Model-free algorithms

In the absence of a model, **model-free (MF)** algorithms run trajectories within a given policy to gain experience and to improve the agent. MF algorithms are made up of three main steps that are repeated until a good policy is created:

1. The generation of new samples by running the policy in the environment. The trajectories are run until a final state is reached or for a fixed number of steps.
2. The estimation of the return function.
3. The improvement of the policy using the samples collected, and the estimation done in step 2.

These three components are at the heart of this type of algorithm, but based on how each step is performed, they generate different algorithms. Value-based algorithms and policy gradient algorithms are two such examples. They seem to be very different, but they are based on similar principles and both use the three-step approach.

Value-based algorithms

Value-based algorithms, also known as **value function algorithms**, use a paradigm that's very similar to the one we saw in the previous section. That is, they use the Bellman equation to learn the Q-function, which in turn is used to learn a policy. In the most common setting, they use deep neural networks as a function approximator and other tricks to deal with high variance and general instabilities. To a certain degree, value-based algorithms are closer to supervised regression algorithms.

Typically, these algorithms are off-policy, meaning they are not required to optimize the same policy that was used to generate the data. This means that these methods can learn from previous experience, as they can store the sampled data in a replay buffer. The ability to use previous samples makes the value function more sample-efficient than other model-free algorithms.

Policy gradient algorithms

The other family of MF algorithms is that of the policy gradient methods (or policy optimization methods). They have a more direct and obvious interpretation of the RL problem, as they learn directly from a parametric policy by updating the parameters in the direction of the improvements. It's based on the RL principle that good actions should be encouraged (by boosting the gradient of the policy upward) while discouraging bad actions.

Contrary to value function algorithms, policy optimization mainly requires on-policy data, making these algorithms more sample inefficient. Policy optimization methods can be quite unstable due to the fact that taking the steepest ascent in the presence of surfaces with high curvature can easily result in moving too far in any given direction, falling down into a bad region. To address this problem, many algorithms have been proposed, such as optimizing the policy only within a trust region, or optimizing a surrogate clipped objective function to limit changes to the policy.

A major advantage of policy gradient methods is that they easily handle environments with continuous action spaces. This is a very difficult thing to approach with value function algorithms as they learn Q-values for discrete pairs of states and actions.

Actor-Critic algorithms

Actor-Critic (AC) algorithms are on-policy policy gradient algorithms that also learn a value function (generally a Q-function) called a critic to provide feedback to the policy, the actor. Imagine that you, the actor, want to go to the supermarket via a new route. Unfortunately, before arriving at the destination, your boss calls you requiring you to go back to work. Because you didn't reach the supermarket, you don't know if the new road is actually faster than the old one. But if you reached a familiar location, you can estimate the time you'll need to go from there to the supermarket and calculate whether the new path is preferable. This estimate is what the critic does. In this way, you can improve the actor even though you didn't reach the final goal.

Combining a critic with an actor has been shown to be very effective and is commonly used in policy gradient algorithms. This technique can also be combined with other ideas used in policy optimization, such as trust-region algorithms.

Hybrid algorithms

Advantages of both value functions and policy gradient algorithms can be merged, creating hybrid algorithms that can be more sample efficient and robust.

Hybrid approaches combine Q-functions and policy gradients to symbiotically and mutually improve each other. These methods estimate the expected Q-function of deterministic actions to directly improve the policy.

Be aware that because AC algorithms learn and use a value function, they are categorized as policy gradients and not as hybrid algorithms. This is because the main underlying objective is that of policy gradient methods. The value function is only an upgrade to provide additional information.

Model-based RL

Having a model of the environment means that the state transitions and the rewards can be predicted for each state-action tuple (without any interaction with the real environment). As we already mentioned, the model is known only in limited cases, but when it is known, it can be used in many different ways. The most obvious application of the model is to use it to plan future actions. Planning is a concept used to express the organization of future moves when the consequences of the next actions are already known. For example, if you know exactly what moves your enemy will make, you can think ahead and plan all your actions before executing the first one. As a downside, planning can be very expensive and isn't a trivial process.

A model can also be learned through interactions with the environment, assimilating the consequences (both in terms of the states and rewards) of an action. This solution is not always the best one because teaching a model could be terribly expensive in the real world. Moreover, if only a rough approximation of the environment is understood by the model, it could lead to disastrous results.

A model, whether known or learned, can be used both to plan and to improve the policy, and can be integrated into different phases of an RL algorithm. Well-known cases of model-based RL involve pure planning, embedded planning to improve the policy, and generated samples from an approximate model.

A set of algorithms that use a model to estimate a value function is called **dynamic programming** (**DP**) and will be studied later in this chapter.

Algorithm diversity

Why are there so many types of RL algorithms? This is because there isn't one that is better than all the others in every context. Each one is designed for different needs and to take care of different aspects. The most notable differences are stability, sample efficiency, and wall clock time (training time). These will be more clear as we progress through the book but as a rule of thumb, policy gradient algorithms are more stable and reliable than value function algorithms. On the other hand, value function methods are more sample efficient as they are off-policy and can use prior experience. In turn, model-based algorithms are more sample efficient than Q-learning algorithms but their computational cost is much higher and they are slower.

Besides the ones just presented, there are other trade-offs that have to be taken into consideration while designing and deploying an algorithm (such as ease of use and robustness), which is not a trivial process.

Dynamic programming

DP is a general algorithmic paradigm that breaks up a problem into smaller chunks of overlapping subproblems, and then finds the solution to the original problem by combining the solutions of the subproblems.

DP can be used in reinforcement learning and is among one of the simplest approaches. It is suited to computing optimal policies by being provided with a perfect model of the environment.

Solving Problems with Dynamic Programming

DP is an important stepping stone in the history of RL algorithms and provides the foundation for the next generation of algorithms, but it is computationally very expensive. DP works with MDPs with a limited number of states and actions as it has to update the value of each state (or action-value), taking into consideration all the other possible states. Moreover, DP algorithms store value functions in an array or in a table. This way of storing information is effective and fast as there isn't any loss of information, but it does require the storage of large tables. Since DP algorithms use tables to store value functions, it is called tabular learning. This is opposed to approximated learning, which uses approximated value functions to store the values in a fixed size function, such as an artificial neural network.

DP uses **bootstrapping**, meaning that it improves the estimation value of a state by using the expected value of the following states. As we have already seen, bootstrapping is used in the Bellman equation. Indeed, DP applies the Bellman equations, (6) and (7), to estimate V^* and/or Q^*. This can be done using the following:

$$V^*(s) = max_a E[r_t + \gamma V^*(s_{t+1}) | s_t = s, a_t = a]$$

Or by using the Q-function:

$$Q^*(s, a) = E[r_t + \gamma max_{a_{t+1}} Q^*(s_{t+1}, a_{t+1}) | s_t = s, a_t = a]$$

Then, once the optimal value and action-value function are found, the optimal policy can be found by just taking the actions that maximize the expectation.

Policy evaluation and policy improvement

To find the optimal policy, you first need to find the optimal value function. An iterative procedure that does this is called **policy evaluation**—it creates a $\{V_0 .. V_k\}$ sequence that iteratively improves the value function for a policy, π, using the state value transition of the model, the expectation of the next state, and the immediate reward. Therefore, it creates a sequence of improving value functions using the Bellman equation:

$$V_{k+1}(s) = E_\pi[r_t + \gamma V_k(s_{t+1}) | s_t = s]$$

$$= \sum_a \pi(s, a) \sum_{s', r} p(s'|s, a)[r + \gamma V_k(s')]$$

(3.8)

This sequence will converge to the optimal value as $k \to \infty$. Figure 3.3 shows the update of $V_{k+1}(s_t)$ using the successive state values:

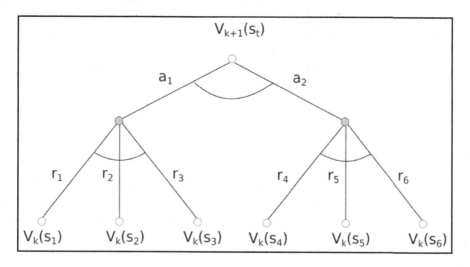

Figure 3.3. The update of $V_{k+1}(s_t)$ using formula (8)

The value function (8) can be updated only if the state transition function, p, and the reward function, r, for every state and action are known, so only if the model of the environment is completely known.

Note that the first summation of the actions in (8) is needed for stochastic policies because the policy outputs a probability for each action. For simplicity from now on, we'll consider only deterministic policies.

Once the value functions are improved, it can be used to find a better policy. This procedure is called *policy improvement* and is about finding a policy, π', as follows:

$$\pi' = argmax_a Q_\pi(s,a) = argmax_a \sum_{s',r} p(s'|s,a)[r + \gamma V_\pi(s')] \qquad (3.9)$$

It creates a policy, π', from the value function, V_π, of the original policy, π. As can be formally demonstrated, the new policy, π', is always better than π, and the policy is optimal if and only if V is optimal. The combination of policy evaluation and policy improvement gives rise to two algorithms to compute the optimal policy. One is called **policy iteration** and the other is called **value iteration**. Both use policy evaluation to monotonically improve the value function and policy improvement to estimate the new policy. The only difference is that policy iteration executes the two phases cyclically, while value iteration combines them in a single update.

Policy iteration

Policy iteration cycles between policy evaluation, which updates V_π under the current policy, π, using formula (8), and policy improvement (9), which computes π' using the improved value function, V_π. Eventually, after n cycles, the algorithm will result in an optimal policy, π^*.

The pseudocode is as follows:

```
Initialize V_π(s) and π(s) for every state s

while π is not stable:

    > policy evaluation
    while V_π is not stable:
        for each state s:
```
$$V_\pi(s) = \sum_{s',r} p(s'|s, \pi(a))[r + \gamma V_\pi(s')]$$

```
    > policy improvement
    for each state s:
```
$$\pi = argmax_a \sum_{s',r} p(s'|s, a)[r + \gamma V_\pi(s')]$$

After an initialization phase, the outer loop iterates through policy evaluation and policy iteration until a stable policy is found. On each of these iterations, policy evaluation evaluates the policy found during the preceding policy improvement steps, which in turn use the estimated value function.

Policy iteration applied to FrozenLake

To consolidate the ideas behind policy iteration, we'll apply it to a game called FrozenLake. Here, the environment consists of a 4 x 4 grid. Using four actions that correspond to the directions (0 is left, 1 is down, 2 is right, and 3 is up), the agent has to move to the opposite side of the grid without falling in the holes. Moreover, movement is uncertain, and the agent has the possibility of movement in other directions. So, in such a situation, it could be beneficial not to move in the intended direction. A reward of +1 is assigned when the end goal is reached. The map of the game is shown in figure 3.4. S is the start position, the star is the end position, and the spirals are the holes:

Figure 3.4 Map of the FrozenLake game

With all the tools needed, let's see how to solve it.

 All the code explained in this chapter is available on the GitHub repository of this book, using the following link: `https://https://github.com/PacktPublishing/Reinforcement-Learning-Algorithms-with-Python`

First, we have to create the environment, initializing the value function and the policy:

```
env = gym.make('FrozenLake-v0')
env = env.unwrapped
nA = env.action_space.n
nS = env.observation_space.n
V = np.zeros(nS)
policy = np.zeros(nS)
```

Then, we have to create the main cycle that does one step of policy evaluation and one step of policy improvement. This cycle finishes whenever the policy is stable. To do this, use the following code:

```
policy_stable = False
it = 0
while not policy_stable:
    policy_evaluation(V, policy)
    policy_stable = policy_improvement(V, policy)
    it += 1
```

Solving Problems with Dynamic Programming

In the end, we can print the number of iterations completed, the value function, the policy, and the score reached running some test games:

```
print('Converged after %i policy iterations'%(it))
run_episodes(env, V, policy)
print(V.reshape((4,4)))
print(policy.reshape((4,4)))
```

Now, before defining `policy_evaluation`, we can create a function to evaluate the expected action-value that will also be used in `policy_improvement`:

```
def eval_state_action(V, s, a, gamma=0.99):
    return np.sum([p * (rew + gamma*V[next_s]) for p, next_s, rew, _ in env.P[s][a]])
```

Here, `env.P` is a dictionary that contains all the information about the dynamics of the environment.

`gamma` is the discount factor, with 0.99 being a standard value to use for simple and medium difficulty problems. The higher it is, the more difficult it is for the agent to predict the value of a state because it should look further into the future.

Next, we can define the `policy_evaluation` function. `policy_evaluation` has to calculate formula (8) under the current policy for every state until it reaches steady values. Because the policy is deterministic, we only evaluate one action:

```
def policy_evaluation(V, policy, eps=0.0001):
    while True:
        delta = 0
        for s in range(nS):
            old_v = V[s]
            V[s] = eval_state_action(V, s, policy[s])
            delta = max(delta, np.abs(old_v - V[s]))
        if delta < eps:
            break
```

We consider the value function stable whenever `delta` is lower than the threshold, `eps`. When these conditions are met, the `while` loop statement is stopped.

`policy_improvement` takes the value function and the policy and iterates them across all of the states to update the policy based on the new value function:

```
def policy_improvement(V, policy):
    policy_stable = True
    for s in range(nS):
        old_a = policy[s]
        policy[s] = np.argmax([eval_state_action(V, s, a) for a in
```

```
        range(nA)])
            if old_a != policy[s]:
                policy_stable = False
    return policy_stable
```

`policy_improvement(V, policy)` returns `False` until the policy changes. That's because it means that the policy isn't stable yet.

The final snippet of code runs some games to test the new policy and prints the number of games won:

```
def run_episodes(env, V, policy, num_games=100):
    tot_rew = 0
    state = env.reset()
    for _ in range(num_games):
        done = False
        while not done:
            next_state, reward, done, _ = env.step(policy[state])
            state = next_state
            tot_rew += reward
            if done:
                state = env.reset()
    print('Won %i of %i games!'%(tot_rew, num_games))
```

That's it.

It converges in about 7 iterations and wins approximately 85% of games:

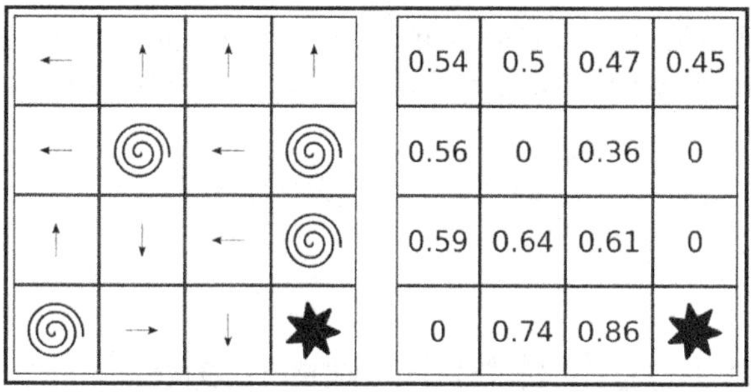

				0.54	0.5	0.47	0.45
				0.56	0	0.36	0
				0.59	0.64	0.61	0
				0	0.74	0.86	

Figure 3.5 Results of the FrozenLake game. The optimal policy is on the left and the optimal state values are on the right

The policy resulting from the code is shown on the left of figure 3.5. You can see that it takes strange directions, but it's only because it follows the dynamics of the environment. On the right of figure 3.5, the final state's values are presented.

Value iteration

Value iteration is the other dynamic programming algorithm to find optimal values in an MDP, but unlike policy iterations that execute policy evaluations and policy iterations in a loop, value iteration combines the two methods in a single update. In particular, it updates the value of a state by selecting the best action immediately:

$$V_{k+1}(s) = max_a \sum_{s',r} p(s'|s,a)[r + \gamma V_k(s')] \qquad (3.10)$$

The code for value iteration is even simpler than the policy iteration code, summarized in the following pseudocode:

```
Initialize V(s) for every state s
while V is not stable:
    > value iteration
    for each state s:
```
$$V(s) = max_a \sum_{s',r} p(s'|s,a)[r + \gamma V(s')]$$

```
    > compute the optimal policy:
```
$$\pi = argmax_a \sum_{s',r} p(s'|s,a)[r + \gamma V(s)]$$

The only difference is in the new value estimation update and in the absence of a proper policy iteration module. The resulting optimal policy is as follows:

$$\pi^* = argmax_a \sum_{s',r} p(s'|s,a)[r + \gamma V^*(s)] \qquad (3.11)$$

Value iteration applied to FrozenLake

We can now apply value iteration to the FrozenLake game in order to compare the two DP algorithms and to see whether they converge to the same policy and value function.

Let's define `eval_state_action` as before to estimate the action state value for a state-action pair:

```
def eval_state_action(V, s, a, gamma=0.99):
    return np.sum([p * (rew + gamma*V[next_s]) for p, next_s, rew, _ in env.P[s][a]])
```

Then, we create the main body of the value iteration algorithm:

```
def value_iteration(eps=0.0001):
    V = np.zeros(nS)
    it = 0
    while True:
        delta = 0
        # update the value for each state
        for s in range(nS):
            old_v = V[s]
            V[s] = np.max([eval_state_action(V, s, a) for a in range(nA)])
# equation 3.10
            delta = max(delta, np.abs(old_v - V[s]))
        # if stable, break the cycle
        if delta < eps:
            break
        else:
            print('Iter:', it, ' delta:', np.round(delta,5))
        it += 1
    return V
```

It loops until it reaches a steady value function (determined by the threshold, `eps`) and for each iteration, it updates the value of each state using formula (10).

As for the policy iteration, `run_episodes` executes some games to test the policy. The only difference is that in this case, the policy is determined at the same time that `run_episodes` is executed (for policy iteration, we defined the action for every state beforehand):

```
def run_episodes(env, V, num_games=100):
    tot_rew = 0
    state = env.reset()

    for _ in range(num_games):
        done = False

        while not done:
            # choose the best action using the value function
            action = np.argmax([eval_state_action(V, state, a) for a in range(nA)]) #(11)
            next_state, reward, done, _ = env.step(action)
```

```
            state = next_state
            tot_rew += reward
            if done:
                state = env.reset()

    print('Won %i of %i games!'%(tot_rew, num_games))
```

Finally, we can create the environment, unwrap it, run the value iteration, and execute some test games:

```
env = gym.make('FrozenLake-v0')
env = env.unwrapped

nA = env.action_space.n
nS = env.observation_space.n

V = value_iteration(eps=0.0001)
run_episodes(env, V, 100)
print(V.reshape((4,4)))
```

The output will be similar to the following:

```
Iter: 0 delta: 0.33333
Iter: 1 delta: 0.1463
Iter: 2 delta: 0.10854
...
Iter: 128 delta: 0.00011
Iter: 129 delta: 0.00011
Iter: 130 delta: 0.0001
Won 86 of 100 games!
[[0.54083394 0.49722378 0.46884941 0.45487071]
 [0.55739213 0.         0.35755091 0.        ]
 [0.5909355  0.64245898 0.61466487 0.        ]
 [0.         0.74129273 0.86262154 0.        ]]
```

The value iteration algorithm converges after 130 iterations. The resulting value function and policy are the same as the policy iteration algorithm.

Summary

An RL problem can be formalized as an MDP, providing an abstract framework for learning goal-based problems. An MDP is defined by a set of states, actions, rewards, and transition probabilities, and solving an MDP means finding a policy that maximizes the expected reward in each state. The Markov property is intrinsic to the MDP and ensures that the future states depend only on the current one, not on its history.

Using the definition of MDP, we formulated the concepts of policy, return function, expected return, action-value function, and value function. The latter two can be defined in terms of the values of the subsequent states, and the equations are called Bellman equations. These equations are useful because they provide a method to compute value functions in an iterative way. The optimal value functions can then be used to find the optimal policy.

RL algorithms can be categorized as model-based or model-free. While the former requires a model of the environment to plan the next actions, the latter is independent of the model and can learn by direct interaction with the environment. Model-free algorithms can be further divided into policy gradient and value function algorithms. Policy gradient algorithms learn directly from the policy through gradient ascent and are typically on-policy. Value function algorithms are usually off-policy, and learn an action-value function or value function in order to create the policy. These two methods can be brought together to give rise to methods that combine the advantages of both worlds.

DP is the first set of model-based algorithms that we looked at in depth. It is used whenever the full model of the environment is known and when it is constituted by a limited number of states and actions. DP algorithms use bootstrapping to estimate the value of a state and they learn the optimal policy through two processes: policy evaluation and policy improvement. Policy evaluation computes the state value function for an arbitrary policy, while policy improvement improves the policy using the value function obtained from the policy evaluation process.

By combining policy improvement and policy evaluation, the policy iteration algorithm and the value iteration algorithm can be created. The main difference between the two is that while policy iteration runs iteratively of policy evaluation and policy improvement, value iteration combines the two processes in a single update.

Though DP suffers from the curse of dimensionality (the complexity grows exponentially with the number of states), the ideas behind policy evaluation and policy iteration are key in almost all RL algorithms because they use a generalized version of them.

Another disadvantage of DP is that it requires the exact model of the environment, limiting its applicability to many other problems.

In the next chapter, you'll see how V-functions and Q-functions can be used to learn a policy, using problems where the model is unknown by sampling directly from the environment.

Questions

1. What's an MDP?
2. What's a stochastic policy?
3. How can a return function be defined in terms of the return at the next time step?
4. Why is the Bellman equation so important?
5. What are the limiting factors of DP algorithms?
6. What is policy evaluation?
7. How do policy iteration and value iteration differ?

Further reading

- Sutton and Barto, *Reinforcement Learning*, Chapters 3 and 4

Section 2: Model-Free RL Algorithms

This section introduces model-free RL algorithms, value-based methods, and policy gradient methods. You will also develop many state-of-the-art algorithms.

This section includes the following chapters:

- Chapter 4, *Q-Learning and SARSA Applications*
- Chapter 5, *Deep Q-Network*
- Chapter 6, *Learning Stochastic and PG Optimization*
- Chapter 7, *TRPO and PPO Implementation*
- Chapter 8, *DDPG and TD3 Applications*

Section 2. Model-Free RL Algorithms

4
Q-Learning and SARSA Applications

Dynamic programming (DP) algorithms are effective for solving **reinforcement learning** (RL) problems, but they require two strong assumptions. The first is that the model of the environment has to be known, and the second is that the state space has to be small enough so that it does not suffer from the curse of dimensionality problem.

In this chapter, we'll develop a class of algorithms that get rid of the first assumption. In addition, it is a class of algorithms that aren't affected by the problem of the curse of dimensionality of DP algorithms. These algorithms learn directly from the environment and from the experience, estimating the value function based on many returns, and do not compute the expectation of the state values using the model, in contrast with DP algorithms. In this new setting, we'll talk about experience as a way to learn value functions. We'll take a look at the problems that arise from learning a policy through mere interactions with the environment and the techniques that can be used to solve them. After a brief introduction to this new approach, you'll learn about **temporal difference** (TD) learning, a powerful way to learn optimal policies from experience. TD learning uses ideas from DP algorithms while using only information gained from interactions with the environment. Two temporal difference learning algorithms are SARSA and Q-learning. Though they are very similar and both guarantee convergence in tabular cases, they have interesting differences that are worth acknowledging. Q-learning is a key algorithm, and many state-of-the-art RL algorithms combined with other techniques use this method, as we will see in later chapters.

Q-Learning and SARSA Applications

To gain a better grasp on TD learning and to understand how to move from theory to practice, you'll implement Q-learning and SARSA in a new game. Then, we'll elaborate on the difference between the two algorithms, both in terms of their performance and use.

The following topics will be covered in this chapter:

- Learning without a model
- TD learning
- SARSA
- Applying SARSA to Taxi-v2
- Q-learning
- Applying Q-learning to Taxi-v2

Learning without a model

By definition, the value function of a policy is the expected return (that is, the sum of discounted rewards) of that policy starting from a given state:

$$V_\pi(s) = E_\pi[G|s_0 = s]$$

Following the reasoning of Chapter 3, *Solving Problems with Dynamic Programming*, DP algorithms update state values by computing expectations for all the next states of their values:

$$V_{k+1}(s) = E_\pi[r_t + \gamma V_k(s_{t+1})|s_t = s] = \sum_a \pi(s,a) \sum_{s',r} p(s'|s,a)[r + \gamma V_k(s')]$$

Unfortunately, computing the value function means that you need to know the state transition probabilities. In fact, DP algorithms use the model of the environment to obtain those probabilities. But the major concern is what to do when it's not available. The best answer is to gain all the information by interacting with the environment. If done well, it works because by sampling from the environment a substantial number of times, you should able to approximate the expectation and have a good estimation of the value function.

Chapter 4

User experience

Now, the first thing we need to clarify is how to sample from the environment, and how to interact with it to get usable information about its dynamics:

Figure 4.1. A trajectory that starts from state s_t

[79]

The simple way to do this is to execute the current policy until the end of the episode. You would end up with a trajectory as shown in figure 4.1. Once the episode terminates, the return values can be computed for each state by backpropagating upward the sum of the rewards, $r_t..r_{t+n}$. Repeating this process multiple times (that is, running multiple trajectories) for every state would have multiple return values. The return values are then averaged for each state to compute the expected returns. The expected returns computed in such a way is an approximated value function. The execution of a policy until a terminal state is called a trajectory or an episode. The more trajectories are run, the more returns are observed and by the law of large numbers, the average of these estimations will converge to the expected value.

Like DP, the algorithms that learn a policy by direct interaction with the environment rely on the concepts of policy evaluation and policy improvement. Policy evaluation is the act of estimating the value function of a policy, while policy improvement uses the estimates made in the previous phase to improve the policy.

Policy evaluation

We just saw how using real experience to estimate the value function is an easy process. It is about running the policy in an environment until a final state is reached, then computing the return value and averaging the sampled return, as can be seen in equation (1):

$$V(s_t) = \frac{1}{N} \sum_{i=0}^{N} (G_t^i) \qquad (1)$$

Thus the expected return of a state can be approximated from the experience by averaging the sampling episodes from that state. The methods that estimate the return function using (1) are called **Monte Carlo methods**. Until all of the state-action pairs are visited and enough trajectory has been sampled, Monte Carlo methods guarantee convergence to the optimal policy.

The exploration problem

How can we guarantee that every action of each state is chosen? And why is that so important? We will first answer the latter question, and then show how we can (at least in theory) explore the environment to reach every possible state.

Why explore?

The trajectories are sampled following a policy that can be stochastic or deterministic. In the case of a deterministic policy, each time a trajectory is sampled, the visited states will always be the same, and the update of the value function will take into account only this limited set of states. This will considerably limit your knowledge about the environment. It is like learning from a teacher that never changes their opinion on a subject—you will be stuck with those ideas without learning about others.

Thus the exploration of the environment is crucial if you want to achieve good results, and it ensures that there are no better policies that could be found.

On the other hand, if a policy is designed in such a way that it explores the environment constantly without taking into consideration what has already been learned, the achievement of a good policy is very difficult, perhaps even impossible. This balance between exploration and exploitation (behaving according to the best policy currently available) is called the exploration-exploitation dilemma and will be considered in greater detail in Chapter 12, *Developing an ESBAS Algorithm*.

How to explore

A very effective method that can be used when dealing with such situations is called ϵ-greedy exploration. It is about acting randomly with probability ϵ while acting greedily (that means choosing the best action) with probability $1 - \epsilon$. For example, if $\epsilon = 0.8$, on average, for every 10 actions, the agent will act randomly 8 times.

To avoid exploring too much in later stages when the agent is confident about its knowledge, ϵ can decrease over time. This strategy is called **epsilon-decay**. With this variation, an initial stochastic policy will gradually converge to a deterministic and, hopefully, optimal policy.

There are many other exploration techniques (such as Boltzmann exploration) that are more accurate, but they are also quite complicated, and for the purpose of this chapter, ϵ-greedy is a perfect choice.

TD learning

Monte Carlo methods are a powerful way to learn directly by sampling from the environment, but they have a big drawback—they rely on the full trajectory. They have to wait until the end of the episode, and only then can they update the state values. Therefore, a crucial factor is knowing what happens when the trajectory has no end, or if it's very long. The answer is that it will produce terrifying results. A similar solution to this problem has already come up in DP algorithms, where the state values are updated at each step, without waiting until the end. Instead of using the complete return accumulated during the trajectory, it just uses the immediate reward and the estimate of the next state value. A visual example of this update is given in figure 4.2 and shows the parts involved in a single step of learning. This technique is called **bootstrapping**, and it is not only useful for long or potentially infinite episodes, but for episodes of any length. The first reason for this is that it helps to decrease the variance of the expected return. The variance is decreased because the state values depend only on the immediate next reward and not on all the rewards of the trajectory. The second reason is that the learning process takes place at every step, making these algorithms learn online. For this reason, it is called one-step learning. In contrast, Monte Carlo methods are offline as they use the information only after the conclusion of the episode. Methods that learn online using bootstrapping are called TD learning methods.

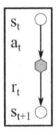

Figure 4.2. One-step learning update with bootstrapping

TD learning can be viewed as a combination of Monte Carlo methods and DP because they use the idea of sampling from the former and the idea of bootstrapping from the latter. TD learning is widely used all across RL algorithms, and it constitutes the core of many of these algorithms. The algorithms that will be presented later in this chapter (namely SARSA and Q-learning) are all one-step, tabular, model-free (meaning that they don't use the model of the environment) TD methods.

TD update

From the previous chapter, *Solving Problems with Dynamic Programming* we know the following:

$$V_\pi(s) = E_\pi[G_t|s_t = s] \qquad (2)$$

Empirically, the Monte Carlo update estimates this value by averaging returns from multiple full trajectories. Developing the equation further, we obtain the following:

$$\begin{aligned} E_\pi[G_t|s_t = s] \\ = E_\pi[r_t + \gamma G_{t+1}|s_t = s] \\ = E_\pi[r_t + \gamma V_\pi(s_{t+1})]|s_t = s] \end{aligned} \qquad (3)$$

The preceding equation is approximated by the DP algorithms. The difference is that TD algorithms estimate the expected value instead of computing it. The estimate is done in the same way as Monte Carlo methods do, by averaging:

$$E_\pi[r_t + \gamma V_\pi(s_{t+1})]|s_t = s] \approx \frac{1}{N}\sum_{i=0}^{N} \pi[r_t^i + \gamma V_\pi(s_{t+1}^i)]|s_t = s]$$

In practice, instead of calculating the average, the TD update is carried out by improving the state value by a small amount toward the optimal value:

$$V(s_t) \leftarrow V(s_t) + \alpha[r + \gamma V(s_{t+1}) - V(s_t)] \qquad (4)$$

α is a constant that establishes how much the state value should change at each update. If $\alpha = 0$, then the state value will not change at all. Instead, if $\alpha = 1$, the state value will be equal to $r + \gamma V(s_{t+1})$ (called the **TD target**) and it will completely forget the previous value. In practice, we don't want these extreme cases, and usually α ranges from 0.5 to 0.001.

Policy improvement

TD learning converges to the optimal condition as long as each action of every state has a probability of greater than zero of being chosen. To satisfy this requirement, TD methods, as we saw in the previous section, have to explore the environment. Indeed, the exploration can be carried out using an ϵ-greedy policy. It makes sure that both greedy actions and random actions are chosen in order to ensure both the exploitation and exploration of the environment.

Comparing Monte Carlo and TD

An important of both Monte Carlo TD methods is that they converge to an optimal solution as long as they deal with tabular cases (meaning that state values are stored in tables or arrays) and have an exploratory strategy. Nonetheless, they differ in the way they update the value function. Overall, TD learning has lower variance but suffers from a higher bias than Monte Carlo learning. In addition to this, TD methods are generally faster in practice and are preferred to Monte Carlo methods.

SARSA

So far, we have presented TD learning as a general way to estimate a value function for a given policy. In practice, TD cannot be used as it is because it lacks the primary component to actually improve the policy. SARSA and Q-learning are two one-step, tabular TD algorithms that both estimate the value functions and optimize the policy, and that can actually be used in a great variety of RL problems. In this section, we will use SARSA to learn an optimal policy for a given MDP. Then, we'll introduce Q-learning.

A concern with TD learning is that it estimates the value of a state. Think about that. In a given state, how can you choose the action with the highest next state value? Earlier, we said that you should pick the action that will move the agent to the state with the highest value. However, without a model of the environment that provides a list of the possible next states, you cannot know which action will move the agent to that state. SARSA, instead of learning the value function, learns and applies the state-action function, Q. $Q(s,a)$ tells the value of a state, s, if the action, a, is taken.

Chapter 4

The algorithm

Basically, all the observations we have done for the TD update are also valid for SARSA. Once we apply them to the definition of Q-function, we obtain the SARSA update:

$$Q(s_t, a_t) \leftarrow Q(s_t, a_t) + \alpha[r_t + \gamma Q(s_{t+1}, a_{t+1}) - Q(s_t, a_t)] \qquad (5)$$

α is a coefficient that determines how much the action value has been updated. γ is the discount factor, a coefficient between 0 and 1 used to give less importance to the values that come from distant future decisions (short-term actions are preferred to long-term ones). A visual interpretation of the SARSA update is given in figure 4.3.

The name SARSA comes from the update that is based on the state, s_t; the action, a_t, the reward, r_t; the next state, s_{t+1}; and finally, the next action, a_{t+1}. Putting everything together, it forms s, a, r, s, a, as can be seen in figure 4.3:

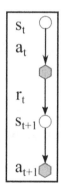

Figure 4.3 SARSA update

SARSA is an on-policy algorithm. On-policy means that the policy that is used to collect experience through interaction with the environment (called a behavior policy) is the same policy that is updated. The on-policy nature of the method is due to the use of the current policy to select the next action, a_{t+1}, to estimate $Q(s_{t+1}, a_{t+1})$, and the assumption that in the following action it will follow the same policy (that is, it acts according to action a_{t+1}).

Q-Learning and SARSA Applications

On-policy algorithms are usually easier than off-policy algorithms, but they are less powerful and usually require more data to learn. Despite this, as for TD learning, SARSA is guaranteed to converge to the optimal policy if it visits every state-action an infinite number of times and the policy, over time, becomes a deterministic one. Practical algorithms use an ϵ-greedy policy with a decay that tends to be zero, or a value close to it. The pseudocode of SARSA is summarized in the following code block. In the pseudocode, we used an ϵ-greedy policy, but any strategy that encourages exploration can be used:

```
Initialize Q(s,a) for every state-action pair
α ∈ (0,1], γ ∈ (0,1]

for N episodes:
    s_t = env_start()
    a_t = egreedy(Q, s_t)

    while s_t is not a final state:
        r_t, s_{t+1} = env(a_t)   # env() take a step in the environment
        a_{t+1} = egreedy(Q, s_{t+1})
        Q(s_t, a_t) ← Q(s_t, a_t) + α[r_t + γQ(s_{t+1}, a_{t+1}) − Q(s_t, a_t)]
        s_t = s_{t+1}
        a_t = a_{t+1}
```

egreedy() is a function that implements the $\epsilon - greedy$ strategy. Note that SARSA executes the same action that has been selected and used in the previous step to update the state-action value.

Applying SARSA to Taxi-v2

After a more theoretical view of TD learning and particularly of SARSA, we are finally able to implement SARSA to solve problems of interest. As we saw previously, SARSA can be applied to environments with unknown models and dynamics, but as it is a tabular algorithm with scalability constraints, it can only be applied to environments with small and discrete action and state spaces. So, we choose to apply SARSA to a gym environment called Taxi-v2 that satisfies all the requirements and is a good test bed for these kinds of algorithm.

Taxi-v2 is a game that was introduced to study hierarchical reinforcement learning (a type of RL algorithm that creates a hierarchy of policies, each with the goal of solving a subtask) where the aim is to pick up a passenger and drop them at a precise location. A reward of +20 is earned when the taxi performs a successful drop-off, but a penalty of -10 is incurred for illegal pickup or drop-off. Moreover, a point is lost for every timestep. The render of the game is given in figure 4.4. There are six legal moves corresponding to the four directions, the pickup, and the drop-off actions. In figure 4.4, the : symbol represents an empty location; the | symbol represents a wall that the taxi can't travel through; and R, G, Y, B are the four locations. The taxi, the yellow rectangle in the diagram, has to pick up a person in the location identified by the light blue color and drop them off in the location identified by the color violet.

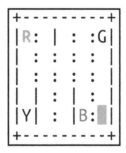

Figure 4.4 Start state of the Taxi-v2 environment

The implementation is fairly straightforward and follows the pseudocode given in the previous section. Though we explain and show all the code here, it is also available on the GitHub repository of the book.

Let's first implement the main function, SARSA(..), of the SARSA algorithm, which does most of the work. After this, we'll implement a couple of auxiliary functions that perform simple but essential tasks.

SARSA needs an environment and a few other hyperparameters as arguments to work:

- A learning rate, lr, previously called α, that controls the amount of learning at each update.
- num_episodes speaks for itself because it is the number of episodes that SARSA will execute before terminating.
- eps is the initial value of the randomness of the ϵ-greedy policy.
- gamma is the discount factor used to give less importance to actions more in the future.
- eps_decay is the linear decrement of eps across episodes.

The first lines of code are as follows:

```
def SARSA(env, lr=0.01, num_episodes=10000, eps=0.3, gamma=0.95,
eps_decay=0.00005):
    nA = env.action_space.n
    nS = env.observation_space.n
    test_rewards = []
    Q = np.zeros((nS, nA))
    games_reward = []
```

Here, some variables are initialized. `nA` and `nS` are the numbers of actions and observations respectively of the environment, `Q` is the matrix that will contain the Q-values of each state-action pair, and `test_rewards` and `games_rewards` are lists used later to hold information about the scores of the games.

Next, we can implement the main loop that learns the Q-values:

```
for ep in range(num_episodes):
    state = env.reset()
    done = False
    tot_rew = 0
    
    if eps > 0.01:
        eps -= eps_decay
    
    action = eps_greedy(Q, state, eps)
```

Line 2 in the preceding code block resets the environment on each new episode and stores the current state of the environment. Line 3 initializes a Boolean variable that will be set to `True` when the environment is in a terminal state. The following two lines update the `eps` variable until it has a value higher than 0.01. We set this threshold to keep, in the long run, a minimum rate of exploration of the environment. The last line chooses an ϵ-greedy action based on the current state and the Q-matrix. We'll define this function later.

Now that we have taken care of the initialization needed at the start of each episode and have chosen the first action, we can loop until the episode (the game) ends. The following piece of code samples from the environment and updates the following Q-function, as per formula (5):

```
while not done:
    next_state, rew, done, _ = env.step(action) # Take one step in the environment
    
    next_action = eps_greedy(Q, next_state, eps)
    Q[state][action] = Q[state][action] + lr*(rew + gamma*Q[next_state][next_action] - Q[state][action]) # (4.5)
```

```
            state = next_state
            action = next_action
        tot_rew += rew
        if done:
            games_reward.append(tot_rew)
```

`done` holds a Boolean value that indicates whether the agent is still interacting with the environment, as can be seen in line 2. Therefore, to loop for a complete episode is the same as iterating as long as `done` is `False` (the first line of the code). Then, as usual, `env.step` returns the next state, the reward, the done flag, and an information string. In the next line, `eps_greedy` chooses the next action based on the `next_state` and the Q-values. The heart of the SARSA algorithm is contained in the subsequent line, which performs the update as per formula (5). Besides the learning rate and the gamma coefficient, it uses the reward obtained in the last step and the values held in the `Q` array.

The final lines set the state and action as the previous one, adds the reward to the total reward of the game, and if the environment is in a final state, the sum of the rewards is appended to `games_reward` and the inner cycle terminates.

In the last lines of the `SARSA` function, every 300 epochs, we run 1,000 test games and print information such as the epoch, the `eps` value, and the mean of the test rewards. Moreover, we return the `Q` array:

```
    if (ep % 300) == 0:
        test_rew = run_episodes(env, Q, 1000)
        print("Episode:{:5d} Eps:{:2.4f} Rew:{:2.4f}".format(ep, eps, test_rew))
        test_rewards.append(test_rew)
return Q
```

We can now implement the `eps_greedy` function, which chooses a random action from those that are allowed with probability, `eps`. To do this, it just samples a uniform number between 0 and 1, and if this is smaller than `eps`, it selects a random action. Otherwise, it selects a greedy action:

```
def eps_greedy(Q, s, eps=0.1):
    if np.random.uniform(0,1) < eps:
        # Choose a random action
        return np.random.randint(Q.shape[1])
    else:
    # Choose the greedy action
    return greedy(Q, s)
```

The greedy policy is implemented by returning the index that corresponds to the maximum Q value in state s:

```
def greedy(Q, s):
    return np.argmax(Q[s])
```

The last function to implement is `run_episodes`, which runs a few episodes to test the policy. The policy used to select the actions is the greedy policy. That's because we don't want to explore while testing. Overall, the function is almost identical to the one implemented in the previous chapter for the dynamic programming algorithms:

```
def run_episodes(env, Q, num_episodes=100, to_print=False):
    tot_rew = []
    state = env.reset()
    for _ in range(num_episodes):
        done = False
        game_rew = 0
        while not done:
            next_state, rew, done, _ = env.step(greedy(Q, state))
            state = next_state
            game_rew += rew
            if done:
                state = env.reset()
                tot_rew.append(game_rew)
    if to_print:
        print('Mean score: %.3f of %i games!'%(np.mean(tot_rew), num_episodes))
    else:
        return np.mean(tot_rew)
```

Great!

Now we're almost done. The last part involves only creating and resetting the environment and the call to the SARSA function, passing the environment along with all the hyperparameters:

```
if __name__ == '__main__':
    env = gym.make('Taxi-v2')
    env.reset()
    Q = SARSA(env, lr=.1, num_episodes=5000, eps=0.4, gamma=0.95, eps_decay=0.001)
```

Chapter 4

As you can see, we start with an `eps` of 0.4. This means that the first actions will be random with a probability of 0.4 and because of the decay, it will decrease until it reaches the minimum value of 0.01 (that is, the threshold we set in the code):

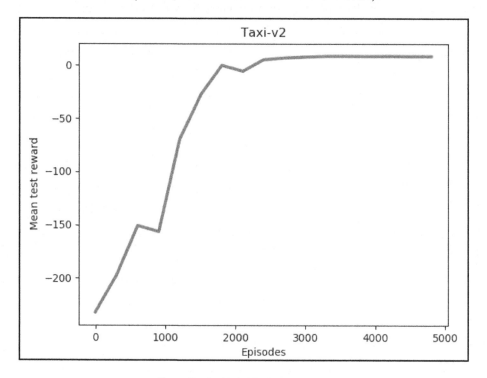

Figure 4.5 Results of the SARSA algorithm on Taxi-v2

Q-Learning and SARSA Applications

The performance plot of the test games' cumulative rewards is shown in figure 4.5. Moreover, figure 4.6 shows a complete episode run with the final policy. It has to be read from left to right and from top to bottom. We can see that the taxi (highlighted in yellow first, and green later) has driven along an optimal path in both directions.

```
+---------+  +---------+  +---------+  +---------+  +---------+  +---------+
|R: | : :G|  |R: | : :G|  |R: | : :G|  |R: | : :G|  |R: | : :G|  |R: | : :G|
| : : : : |  | : : : : |  | : : : : |  | : : : : |  | : : : : |  | : : : : |
| : : : : |  | : : :▌: |  | : : :▌: |  | : :▌: : |  | :▌: : : |  |▌: : : : |
| | : | : |  | | : |▌ |  | | : | : |  | | : | : |  | | : | : |  | | : | : |
|Y| : |▌: |  |Y| : |B: |  |Y| : |B: |  |Y| : |B: |  |Y| : |B: |  |Y| : |B: |
+---------+  +---------+  +---------+  +---------+  +---------+  +---------+
  (North)      (North)      (West)       (West)       (West)

+---------+  +---------+  +---------+  +---------+  +---------+  +---------+
|R: | : :G|  |R: | : :G|  |R: | : :G|  |R: | : :G|  |R: | : :G|  |R: | : :G|
| : : : : |  | : : : : |  | : : : : |  | : : : : |  |▌: : : : |  | :▌: : : |
|▌: : : : |  | : : : : |  | : : : : |  |▌: : : : |  | | : | : |  | | : | : |
|▌| : | : |  | |▌: | : |  | |▌: | : |  |▌| : | : |  |Y| : |B: |  |Y| : |B: |
|Y| : |B: |  |▌| : |B: |  |Y| : |B: |  |Y| : |B: |  |Y| : |B: |  |Y| : |B: |
+---------+  +---------+  +---------+  +---------+  +---------+  +---------+
  (South)      (South)     (Pickup)     (North)      (North)      (East)

+---------+  +---------+  +---------+  +---------+
|R: | : :G|  |R: | : :G|  |R: | : :G|  |R: | : :G|
| : : : : |  | : : : : |  | : : : : |  | : : : : |
| : :▌: : |  | : : :▌: |  | : : : : |  | : : : : |
| | : | : |  | | : | : |  | | : |▌: |  | | : |▌: |
|Y| : |B: |  |Y| : |B: |  |Y| : |B: |  |Y| : |▌: |
+---------+  +---------+  +---------+  +---------+
  (East)       (East)       (South)      (South)
```

Figure 4.6 Render of the Taxi game. The policy derives from the Q-values trained with SARSA

 For all the color references mentioned in the chapter, please refer to the color images bundle at `http://www.packtpub.com/sites/default/files/downloads/9781789131116_ColorImages.pdf`.

To have a better view of the algorithm and all the hyperparameters, we suggest you play with them, change them, and observe the results. You can also try to use an exponential ϵ-decay rate instead of a linear one. You learn by doing just as RL algorithms do, by trial and error.

Q-learning

Q-learning is another TD algorithm with some very useful and distinct features from SARSA. Q-learning inherits from TD learning all the characteristics of one-step learning (from TD learning, that is, the ability of learning at each step) and the characteristic to learn from experience without a proper model of the environment.

The most distinctive feature about Q-learning compared to SARSA is that it's an off-policy algorithm. As a reminder, off-policy means that the update can be made independently from whichever policy has gathered the experience. This means that off-policy algorithms can use old experiences to improve the policy. To distinguish between the policy that interacts with the environment and the one that actually improves, we call the former a behavior policy and the latter a target policy.

Here, we'll explain the more primitive version of the algorithm that copes with tabular cases, but it can easily be adapted to work with function approximators such as artificial neural networks. In fact, in the next chapter, we'll implement a more sophisticated version of this algorithm that is able to use deep neural networks and that also uses previous experiences to exploit the full capabilities of the off-policy algorithms.

But first, let's see how Q-learning works, formalize the update rule, and create a pseudocode version of it to unify all the components.

Theory

The idea of Q-learning is to approximate the Q-function by using the current optimal action value. The Q-learning update is very similar to the update done in SARSA, with the exception that it takes the maximum state-action value:

$$Q(s_t, a_t) \leftarrow Q(s_t, a_t) + \alpha[r_t + \gamma max_a Q(s_{t+1}, a) - Q(s_t, a_t)] \qquad (6)$$

α is the usual learning rate and γ is the discount factor.

Q-Learning and SARSA Applications

While the SARSA update is done on the behavior policy (like a ϵ-greedy policy), the Q-update is done on the greedy target policy that results from the maximum action value. If this concept is not clear yet, take a look at figure 4.7. While in SARSA we had figure 4.3, where both actions a_t and a_{t+1} come from the same policy, in Q-learning, action a_{t+1} is chosen based on the next maximum state-action value. Because an update in Q-learning is not more dependent on the behavior policy (which is used only for sampling from the environment), it becomes an off-policy algorithm.

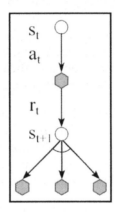

Figure 4.7. Q-learning update

The algorithm

As Q-learning is a TD method, it needs a behavior policy that, as time passes, will converge to a deterministic policy. A good strategy is to use an ϵ-greedy policy with linear or exponential decay (as has been done for SARSA).

To recap, the Q-learning algorithm uses the following:

- A target greedy policy that constantly improves
- A behavior ϵ-greedy policy to interact with and explore the environment

After these conclusive observations, we can finally come up with the following pseudocode for the Q-learning algorithm:

```
Initialize Q(s,a) for every state-action pair
α ∈ (0, 1], γ ∈ (0, 1]

for N episodes:
    s_t = env_start()
```

```
while s_t is not a final state:
    a_t = εgreedy(Q, s_t)
```
$r_t, s_{t+1} = env(a_t)$ `# env() take a step in the environment`
$Q(s_t, a_t) \leftarrow Q(s_t, a_t) + \alpha[r_t + \gamma max_a Q(s_{t+1}, a) - Q(s_t, a_t)]$
$s_t = s_{t+1}$

In practice, α usually has values between 0.5 and 0.001 and γ ranges from 0.9 to 0.999.

Applying Q-learning to Taxi-v2

In general, Q-learning can be used to solve the same kinds of problems that can be tackled with SARSA, and because they both come from the same family (TD learning), they generally have similar performances. Nevertheless, in some specific problems, one approach can be preferred to the other. So it's useful to also know how Q-learning is implemented.

For this reason, here we'll implement Q-learning to solve Taxi-v2, the same environment that was used for SARSA. But be aware that with just a few adaptations, it can be used with every other environment with the correct characteristics. Having the results from both Q-learning and SARSA from the same environment we'll have the opportunity to compare their performance.

To be as consistent as possible, we kept some functions unchanged from the SARSA implementation. These are as follows:

- `eps_greedy(Q, s, eps)` is the ϵ-greedy policy that takes a Q matrix, a state s, and the eps value. It returns an action.
- `greedy(Q, s)` is the greedy policy that takes a Q matrix and a state s. It returns the action associated with the maximum Q-value in the state s.
- `run_episodes(env, Q, num_episodes, to_print)` is a function that runs num_episodes games to test the greedy policy associated with the Q matrix. If to_print is True it prints the results. Otherwise, it returns the mean of the rewards.

Q-Learning and SARSA Applications

To see the implementation of those functions, you can refer to the *SARSA applied to Taxi-v2* section or the GitHub repository of the book, which can be found at https://github.com/PacktPublishing/Reinforcement-Learning-Algorithms-with-Python.

The main function that executes the Q-learning algorithm takes an environment, env; a learning rate, lr (the α variable used in (6)); the number of episodes to train the algorithm, num_episodes; the initial ϵ value, eps, used by the ϵ-greedy policy; the decay rate, eps_decay; and the discount factor, gamma, as arguments:

```python
def Q_learning(env, lr=0.01, num_episodes=10000, eps=0.3, gamma=0.95, eps_decay=0.00005):
    nA = env.action_space.n
    nS = env.observation_space.n

    # Q(s,a) -> each row is a different state and each columns represent a different action
    Q = np.zeros((nS, nA))

    games_reward = []
    test_rewards = []
```

The first lines of the function initialize the variables with the dimensions of the action and observation space, initialize the array Q that contains the Q-value of each state-action pair, and create empty lists used to keep track of the progress of the algorithm.

Then, we can implement the cycle that iterates num_episodes times:

```python
    for ep in range(num_episodes):
        state = env.reset()
        done = False
        tot_rew = 0
        if eps > 0.01:
            eps -= eps_decay
```

Each iteration (that is, each episode) starts by resetting the environment, initializing the done and tot_rew variables, and decreasing eps linearly.

Then, we have to iterate across all of the timesteps of an episode (that correspond to an episode) because that is where the Q-learning update takes place:

```python
        while not done:
            action = eps_greedy(Q, state, eps)
            next_state, rew, done, _ = env.step(action) # Take one step in the environment

            # get the max Q value for the next state
```

```
            Q[state][action] = Q[state][action] + lr*(rew +
gamma*np.max(Q[next_state]) - Q[state][action]) # (4.6)
            state = next_state
            tot_rew += rew

            if done:
                games_reward.append(tot_rew)
```

This is the main body of the algorithm. The flow is fairly standard:

1. The action is chosen following the ϵ-greedy policy (the behavior policy).
2. The action is executed in the environment, which returns the next state, a reward, and the done flag.
3. The action-state value is updated based on formula (6).
4. `next_state` is assigned to the `state` variable.
5. The reward of the last step is added up to the cumulative reward of the episode.
6. If it was the final step, the reward is stored in `games_reward` and the cycle terminates.

In the end, every 300 iterations of the outer cycle, we can run 1,000 games to test the agent, print some useful information, and return the Q array:

```
        if (ep % 300) == 0:
            test_rew = run_episodes(env, Q, 1000)
            print("Episode:{:5d} Eps:{:2.4f} Rew:{:2.4f}".format(ep, eps, test_rew))
            test_rewards.append(test_rew)
    return Q
```

That's everything. As a final step, in the `main` function, we can create the environment and run the algorithm:

```
if __name__ == '__main__':
    env = gym.make('Taxi-v2')
    Q = Q_learning(env, lr=.1, num_episodes=5000, eps=0.4, gamma=0.95, eps_decay=0.001)
```

The algorithm reaches steady results after about 3,000 episodes, as can be deduced from figure 4.8. This plot can be created by plotting `test_rewards`:

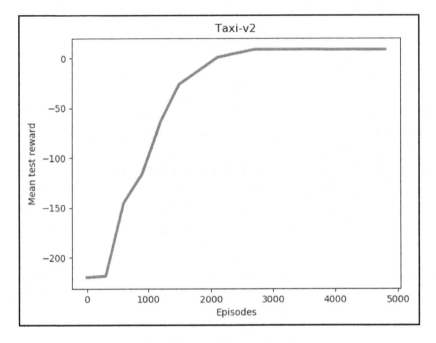

Figure 4.8 The results of Q-learning on Taxi-v2

As usual, we suggest that you tune the hyperparameters and play with the implementation to gain better insight into the algorithm.

Overall, the algorithm has found a policy similar to the one found by the SARSA algorithm. To find it by yourself, you can render some episodes or print the greedy action resulting from the Q array.

Comparing SARSA and Q-learning

We will now look at a quick comparison of the two algorithms. In figure 4.9, the performance of Q-learning and SARSA in the Taxi-v2 environment is plotted as the episode progresses. We can see that both are converging to the same value (and to the same policy) with comparable speed. While doing these comparisons, you have to consider that the environment and the algorithms are stochastic and they may produce different results. We can also see from plot 4.9 that Q-learning has a more regular shape. This is due to the fact that it is more robust and less sensitive to change:

Chapter 4

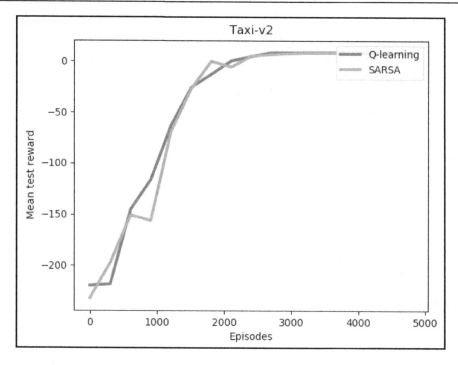

Figure 4.9 Comparison of the results between SARSA and Q-learning on Taxi-v2

So, is it better to use Q-learning? Overall, the answer is yes, and in most cases, Q-learning outperforms the other algorithms, but there are some environments in which SARSA works better. The choice between the two is dependent on the environment and the task.

Summary

In this chapter, we introduced a new family of RL algorithms that learn from experience by interacting with the environment. These methods differ from dynamic programming in their ability to learn a value function and consequently a policy without relying on the model of the environment.

Initially, we saw that Monte Carlo methods are a simple way to sample from the environment but because they need the full trajectory before starting to learn, they are not applicable in many real problems. To overcome these drawbacks, bootstrapping can be combined with Monte Carlo methods, giving rise to so-called temporal difference (TD) learning. Thanks to the bootstrapping technique, these algorithms can learn online (one-step learning) and reduce the variance while still converging to optimal policies. Then, we learned two one-step, tabular, model-free TD methods, namely SARSA and Q-learning. SARSA is on-policy because it updates a state value by choosing the action based on the current policy (the behavior policy). Q-learning, instead, is off-policy because it estimates the state value of a greedy policy while collecting experience using a different policy (the behavior policy). This difference between SARSA and Q-learning makes the latter slightly more robust and efficient than the former.

Every TD method needs to explore the environment in order to know it well and find the optimal policies. The exploration of the environment is in the hands of the behavior policy, which occasionally has to act non-greedily, for example, by following an ϵ-greedy policy.

We implemented both SARSA and Q-learning and applied them to a tabular game called Taxi. We saw that both converge to the optimal policy with similar results.

The Q-learning algorithm is key in RL because of its qualities. Moreover, through careful design, it can be adapted to work with very complex and high-dimensional games. All of this is possible thanks to the use of function approximations such as deep neural networks. In the next chapter, we'll elaborate on this, and introduce a deep Q-network that can learn to play Atari games directly from pixels.

Questions

- What's the main property of the Monte Carlo method used in RL?
- Why are Monte Carlo methods offline?
- What are the two main ideas of TD learning?
- What are the differences between Monte Carlo and TD?
- Why is exploration important in TD learning?
- Why is Q-learning off-policy?

5
Deep Q-Network

So far, we've approached and developed reinforcement learning algorithms that learn about a value function, V, for each state, or an action-value function, Q, for each action-state pair. These methods involve storing and updating each value separately in a table (or an array). These approaches do not scale because, for a large number of states and actions, the table's dimensions increase exponentially and can easily exceed the available memory capacity.

In this chapter, we will introduce the use of function approximation in reinforcement learning algorithms to overcome this problem. In particular, we will focus on deep neural networks that are applied to Q-learning. In the first part of this chapter, we'll explain how to extend Q-learning with function approximation to store Q values, and we'll explore some major difficulties that we may face. In the second part, we will present a new algorithm called **Deep Q-network (DQN)**, which using new ideas, offers an elegant solution to some challenges that are found in the vanilla version of Q-learning with neural networks. You'll see how this algorithm achieves surprising results on a wide variety of games that learn only from pixels. Moreover, you'll implement this algorithm and apply it to Pong, and see some of its strengths and vulnerabilities for yourself.

Since DQN was proposed, other researchers have proposed many variations that provide more stability and efficiency for the algorithm. We'll quickly look at and implement some of them so that we have a better understanding of the weaknesses of the basic version of DQN and so that we can provide you with some ideas so that you can improve it yourself.

The following topics will be covered in this chapter:

- Deep neural networks and Q-learning
- DQN
- DQN applied to Pong
- DQN variations

Deep neural networks and Q-learning

The Q-learning algorithm, as we saw in Chapter 4, *Q-Learning and SARSA Applications*, has many qualities that enable its application in many real-world contexts. A key ingredient of this algorithm is that it makes use of the Bellman equation for learning the Q-function. The Bellman equation, as used by the Q-learning algorithm, enables the updating of Q-values from subsequent state-action values. This makes the algorithm able to learn at every step, without waiting until the trajectory is completed. Also, every state or action-state pair has its own values stored in a lookup table that saves and retrieves the corresponding values. Being designed in this way, Q-learning converges to optimal values as long as all the state-action pairs are repeatedly sampled. Furthermore, the method uses two policies: a non-greedy behavior policy to gather experience from the environment (for example, ϵ-greedy) and a target greedy policy that follows the maximum Q-value.

Maintaining a tabular representation of values can be contraindicated and in some cases, harmful. That's because most problems have a very high number of states and actions. For example, images (including small ones) have more state than the atoms in the universe. You can easily guess that, in this situation, tables cannot be used. Besides the infinite memory that the storage of such a table requires, only a few states will be visited more than once, making learning about the Q-function or V-function extremely difficult. Thus, we may want to generalize across states. In this case, generalization means that we are not only interested in the precise value of a state, $V(s)$, but also in the values in similar and near states. If a state has never been visited, we could approximate it with the value of a state near it. Generally speaking, the concept of generalization is incredibly important in all machine learning, including reinforcement learning.

The concept of generalization is fundamental in circumstances where the agent doesn't have a complete view of the environment. In this case, the full state of the environment will be hidden by the agent that has to make decisions based solely on a restricted representation of the environment. This is known as **observation**. For example, think about a humanoid agent that deals with basic interactions in the real world. Obviously, it doesn't have a view of the complete state of the universe and of all the atoms. It only has a limited viewpoint, that is, observation, which is perceived by its sensors (such as video cameras). For this reason, the humanoid agent should generalize what's happening around it and behave accordingly.

Function approximation

Now that we have talked about the main constraints of tabular algorithms and expressed the need for generalization capabilities in RL algorithms, we have to deal with the tools that allow us to get rid of these tabular constraints and address the generalization problem.

Chapter 5

We can now dismiss tables and represent value functions with a function approximator. Function approximation allows us to represent value functions in a constraint domain using only a fixed amount of memory. Resource allocation is only dependent on the function that's used to approximate the problem. The choice of function approximator is, as always, task-dependent. Examples of function approximation are linear functions, decision trees, nearest neighbor algorithms, artificial neural networks, and so on. As you may expect, artificial neural networks are preferred over all the others – it is not a coincidence that it is widespread across all kinds of RL algorithms. In particular, deep artificial neural networks, or for brevity, **deep neural networks** (**DNNs**), are used. Their popularity is due to their efficiency and ability to learn features by themselves, creating a hierarchical representation as the hidden layers of the network increase. Also, deep neural networks, and in particular, **convolutional neural networks** (**CNNs**), deal incredibly well with images, as demonstrated by recent breakthroughs, especially in supervised tasks. But despite the fact that almost all studies of deep neural networks have been done in supervised learning, their integration in an RL framework has produces very interesting results. However, as we'll see shortly, this is not easy.

Q-learning with neural networks

In Q-learning, a deep neural network learns a set of weights to approximate the Q-value function. Thereby, the Q-value function is parametrized by θ (the weights of the network) and written as follows:

$$Q_\theta(s, a)$$

To adapt Q-learning with deep neural networks (this combination takes the name of deep Q-learning), we have to come up with a loss function (or objective) to minimize.

As you may recall, the tabular Q-learning update is as follows:

$$Q(s, a) \leftarrow Q(s, a) + \alpha[r + \gamma max_{a'} Q(s', a') - Q(s, a)]$$

Here, s' is the state at the next step. This update is done online on each sample that's collected by the behavior policy.

Compared to the previous chapters, to simplify the notation, here, we refer to s, a as the state and action in the present step, while s', a' is referred to as the state and action in the next step.

[103]

Deep Q-Network

With the neural network, our objective is to optimize the weight, θ, so that Q_θ resembles the optimal Q-value function. But since we don't have the optimal Q-function, we can only make small steps toward it by minimizing the Bellman error for one step, $r + \gamma max_{a'} Q(s', a') - Q(s, a)$. This step is similar to what we've done in tabular Q-learning. However, in deep Q-learning, we don't update the single value, $Q(s, a)$. Instead, we take the gradient of the Q-function with respect to the parameters, θ:

$$\theta \leftarrow \theta - \alpha [r + \gamma max_{a'} Q_\theta(s', a') - Q_\theta(s, a)] \nabla_\theta Q_\theta(s, a) \quad (5.1)$$

Here, $\nabla_\theta Q_\theta(s, a)$ is the partial derivate of Q with respect to θ. α is called the learning rate, which is the size of the step to take toward the gradient.

In reality, the smooth transition that we just saw from tabular Q-learning to deep Q-learning doesn't yield a good approximation. The first fix involves the use of the **Mean Square Error (MSE)** as a loss function (instead of the Bellman error). The second fix is to migrate from an online Q-iteration to a batch Q-iteration. This means that the parameters of the neural network are updated using multiple transitions at once (such as using a mini-batch of size greater than 1 in supervised settings). These changes produce the following loss function:

$$L(\theta) = E_{(s,a,r,s')}[(y_i - Q_\theta(s_i, a_i))^2] \quad (5.2)$$

Here, y isn't the true action-value function since we haven't used it. Instead, it is the Q-target value:

$$y_i = r_i + \gamma max_{a'_i} Q_\theta(s'_i, a'_i) \quad (5.3)$$

Then, the network parameter, θ, is updated by gradient descent on the MSE loss function, $L(\theta)$:

$$\theta = \theta - \alpha \nabla_\theta L(\theta)$$

It's very important to note that y_i is treated as a constant and that the gradient of the loss function isn't propagated further.

> Since, in the previous chapter, we introduced MC algorithms, we want to highlight that these algorithms can also be adapted to work with neural networks. In this case, y_i will be the return, G. Since the MC update isn't biased, it's asymptotically better than TD, but the latter has better results in practice.

Deep Q-learning instabilities

With the loss function and the optimization technique we just presented, you should be able to develop a deep Q-learning algorithm. However, the reality is much more subtle. Indeed, if we try to implement it, it probably won't work. Why? Once we introduce neural networks, we can no longer guarantee improvement. Although tabular Q-learning has convergence capabilities, its neural network counterpart does not.

Sutton and Barto in *Reinforcement Learning: An Introduction*, introduced a problem called the deadly triad, which arises when the following three factors are combined:

- Function approximation
- Bootstrapping (that is, the update used by other estimates)
- Off-policy learning (Q-learning is an off-policy algorithm since its update is independent on the policy that's being used)

But these are exactly the three main ingredients of the deep Q-learning algorithm. As the authors noted, we cannot get rid of bootstrapping without affecting the computational cost or data efficiency. Moreover, off-policy learning is important for creating more intelligent and powerful agents. And clearly, without deep neural networks, we'll lose an extremely important component. Therefore, it is very important to design algorithms that preserve these three components but at the same time mitigate the deadly triad problem.

Besides, from equations (5.2) and (5.3), the problem may seem similar to supervised regression, but it's not. In supervised learning, when performing SGD, the mini-batches are always sampled randomly from a dataset to make sure that they are **independent and identically distributed** (**IID**). In RL, it is the policy that gathers the experience. And because the states are sequential and strongly related to each other, the i.i.d assumption is immediately lost, causing severe instabilities when performing SGD.

Another cause of instability is due to the non-stationarity of the Q-learning process. From equation, (5.2) and (5.3), you can see that the same neural network that is updated is also the one that computes the target values, y. This is dangerous, considering that the target values will also be updated during training. It's like shooting at a moving circular target without taking into consideration its movement. These behaviors are only due to the generalization capabilities of the neural network; in fact, they are not a problem in a tabular case.

Deep Q-learning is poorly understood theoretically but, as we'll soon see, there is an algorithm that deploys a few tricks to increase the i.i.d of the data and alleviate the moving target problem. These tricks make the algorithm much more stable and flexible.

DQN

DQN, which was introduced for the first time in the paper *Human-level control through deep reinforcement learning* by Mnih and others from DeepMind, is the first scalable reinforcement learning algorithm that combines Q-learning with deep neural networks. To overcome stability issues, DQN adopts two novel techniques that turned out to be essential for the balance of the algorithm.

DQN has proven itself to be the first artificial agent capable of learning in a diverse array of challenging tasks. Furthermore, it has learned how to control many tasks using only high-dimensional row pixels as input and using an end-to-end RL approach.

The solution

The key innovations brought by DQN involve a **replay buffer** to get over the data correlation drawback, and a separate *target network* to get over the non-stationarity problem.

Replay memory

To use more IID data during SGD iterations, DQN introduced a replay memory (also called experienced replay) to collect and store the experience in a large buffer. This buffer ideally contains all the transitions that have taken place during the agent's lifetime. When doing SGD, a random mini-batch will be gathered from the experienced replay and used in the optimization procedure. Since the replay memory buffer holds varied experience, the mini-batch that's sampled from it will be diverse enough to provide independent samples. Another very important feature behind the use of an experience replay is that it enables the reusability of the data as the transitions will be sampled multiple times. This greatly increases the data efficiency of the algorithm.

The target network

The moving target problem is due to continuously updating the network during training, which also modifies the target values. Nevertheless, the neural network has to update itself in order to provide the best possible state-action values. The solution that's employed in DQNs is to use two neural networks. One is called the *online network*, which is constantly updated, while the other is called the *target network*, which is updated only every N iterations (with N usually being between 1,000 and 10,000). The online network is used to interact with the environment while the target network is used to predict the target values. In this way, for N iterations, the target values that are produced by the target network remain fixed, preventing the propagation of instabilities and decreasing the risk of divergence. A potential disadvantage is that the target network is an old version of the online network. Nonetheless, in practice, the advantages greatly outweigh the disadvantages and the stability of the algorithm will improve significantly.

The DQN algorithm

The introduction of a replay buffer and of a separate target network in a deep Q-learning algorithm has been able to control Atari games (such as Space Invaders, Pong, and Breakout) from nothing but images, a reward, and a terminal signal. DQN learns completely end to end with a combination of CNN and fully connected neural networks.

Deep Q-Network

DQN has been trained separately on 49 Atari games with the same algorithm, network architecture, and hyperparameters. It performed better than all the previous algorithms, achieving a level comparable to or better than professional gamers on many games. The Atari games are not easy to solve and many of them demand complex planning strategies. Indeed, a few of them (such as the well-known Montezuma's Revenge) required a level that even DQN hasn't been able to achieve.

A particularity of these games is that, as they provide only images to the agent, they are partially observable. They don't show the full state of the environment. In fact, a single image isn't enough to fully understand the current situation. For example, can you deduce the direction of the ball in the following image?

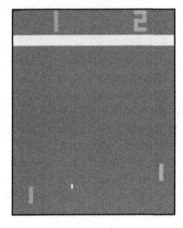

Figure 5.1. Rendering of pong

You can't, and neither can the agent. To overcome this situation, at each point in time, a sequence of the previous observations is considered. Usually the last two to five frames are used, and in most cases, they give a pretty accurate approximation of the actual overall state.

The loss function

The deep Q-network is trained by minimizing the loss function (5.2) that we have already presented, but with the further employment of a separate Q-target network, $\hat{Q}$, with a weight, θ', putting everything together, the loss function becomes:

$$L(\theta) = E_{(s,a,r,s')}[(r + \gamma max_{a'} \hat{Q}_{\theta'}(s',a') - Q_\theta(s,a))^2] \quad (5.4)$$

Here, θ is the parameters of the online network.

The optimization of the differentiable loss function (5.4) is performed with our favorite iterative method, namely mini-batch gradient descent. That is, the learning update is applied to mini-batches that have been drawn uniformly from the experienced buffer. The derivative of the loss function is as follows:

$$\nabla_\theta L(\theta) = E_{(s,a,r,s')}[(r + \gamma max_{a'} \hat{Q}_{\theta'}(s',a') - Q_\theta(s,a))\nabla_\theta Q_\theta(s,a)] \quad (5.5)$$

Unlike the problem framed in the case of deep Q-learning, in DQN, the learning process is more stable. Furthermore, because the data is more i.i.d. and the target is (somehow) fixed, it's very similar to a regression problem. But on the other hand, the targets still depend on the network weights.

> If you optimize the loss function (5.4) at each step and only on a single sample, you would obtain the Q-learning algorithm with function approximation.

Pseudocode

Now that all the components of DQN have been explained, we can put all the pieces together and show you the pseudocode version of the algorithm to clarify any uncertainties (don't worry if it doesn't – in the next section, you'll implement it and everything will be clearer).

The DQN algorithm involves three main parts:

- Data collection and storage. The data is collected by following a behavior policy (for example, ϵ-greedy).
- Neural network optimization (performing SGD on mini-batches that have been sampled from the buffer).
- Target update.

Deep Q-Network

The pseudocode of DQN is as follows:

```
Initialize Q function with random weight θ
Initialize Q̂ function with random weight θ' = θ
Initialize empty replay memory D
for episode = 1..M do
    Initialize environment s ← env.reset()
    for t = 1..T do
        > Collect observation from the env:
        a ← εgreedy(φ(s))
        s', r, d ← env(a)
        > Store the transition in the replay buffer:
        φ ← φ(s), φ' ← φ(s')
        D ← D ∪ (φ, a, r, φ', d)
        > Update the model using (5.4):
        Sample a random minibatch (φ_j, a_j, r_j, φ'_j, d_j) from D
```

$$y_j = \begin{cases} r_j & \text{if } d_{j+1} = True \\ r_j + \gamma max_{a'} \hat{Q}_{\theta'}(\phi_{j+1}, a') & \text{otherwise} \end{cases}$$

```
        Perform a step of GD on (y_j - Q_θ(φ_j, a_j))² on θ
        > Update target network:
        Every C steps θ' ← θ  (i.e. Q̂ ← Q)
        s ← s'
    end for
end for
```

Here, d is a flag that's returned by the environment that signals whether the environment is in its final state. If d=True, that is, the episode has ended, the environment has to be reset. ϕ is a preprocessing step that changes the images to reduce their dimensionality (it converts the images into grayscale and resizes them into smaller images) and adds the last n frames to the current frame. Usually, n is a value between 2 and 4. The preprocessing part will be explained in more detail in the next section, where we'll implement DQN.

In DQN, the experienced replay, D, is a dynamic buffer that stores a limited number of frames. In the paper, the buffer contains the last 1 million transitions and when it exceeds this dimension, it discards the older experiences.

All the other parts have already been described. If you are wondering why the target value, y_j, takes the r_j if $d_{j+1} = True$ value, it is because there won't be any other interactions with the environment after and so r_j is its actual unbiased Q-value.

Model architecture

So far, we have talked about the algorithm itself, but we haven't explained the architecture of the DQN. Besides the new ideas that have been adopted to stabilize its training, the architecture of the DQN plays a crucial role in the final performance of the algorithm. In the *DQN* paper, a single model architecture is used in all of the Atari environments. It combines CNNs and FNNs. In particular, as observation images are given as input, it employs a CNN to learn about feature maps from those images. CNNs have been widely used with images for their translation invariance characteristics and for their property of sharing weights, which allows the network to learn with fewer weights compared to other deep neural network types.

The output of the model corresponds to the state-action values, with one for each action. Thus, to control an agent with five actions, the model will output a value for each of those five actions. Such a model architecture allows us to compute all the Q-values with only one forward pass.

There are three convolutional layers. Each layer includes a convolution operation with an increasing number of filters and a decreasing dimension, as well as a non-linear function. The last hidden layer is a fully connected layer, followed by a rectified activation function and a fully-connected linear layer with an output for each action. A simple representation of this architecture is shown in the following illustration:

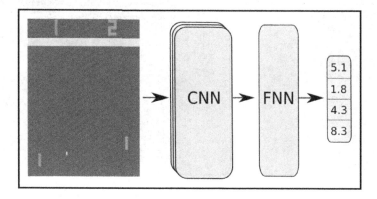

Figure 5.2. Illustration of a DNN architecture for DQN composed with a CNN and FNN

DQN applied to Pong

Equipped with all the technical knowledge about Q-learning, deep neural networks, and DQN, we can finally put it to work and start to warm up the GPU. In this section, we will apply DQN to an Atari environment, Pong. We have chosen Pong rather than all the other Atari environments because it's simpler to solve and thus requires less time, computational power, and memory. That being said, if you have a decent GPU available, you can apply the same exact configuration to almost all the other Atari games (some may require a little bit of fine-tuning). For the same reason, we adopted a lighter configuration compared to the original DQN paper, both in terms of the capacity of the function approximator (that is, fewer weights) and hyperparameters such as a smaller buffer size. This does not compromise the results rather on Pong but might degrade the performance of other games.

First, we will briefly introduce the Atari environment and the preprocessing pipeline before moving on to the DQN implementation.

Atari games

Atari games became a standard testbed for deep RL algorithms since their introduction in the DQN paper. These were first provided in the **Arcade Learning Environment** (**ALE**) and subsequently wrapped by OpenAI Gym to provide a standard interface. ALE (and Gym) includes 57 of the most popular Atari 2600 video games, such as Montezuma's Revenge, Pong, Breakout, and Space Invaders, as shown in the following illustration. These games have been widely used in RL research for their high-dimensional state space (210 x 160 pixels) and their task diversity between games:

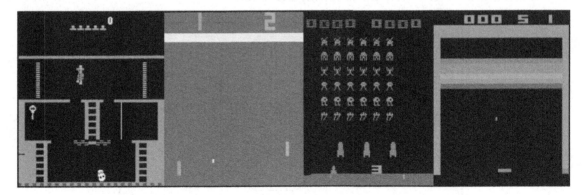

Figure 5.3 The Montezuma's Revenge, Pong, Breakout, and Space Invaders environments

A very important note about Atari environments is that they are deterministic, meaning that, given a fixed set of actions, the results will be the same across multiple matches. From an algorithm perspective, this determinism holds true until all the history is used to choose an action from a stochastic policy.

Preprocessing

The frames in Atari are 210 x 160 pixels with RGB color, thus having an overall size of 210 x 160 x 3. If a history of 4 frames was used, the input would have a dimension of 210 x 160 x 12. Such dimensionality can be computationally demanding and it could be difficult to store a large number of frames in the experienced buffer. Therefore, a preprocessing step to reduce the dimensionality is necessary. In the original DQN implementation, the following preprocessing pipeline is used:

- RGB colors are converted into grayscale
- The images are downsampled to 110 x 84 and then cropped to 84 x 84
- The last three to four frames are concatenated to the current frame
- The frames are normalized

Furthermore, because the games are run at a high frame rate, a technique called frame-skipping is used to skip k consecutive frames. This technique allows the agent to store and train on fewer frames for each game without significantly degrading the performance of the algorithms. In practice, with the frame-skipping technique, the agent selects an action every k frames and repeats the action on the skipped frames.

In addition, in some environments, at the start of each game, the agent has to push the fire button in order to start the game. Also, because of the determinism of the environment, some no-ops are taken on the reset of the environment to start the agent in a random position.

Luckily for us, OpenAI released an implementation of the preprocessing pipeline that is compatible with the Gym interface. You can find it in this book's GitHub repository in the `atari_wrappers.py` file. Here, we will give just a brief explanation of the implementation:

- `NoopResetEnv(n)`: Takes n no-ops on reset of the environment to provide a random starting position for the agent.
- `FireResetEnv()`: Fires on reset of the environment (required only in some games).

Deep Q-Network

- `MaxAndSkipEnv(skip)`: Skips `skip` frames while taking care of repeating the actions and summing the rewards.
- `WarpFrame()`: Resizes the frame to 84 x 84 and converts it into grayscale.
- `FrameStack(k)`: Stacks the last `k` frames.

All of these functions are implemented as a wrapper. A wrapper is a way to easily transform an environment by adding a new layer on top of it. For example, to scale the frames on Pong, we would use the following code:

```
env = gym.make('Pong-v0')
env = ScaledFloatFrame(env)
```

A wrapper has to inherit the `gym.Wrapper` class and override at least one of the following methods: `__init__(self, env)`, `step`, `reset`, `render`, `close`, or `seed`.

We won't show the implementation of all the wrappers listed here as they are outside of the scope of this book, but we will use `FireResetEnv` and `WrapFrame` as examples to give you a general idea of their implementation. The complete code is available in this book's GitHub repository:

```
class FireResetEnv(gym.Wrapper):
    def __init__(self, env):
        """Take action on reset for environments that are fixed until firing."""
        gym.Wrapper.__init__(self, env)
        assert env.unwrapped.get_action_meanings()[1] == 'FIRE'
        assert len(env.unwrapped.get_action_meanings()) >= 3

    def reset(self, **kwargs):
        self.env.reset(**kwargs)
        obs, _, done, _ = self.env.step(1)
        if done:
            self.env.reset(**kwargs)
        obs, _, done, _ = self.env.step(2)
        if done:
            self.env.reset(**kwargs)
        return obs

    def step(self, ac):
        return self.env.step(ac)
```

First, `FireResetEnv` inherits the `Wrapper` class from Gym. Then, during the initialization, it checks the availability of the `fire` action by unwrapping the environment through `env.unwrapped`. The function overrides the `reset` function by calling `reset`, which was defined in the previous layer with `self.env.reset`, then takes a fire action by calling `self.env.step(1)` and an environment-dependent action, `self.env.step(2)`.

`WrapFrame` has a similar definition:

```python
class WarpFrame(gym.ObservationWrapper):
    def __init__(self, env):
        """Warp frames to 84x84 as done in the Nature paper and later work."""
        gym.ObservationWrapper.__init__(self, env)
        self.width = 84
        self.height = 84
        self.observation_space = spaces.Box(low=0, high=255,
                shape=(self.height, self.width, 1), dtype=np.uint8)
    def observation(self, frame):
        frame = cv2.cvtColor(frame, cv2.COLOR_RGB2GRAY)
        frame = cv2.resize(frame, (self.width, self.height),
interpolation=cv2.INTER_AREA)
        return frame[:, :, None]
```

This time, `WarpFrame` inherits the properties from `gym.ObservationWrapper` and creates a `Box` space with values between 0 and 255 and with the shape 84 x 84.
When `observation()` is called, it converts the RGB frames into grayscale and resizes the images to the chosen shape.

We can then create a function, `make_env`, to apply every wrapper to an environment:

```python
def make_env(env_name, fire=True, frames_num=2, noop_num=30,
skip_frames=True):
    env = gym.make(env_name)
    if skip_frames:
        env = MaxAndSkipEnv(env) # Return only every `skip`-th frame
    if fire:
        env = FireResetEnv(env) # Fire at the beginning
    env = NoopResetEnv(env, noop_max=noop_num)
    env = WarpFrame(env) # Reshape image
    env = FrameStack(env, frames_num) # Stack last 4 frames
    return env
```

Deep Q-Network

The only preprocessing step that is missing is the scaling of the frame. We'll take care of scaling immediately before giving the observation frame as input to the neural network. This is because `FrameStack` uses a particular memory-efficient array called a lazy array, which is lost whenever scaling is applied as a wrapper.

DQN implementation

Though DQN is a pretty simple algorithm, it requires particular attention when it comes to its implementation and design choices. This algorithm, like every other deep RL algorithm, is not easy to debug and tune. Therefore, throughout this book, we'll give you some techniques and suggestions for how to do this.

The DQN code contains four main components:

- DNNs
- An experienced buffer
- A computational graph
- A training (and evaluation) loop

The code, as usual, is written in Python and TensorFlow, and we'll use TensorBoard to visualize the training and the performance of the algorithm.

All the code is available in this book's GitHub repository. Make sure to check it out there. We don't provide the implementation of some simpler functions here to avoid weighing down the code.

Let's immediately jump into the implementation by importing the required libraries:

```
import numpy as np
import tensorflow as tf
import gym
from datetime import datetime
from collections import deque
import time
import sys

from atari_wrappers import make_env
```

`atari_wrappers` includes the `make_env` function we defined previously.

DNNs

The DNN architecture is as follows (the components are built in sequential order):

1. A convolution of 16 filters of dimension 8 x 8 with 4 strides and rectifier nonlinearity.
2. A convolution of 32 filters of dimension 4 x 4 with 2 strides and rectifier nonlinearity.
3. A convolution of 32 filters of dimension 3 x 3 with 1 strides and rectifier nonlinearity.
4. A dense layer of 128 units and ReLU activation.
5. A dense layer with a number of units equal to the actions that are allowed in the environment and a linear activation.

In `cnn`, we define the first three convolutional layers, while in `fnn`, we define the last two dense layers:

```
def cnn(x):
    x = tf.layers.conv2d(x, filters=16, kernel_size=8, strides=4, padding='valid', activation='relu')
    x = tf.layers.conv2d(x, filters=32, kernel_size=4, strides=2, padding='valid', activation='relu')
    return tf.layers.conv2d(x, filters=32, kernel_size=3, strides=1, padding='valid', activation='relu')

def fnn(x, hidden_layers, output_layer, activation=tf.nn.relu, last_activation=None):
    for l in hidden_layers:
        x = tf.layers.dense(x, units=l, activation=activation)
    return tf.layers.dense(x, units=output_layer, activation=last_activation)
```

In the preceding code, `hidden_layers` is a list of integer values. In our implementation, this is `hidden_layers=[128]`. On the other hand, `output_layer` is the number of agent actions.

In `qnet`, the CNN and FNN layers are connected with a layer that flattens the 2D output of the CNN:

```
def qnet(x, hidden_layers, output_size, fnn_activation=tf.nn.relu, last_activation=None):
    x = cnn(x)
    x = tf.layers.flatten(x)
    return fnn(x, hidden_layers, output_size, fnn_activation, last_activation)
```

Deep Q-Network

The deep neural network is now fully defined. All we need to do is connect it to the main computational graph.

The experienced buffer

The experienced buffer is a class of the `ExperienceBuffer` type and stores a queue of type **FIFO (First In, First Out)** for each of the following components: observation, reward, action, next observation, and done. FIFO means that once it reaches the maximum capacity specified by `maxlen`, it discards the elements starting from the oldest one. In our implementation, the capacity is `buffer_size`:

```python
class ExperienceBuffer():
    def __init__(self, buffer_size):
        self.obs_buf = deque(maxlen=buffer_size)
        self.rew_buf = deque(maxlen=buffer_size)
        self.act_buf = deque(maxlen=buffer_size)
        self.obs2_buf = deque(maxlen=buffer_size)
        self.done_buf = deque(maxlen=buffer_size)

    def add(self, obs, rew, act, obs2, done):
        self.obs_buf.append(obs)
        self.rew_buf.append(rew)
        self.act_buf.append(act)
        self.obs2_buf.append(obs2)
        self.done_buf.append(done)
```

The `ExperienceBuffer` class also manages the sampling of mini-batches, which are used to train the neural network. These are uniformly sampled from the buffer and have a predefined `batch_size` size:

```python
    def sample_minibatch(self, batch_size):
        mb_indices = np.random.randint(len(self.obs_buf), size=batch_size)

        mb_obs = scale_frames([self.obs_buf[i] for i in mb_indices])
        mb_rew = [self.rew_buf[i] for i in mb_indices]
        mb_act = [self.act_buf[i] for i in mb_indices]
        mb_obs2 = scale_frames([self.obs2_buf[i] for i in mb_indices])
        mb_done = [self.done_buf[i] for i in mb_indices]

        return mb_obs, mb_rew, mb_act, mb_obs2, mb_done
```

Lastly, we override the `_len` method to provide the length of the buffers. Note that because every buffer is the same size as the others, we only return the length of `self.obs_buf`:

```
def __len__(self):
    return len(self.obs_buf)
```

The computational graph and training loop

The core of the algorithm, namely the computational graph and the training (and evaluation) loop, is implemented in the DQN function, which takes the name of the environment and all the other hyperparameters as arguments:

```
def DQN(env_name, hidden_sizes=[32], lr=1e-2, num_epochs=2000,
buffer_size=100000, discount=0.99, update_target_net=1000, batch_size=64,
update_freq=4, frames_num=2, min_buffer_size=5000, test_frequency=20,
start_explor=1, end_explor=0.1, explor_steps=100000):

    env = make_env(env_name, frames_num=frames_num, skip_frames=True,
noop_num=20)
    env_test = make_env(env_name, frames_num=frames_num, skip_frames=True,
noop_num=20)
    env_test = gym.wrappers.Monitor(env_test,
"VIDEOS/TEST_VIDEOS"+env_name+str(current_milli_time()),force=True,
video_callable=lambda x: x%20==0)

    obs_dim = env.observation_space.shape
    act_dim = env.action_space.n
```

In the first few lines of the preceding code, two environments are created: one for training and one for testing. Moreover, `gym.wrappers.Monitor` is a Gym wrapper that saves the games of an environment in video format, while `video_callable` is a function parameter that establishes how often the videos are saved, which in this case is every 20 episodes.

Then, we can reset the TensorFlow graph and create placeholders for the observations, the actions, and the target values. This is done with the following lines of code:

```
    tf.reset_default_graph()
    obs_ph = tf.placeholder(shape=(None, obs_dim[0], obs_dim[1],
obs_dim[2]), dtype=tf.float32, name='obs')
    act_ph = tf.placeholder(shape=(None,), dtype=tf.int32, name='act')
    y_ph = tf.placeholder(shape=(None,), dtype=tf.float32, name='y')
```

Deep Q-Network

Now, we can create a target and an online network by calling the `qnet` function that we defined previously. Because the target network has to update itself sometimes and take the parameters of the online network, we create an operation called `update_target_op`, which assigns every variable of the online network to the target network. This assignment is done by the TensorFlow `assign` method. `tf.group`, on the other hand, aggregates every element of the `update_target` list as a single operation. The implementation is as follows:

```
with tf.variable_scope('target_network'):
    target_qv = qnet(obs_ph, hidden_sizes, act_dim)
target_vars = tf.trainable_variables()

with tf.variable_scope('online_network'):
    online_qv = qnet(obs_ph, hidden_sizes, act_dim)
train_vars = tf.trainable_variables()

update_target = [train_vars[i].assign(train_vars[i+len(target_vars)])
    for i in range(len(train_vars) - len(target_vars))]
update_target_op = tf.group(*update_target)
```

Now that we have defined the placeholder that's created the deep neural network and defined the target update operation, all that remains is to define the loss function. The loss function is $(y_j - Q_\theta(\varphi_j, a_j))^2$ (or, equivalently, (5.5)). It requires the target values, y_j, computed as they are in formula (5.6), which are passed through the `y_ph` placeholder and the Q-values of the online network, $Q_\theta(\varphi_j, a_j)$. A Q-value is dependent on the action, a_j, but since the online network outputs a value for each action, we have to find a way to retrieve only the Q-value of a_j while discarding the other action-values. This operation can be achieved by using a one-hot encoding of the action, a_j, and then multiplying it by the output of the online network. For example, if there are five possible actions and $a_j = 3$, then the one-hot encoding will be $[0, 0, 0, 1, 0]$. Then, supposing that the network outputs $[3.4, 3.7, 5.4, 2.1]$, the results of the multiplication with the one-hot encoding will be $[0, 0, 0, 5.4, 0]$. After, the q-value is obtained by summing this vector. The result will be $[5.4]$. All of this is done in the following three lines of code:

```
act_onehot = tf.one_hot(act_ph, depth=act_dim)
q_values = tf.reduce_sum(act_onehot * online_qv, axis=1)
v_loss = tf.reduce_mean((y_ph - q_values)**2)
```

To minimize the loss function we just defined, we will use Adam, a variant of SGD:

```
v_opt = tf.train.AdamOptimizer(lr).minimize(v_loss)
```

This concludes the creation of the computation graph. Before going through the main DQN cycle, we have to prepare everything so that we can save the scalars and the histograms. By doing this, we will be able to visualize them later in TensorBoard:

```
now = datetime.now()
clock_time = "{}_{}.{}.{}".format(now.day, now.hour, now.minute, int(now.second))

mr_v = tf.Variable(0.0)
ml_v = tf.Variable(0.0)

tf.summary.scalar('v_loss', v_loss)
tf.summary.scalar('Q-value', tf.reduce_mean(q_values))
tf.summary.histogram('Q-values', q_values)

scalar_summary = tf.summary.merge_all()
reward_summary = tf.summary.scalar('test_rew', mr_v)
mean_loss_summary = tf.summary.scalar('mean_loss', ml_v)

hyp_str = "-lr_{}-upTN_{}-upF_{}-frms_{}".format(lr, update_target_net, update_freq, frames_num)
file_writer = tf.summary.FileWriter('log_dir/'+env_name+'/DQN_'+clock_time+'_'+hyp_str, tf.get_default_graph())
```

Everything is quite self-explanatory. The only things that you may question are the `mr_v` and `ml_v` variables. These are variables we want to track with TensorBoard. However, because they aren't defined internally by the computation graph, we have to declare them separately and assign them in `session.run` later. `FileWriter` is created with a unique name and associated with the default graph.

We can now define the `agent_op` function that computes the forward pass on a scaled observation. The observation has already passed through the preprocessing pipeline (built in the environment with the wrappers), but we left the scaling aside:

```
def agent_op(o):
    o = scale_frames(o)
    return sess.run(online_qv, feed_dict={obs_ph:[o]})
```

Then, the session is created, the variables are initialized, and the environment is reset:

```
sess = tf.Session()
sess.run(tf.global_variables_initializer())

step_count = 0
last_update_loss = []
ep_time = current_milli_time()
```

Deep Q-Network

```
batch_rew = []

obs = env.reset()
```

The next move involves instantiating the replay buffer, updating the target network so that it has the same parameters as the online network, and initializing the decay rate with `eps_decay`. The policy for the epsilon decay is the same as the one that was adopted in the DQN paper. A decay rate has been chosen so that, when it's applied linearly to the `eps` variable, it reaches a terminal value, `end_explor`, in about `explor_steps` steps. For example, if you want to decrease from 1.0 to 0.1 in 1,000 steps, you have to decrement the variable by a value equal to $(1-0.1)/1000 = 0.0009$ on each step. All of this is accomplished in the following lines of code:

```
obs = env.reset()

buffer = ExperienceBuffer(buffer_size)

sess.run(update_target_op)

eps = start_explor
eps_decay = (start_explor - end_explor) / explor_steps
```

As you may recall, the training loop comprises two inner cycles: the first iterates across the epochs while the other iterates across each transition of the epoch. The first part of the innermost cycle is quite standard. It selects an action following an ϵ-greedy behavior policy that uses the online network, takes a step in the environment, adds the new transition to the buffer, and finally, updates the variables:

```
for ep in range(num_epochs):
    g_rew = 0
    done = False

    while not done:
        act = eps_greedy(np.squeeze(agent_op(obs)), eps=eps)
        obs2, rew, done, _ = env.step(act)
        buffer.add(obs, rew, act, obs2, done)

        obs = obs2
        g_rew += rew
        step_count += 1
```

In the preceding code, `obs` takes the value of the next observation and the cumulative game reward is incremented.

Then, in the same cycle, `eps` is decayed and if some of the conditions are met, it trains the online network. These conditions make sure that the buffer has reached a minimal size and that the neural network is trained only once every `update_freq` steps. To train the online network, first, a minibatch is sampled from the buffer and the target values are calculated. Then, the session is run to minimize the loss function, `v_loss`, which feeds the dictionary with the target values, the actions, and the observations of the minibatch. While the session is running, it also returns `v_loss` and `scalar_summary` for statistics purposes. `scalar_summary` is then added to `file_writer` to be saved in the TensorBoard logging file. Finally, every `update_target_net` epochs, the target network is updated. A summary with the mean losses is also run and added to the TensorBoard logging file. All of this is done by the following snippet of code:

```
if eps > end_explor:
    eps -= eps_decay

if len(buffer) > min_buffer_size and (step_count % update_freq == 0):
    mb_obs, mb_rew, mb_act, mb_obs2, mb_done = buffer.sample_minibatch(batch_size)
    mb_trg_qv = sess.run(target_qv, feed_dict={obs_ph:mb_obs2})
    y_r = q_target_values(mb_rew, mb_done, mb_trg_qv, discount)
    # Compute the target values
    train_summary, train_loss, _ = sess.run([scalar_summary, v_loss, v_opt], feed_dict={obs_ph:mb_obs, y_ph:y_r, act_ph: mb_act})

    file_writer.add_summary(train_summary, step_count)
    last_update_loss.append(train_loss)

    if (len(buffer) > min_buffer_size) and (step_count % update_target_net) == 0:
        _, train_summary = sess.run([update_target_op, mean_loss_summary], feed_dict={ml_v:np.mean(last_update_loss)})
        file_writer.add_summary(train_summary, step_count)
        last_update_loss = []
```

When an epoch terminates, the environment is reset, the total reward of the game is appended to `batch_rew`, and the latter is set to zero. Moreover, every `test_frequency` epochs, the agent is tested for 10 games, and the statistics are added to `file_writer`. At the end of the training, the environments and the writer are closed. The code is as follows:

```
if done:
    obs = env.reset()
    batch_rew.append(g_rew)
    g_rew = 0
    if ep % test_frequency == 0:
        test_rw = test_agent(env_test, agent_op, num_games=10)
```

Deep Q-Network

```
            test_summary = sess.run(reward_summary, feed_dict={mr_v:
np.mean(test_rw)})
            file_writer.add_summary(test_summary, step_count)
            print('Ep:%4d Rew:%4.2f, Eps:%2.2f -- Step:%5d -- Test:%4.2f
%4.2f' % (ep,np.mean(batch_rew), eps, step_count, np.mean(test_rw),
np.std(test_rw))
            batch_rew = []
    file_writer.close()
    env.close()
    env_test.close()
```

That's it. We can now call the DQN function with the name of the Gym environment and all the hyperparameters:

```
if __name__ == '__main__':
    DQN('PongNoFrameskip-v4', hidden_sizes=[128], lr=2e-4,
buffer_size=100000, update_target_net=1000, batch_size=32, update_freq=2,
frames_num=2, min_buffer_size=10000)
```

There's one last note before reporting the results. The environment that's being used here isn't the default version of Pong-v0 but a modified version of it. The reason for this is that in the regular version, each action is performed 2, 3, or 4 times where this number is sampled uniformly. But because we want to skip a fixed number of times, we opted for the version without the built-in skip feature, NoFrameskip, and added the custom MaxAndSkipEnv wrapper.

Results

Evaluating the progress of an RL algorithm is very challenging. The most obvious way to do this is to keep track of its end goal; that is, monitoring the total reward that's accumulated during the epochs. This is a good metric. However, training the average reward can be very noisy due to changes in the weights. This leads to large changes in the distribution of the state that's being visited.

For these reasons, we evaluated the algorithm on 10 test games every 20 training epochs and kept track of the average of the total (non-discounted) reward that was accumulated throughout the games. Moreover, because of the determinism of the environment, we tested the agent on an ϵ-greedy policy (with $\epsilon = 0.05$) so that we have a more robust evaluation. The scalar summary is called test_rew. You can see it in TensorBoard if you access the directory where the logs have been saved, and execute the following command:

```
tensorboard --logdir .
```

The plot, which should be similar to yours (if you run the DQN code), is shown in the following diagram. The x axis represents the number of steps. You can see that it reaches a steady score of ± 19 after a linear increase in the first 250,000 steps and a more significant growth in the next 300,000 steps:

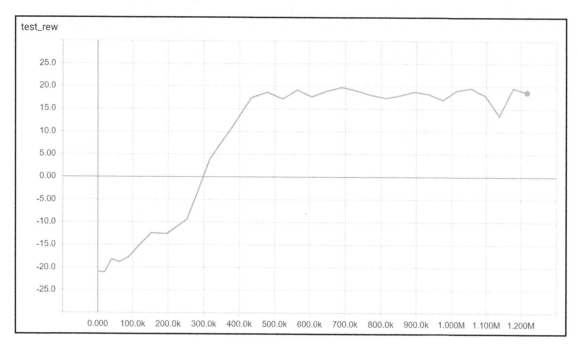

Figure 5.4. A plot of the mean total reward across 10 games. The x axis represents the number of steps

Pong is a relatively simple task to complete. In fact, our algorithm has been trained on around 1.1 million steps, whereas in the DQN paper, all the algorithms were trained on 200 million steps.

Deep Q-Network

An alternative way to evaluate the algorithm involves the estimated action-values. Indeed, the estimated action-values are a valuable metric because they measure the belief of the quality of the state-action pair. Unfortunately, this option is not optimal as some algorithms tend to overestimate the Q-values, as we will soon learn. Despite this, we tracked it during training. The plot is visible in the following diagram and, as we expected, the Q-value increases throughout the training in a similar way to the plot in the preceding diagram:

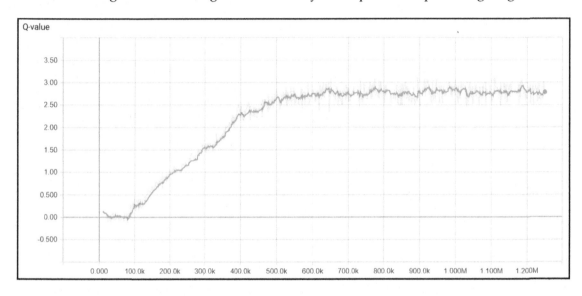

Figure 5.5. A plot of the estimated training Q-values. The x axis represents the number of steps

Another important plot, shown in the following diagram, shows the loss function through time. It's not as useful as in supervised learning as the target values aren't the ground truth, but it can always provide a good insight into the quality of the model:

Chapter 5

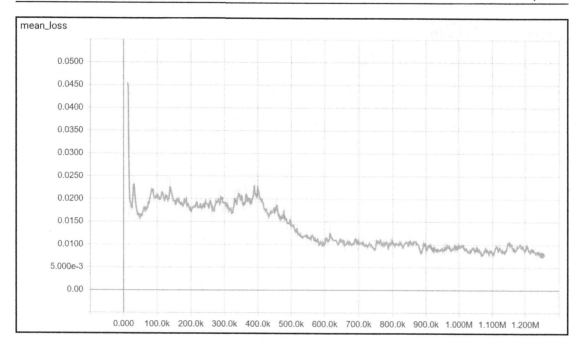

Figure 5.6. A plot of the loss function

DQN variations

Following the amazing results of DQN, many researchers have studied it and come up with integrations and changes to improve its stability, efficiency, and performance. In this section, we will present three of these improved algorithms, explain the idea and solution behind them, and provide their implementation. The first is Double DQN or DDQN, which deals with the over-estimation problem we mentioned in the DQN algorithm. The second is Dueling DQN, which decouples the Q-value function in a state value function and an action-state advantage value function. The third is n-step DQN, an old idea taken from TD algorithms, which spaces the step length between one-step learning and MC learning.

Double DQN

The over-estimation of the Q-values in Q-learning algorithms is a well-known problem. The cause of this is the max operator, which over-estimates the actual maximum estimated values. To comprehend this problem, let's assume that we have noisy estimates with a mean of 0 but a variance different from 0, as shown in the following illustration. Despite the fact that, asymptotically, the average value is 0, the max function will always return values greater than 0:

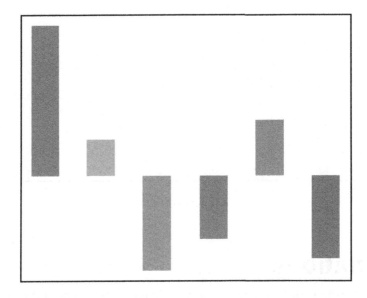

Figure 5.7. Six values sampled from a normal distribution with a mean of 0

In Q-learning, this over-estimation is not a real problem until the higher values are uniformly distributed. If, however, the over-estimation is not uniform and the error differs from states and actions, this over-estimation negatively affects the DQN algorithm, which degrades the resulting policy.

To address this problem, in the paper `Deep Reinforcement Learning with Double Q-learning`, the authors suggest using two different estimators (that is, two neural networks): one for the action selection and one for the Q-values estimation. But instead of using two different neural networks and increasing the complexity, the paper proposes the use of the online network to choose the best action with the max operation, and the use of the target network to compute its Q-values. With this solution, the target value, y, will change from being as follows for standard Q-learning:

$$y = r + \gamma max_{a'} \hat{Q}_{\theta'}(\phi', a') = r + \gamma \hat{Q}_{\theta'}(\phi', argmax_{a'} \hat{Q}_{\theta'}(s', a'))$$

Now, it's as follows:

$$y = r + \gamma \hat{Q}_{\theta'}(\phi', argmax_{a'} Q_{\theta}(s', a')) \quad (5.7)$$

This uncoupled version significantly reduces over-estimation problems and improves the stability of the algorithm.

DDQN implementation

From an implementation perspective, the only change to make in order to implement DDQN is in the training phase. You just need to replace the following lines of code in the DDQN implementation itself:

```
mb_trg_qv = sess.run(target_qv, feed_dict={obs_ph:mb_obs2})
y_r = q_target_values(mb_rew, mb_done, mb_trg_qv, discount)
```

Replace this with the following code:

```
mb_onl_qv, mb_trg_qv = sess.run([online_qv,target_qv],
feed_dict={obs_ph:mb_obs2})
y_r = double_q_target_values(mb_rew, mb_done, mb_trg_qv, mb_onl_qv,
discount)
```

Here, `double_q_target_values` is a function that computes (5.7) for each transition of the minibatch.

Results

To see if DQN actually overestimates the Q-values in respect to DDQN, we reported the Q-value plot in the following diagram. We also included the results of DQN (the orange line) so that we have a direct comparison between the two algorithms:

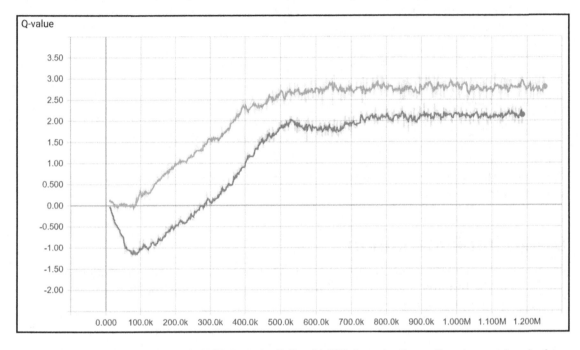

Figure 5.8. A plot of the estimated training Q-values. The DDQN values are plotted in blue and the DQN values are plotted in orange. The x axis represents the number of steps

The performance of both DDQN (the blue line) and DQN (the orange line), which are represented by the average reward of the test games, is as follows:

 For all the color references mentioned in the chapter, please refer to the color images bundle at `http://www.packtpub.com/sites/default/files/downloads/9781789131116_ColorImages.pdf`.

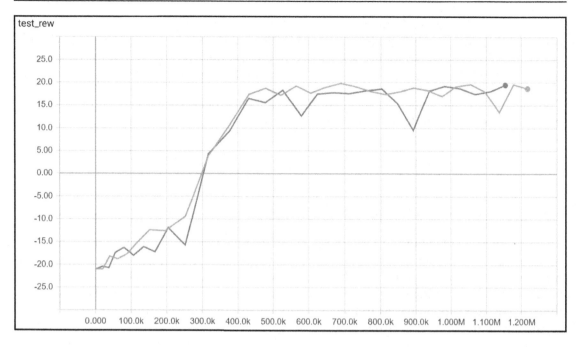

Figure 5.9. A plot of the mean test rewards. The DDQN values are plotted in blue and the DQN values are plotted in orange. The x axis represents the number of steps

As we expected, the Q-values are always smaller in DDQN than in DQN, meaning that the latter was actually over-estimating the values. Nonetheless, the performance on the test games doesn't seem to be impacted, meaning that those over-estimations were probably not hurting the performance of the algorithm. However, be aware that we only tested the algorithm on Pong. The effectiveness of an algorithm shouldn't be evaluated in a single environment. In fact, in the paper, the authors apply it to all 57 ALE games and reported that DDQN not only yields more accurate value estimates but leads to much higher scores on several games.

Dueling DQN

In the paper *Dueling Network Architectures for Deep Reinforcement Learning* (https://arxiv.org/abs/1511.06581), a novel neural network architecture with two separate estimators was proposed: one for the state value function and the other for the state-action advantage value function.

The advantage function is used everywhere in RL and is defined as follows:

$$A(s,a) = Q(s,a) - V(s)$$

Deep Q-Network

The advantage function tells us the improvement of an action, a, compared to the average action in a given state, s. Thus, if $A(s,a)$ is a positive value, this means that the action, a, is better then the average action in the state, s. On the contrary, if $A(s,a)$ is a negative value, this means that a is worse than the average action in the state, s.

Thus, estimating the value function and the advantage function separately, as done in the paper, allows us to rebuild the Q-function, like so:

$$Q(s,a) = V(s) + A(s,a) - \frac{1}{|A|}\sum_{a'} A(s,a') \qquad (5.8)$$

Here, the mean of the advantage has been added to increase the stability of the DQN.

The architecture of Dueling DQN consists of two heads (or streams): one for the value function and one for the advantage function, all while sharing a common convolutional module. The authors reported that this architecture can learn which states are or are not valuable, without having to learn the absolute value of each action in a state. They tested this new architecture on the Atari games and obtained considerable improvements regarding their overall performance.

Dueling DQN implementation

One of the benefits of this architecture and of formula (5.8) is that it doesn't impose any changes on the underlying RL algorithm. The only changes are in the construction of the Q-network. Thus, we can replace `qnet` with the `dueling_qnet` function, which can be implemented as follows:

```
def dueling_qnet(x, hidden_layers, output_size, fnn_activation=tf.nn.relu, last_activation=None):
    x = cnn(x)
    x = tf.layers.flatten(x)
    qf = fnn(x, hidden_layers, 1, fnn_activation, last_activation)
    aaqf = fnn(x, hidden_layers, output_size, fnn_activation, last_activation)
    return qf + aaqf - tf.reduce_mean(aaqf)
```

Two forward neural networks are created: one with only one output (for the value function) and one with as many outputs as the actions of the agent (for the state-dependent action advantage function). The last line returns formula (5.8).

Results

The results of the test rewards, as shown in the following diagram, are promising, proving a clear benefit in the use of a dueling architecture:

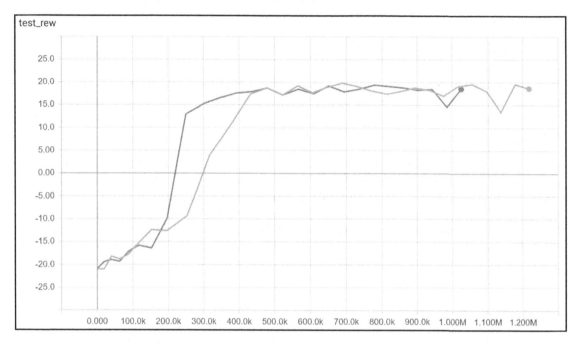

Figure 5.10. A plot of the test rewards. The dueling DQN values are plotted in red and the DQN values are plotted in orange. The x axis represents the number of steps

N-step DQN

The idea behind n-step DQN is old and comes from the shift between temporal difference learning and Monte Carlo learning. These algorithms, which were introduced in Chapter 4, *Q-Learning and SARSA Applications*, are at the opposite extremes of a common spectrum. TD learning learns from a single step, while MC learns from the complete trajectory. TD learning exhibits a minimal variance but a maximal bias, where as MC exhibits high variance but a minimal bias. The variance-bias problem can be balanced using an n-step return. An n-step return is a return computed after n steps. TD learning can be viewed as a 0-step return while MC can be viewed as a ∞-step return.

Deep Q-Network

With the n-step return, we can update the target value, as follows:

$$y_t = \sum_{t'=t}^{t'+N-1} r_{t'} + \gamma^N \max_{a'_{t+N}} \hat{Q}_{\theta'}(\phi'_{t+N}, a'_{t+N}) \tag{5.9}$$

Here, N is the number of steps.

An n-step return is like looking ahead n steps, but in practice, as it's impossible to actually look into the future, it's done in the opposite way, that is, by computing the y value of n-steps ago. This leads to values that are only available at time $t+n$, delaying the learning process.

The main advantage of this approach is that the target values are less biased and this can lead to faster learning. An important problem that arises is that the target values that are calculated in this way are correct, but only when the learning is on-policy (DQN is off-policy). This is because formula (5.9) assumes that the policy that the agent will follow for the next n-steps is the same policy that collected the experience. There are some ways to adjust for the off-policy case, but they are generally complicated to implement and the best general practice is just to keep a small n and ignore the problem.

Implementation

To implement n-step DQN, only a few changes in the buffer are required. When sampling from the buffer, the n-step reward, the n-step next state, and the n-step done flag have to be returned. We will not provide the implementation here as it is quite simple but you can look at it in the code provided in this book's GitHub repository. The code to support n-step return is in the `MultiStepExperienceBuffer` class.

Results

For off-policy algorithms (such as DQN), n-step learning works well with small values of n. In DQN, it has been shown that the algorithm works well with values of n between 2 and 4, leading to improvements in a wide range of Atari games.

Chapter 5

In the following graph, the results of our implementation are visible. We tested DQN with a three-step return. From the results, we can see that it requires more time before taking off. Afterward, it has a steeper learning curve but with an overall similar learning curve compared to DQN:

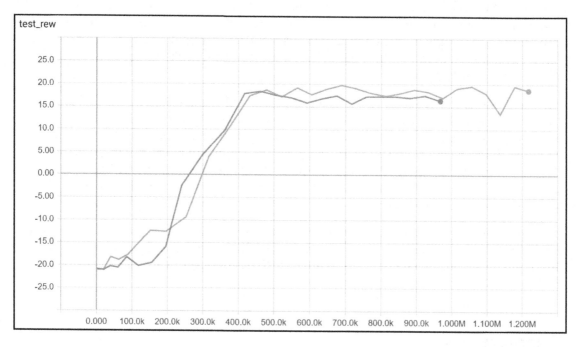

Figure 5.11. A plot of the mean test total reward. The three-step DQN values are plotted in violet and the DQN values are plotted in orange. The x axis represents the number of steps

Summary

In this chapter, we went further into RL algorithms and talked about how these can be combined with function approximators so that RL can be applied to a broader variety of problems. Specifically, we described how function approximation and deep neural networks can be used in Q-learning and the instabilities that derive from it. We demonstrated that, in practice, deep neural networks cannot be combined with Q-learning without any modifications.

Deep Q-Network

The first algorithm that was able to use deep neural networks in combination with Q-learning was DQN. It integrates two key ingredients to stabilize learning and control complex tasks such as Atari 2600 games. The two ingredients are the replay buffer, which is used to store the old experience, and a separate target network, which is updated less frequently than the online network. The former is employed to exploit the off-policy quality of Q-learning so that it can learn from the experiences of different policies (in this case, old policies) and to sample more i.i.d mini-batches from a larger pool of data to perform stochastic gradient descent. The latter is introduced to stabilize the target values and reduce the non-stationarity problem.

After this formal introduction to DQN, we implemented it and tested it on Pong, an Atari game. Moreover, we showed more practical aspects of the algorithm, such as the preprocessing pipeline and the wrappers. Following the publication of DQN, many other variations have been introduced to improve the algorithm and overcome its instabilities. We took a look at them and implemented three variations, namely Double DQN, Dueling DQN, and n-step DQN. Despite the fact that, in this chapter, we applied these algorithms exclusively to Atari games, they can be employed in many real-world problems.

In the next chapter, we'll introduce a different category of deep RL algorithms called policy gradient algorithms. These are on-policy and, as we'll soon see, they have some very important and unique characteristics that widen their applicability to a larger set of problems.

Questions

1. What is the cause of the deadly triad problem?
2. How does DQN overcome instabilities?
3. What's the moving target problem?
4. How is the moving target problem mitigated in DQN?
5. What's the optimization procedure that's used in DQN?
6. What's the definition of a state-action advantage value function?

Further reading

- For a comprehensive tutorial regarding OpenAI Gym wrappers, read the following article: https://hub.packtpub.com/openai-gym-environments-wrappers-and-monitors-tutorial/.
- For the original *Rainbow* paper, go to https://arxiv.org/abs/1710.02298.

6
Learning Stochastic and PG Optimization

So far, we've addressed and developed value-based reinforcement learning algorithms. These algorithms learn a value function in order to be able to find a good policy. Despite the fact that they exhibit good performances, their application is constrained by some limits that are embedded in their inner workings. In this chapter, we'll introduce a new class of algorithms called policy gradient methods, which are used to overcome the constraints of value-based methods by approaching the RL problem from a different perspective.

Policy gradient methods select an action based on a learned parametrized policy, instead of relying on a value function. In this chapter, we will also elaborate on the theory and intuition behind these methods, and with this background, develop the most basic version of a policy gradient algorithm, named **REINFORCE**.

REINFORCE exhibits some deficiencies due to its simplicity, but these can be mitigated with only a small amount of additional effort. Thus, we'll present two improved versions of REINFORCE, called **REINFORCE** with baseline and **actor-critic** (**AC**) models.

Learning Stochastic and PG Optimization

The following topics will be covered in this chapter:

- Policy gradient methods
- Understanding the REINFORCE algorithm
- REINFORCE with a baseline
- Learning the AC algorithm

Policy gradient methods

The algorithms that have been learned and developed so far are value-based, which, at their core, learn a value function, *V(s)*, or action-value function, *Q(s, a)*. A value function is a function that defines the total reward that can be accumulated from a given state or state-action pair. An action can then be selected, based on the estimated action (or state) values.

Therefore, a greedy policy can be defined as follows:

$$\pi(s) = argmax_a Q(s, a)$$

Value-based methods, when combined with deep neural networks, can learn very sophisticated policies in order to control agents that operate in high-dimensionality spaces. Despite these great qualities, they suffer when dealing with problems with a large number of actions, or when the action space is continuous.

In such cases, maximum operation is not feasible. **Policy gradient** (**PG**) algorithms exhibit incredible potential in such contexts, as they can be easily adapted to continuous action spaces.

PG methods belong to the broader class of policy-based methods, including evolution strategies, which are studied later in Chapter 11, *Understanding Black-Box Optimization Algorithms*. The distinctiveness of PG algorithms is in their use of the gradient of the policy, hence the name **policy gradient**.

A more concise categorization of RL algorithms, with respect to the one reported in Chapter 3, *Solving Problems with Dynamic Programming*, is shown in the following diagram:

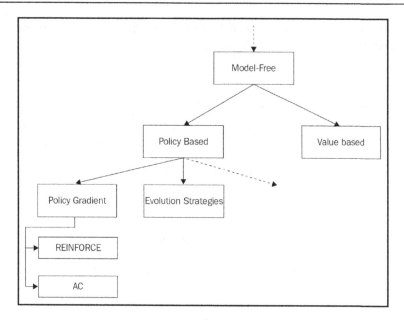

Examples of policy gradient methods are **REINFORCE** and **AC** that will be introduced in the next sections.

The gradient of the policy

The objective of RL is to maximize the expected return (the total reward, discounted or undiscounted) of a trajectory. The objective function, can then be expressed as:

$$J(\theta) = E_{\tau \sim \pi_\theta}[R(\tau)] \quad (6.1)$$

Where θ is the parameters of the policy, such as the trainable variables of a deep neural network.

In PG methods, the maximization of the objective function is done through the gradient of the objective function $\nabla_\theta J(\theta)$. Using gradient ascent, we can improve $J(\theta)$ by moving the parameters toward the direction of the gradient, as the gradient points in the direction in which the function increases.

Learning Stochastic and PG Optimization

 We have to take the same direction of the gradient, because we aim to maximize the objective function (6.1).

Once the maximum is found, the policy, π_θ, will produce trajectories with the highest possible return. On an intuitive level, policy gradient incentivizes good policies by increasing their probability while punishing bad policies by reducing their probabilities.

Using equation (6.1), the gradient of the objective function is defined as follows:

$$\nabla_\theta J(\theta) = \nabla_\theta E_{\tau \sim \pi_\theta}[R(\tau)] \qquad (6.2)$$

By relating to the concepts from the previous chapters, in policy gradient methods, policy evaluation is the estimation of the return, R. Instead, policy improvement is the optimization step of the parameter θ. Thus, policy gradient methods have to symbiotically carry on both phases in order to improve the policy.

Policy gradient theorem

An initial problem is encountered when looking at equation (6.2), because, in its formulation, the gradient of the objective function depends on the distribution of the states of a policy; that is:

$$\nabla_\theta J(\theta) = \nabla_\theta E_{\tau \sim \pi_\theta}[R(\tau)] = \nabla_\theta \sum_s d(s) \sum_a \pi_\theta(a|s) R(s,a) \qquad (6.3)$$

We would use a stochastic approximation of that expectation, but to compute the distribution of the states, $d(s)$, we still need a complete model of the environment. Thus, this formulation isn't suitable for our purposes.

The policy gradient theorem comes to the rescue here. Its purpose is to provide an analytical formulation to compute the gradient of the objective function, with respect to the parameters of the policy, without involving the derivative of the state distribution. Formally, the policy gradient theorem, enables us to express the gradient of the objective function as:

$$\nabla_\theta J(\theta) = E_{\tau \sim \pi_\theta}[\nabla_\theta \log \pi_\theta(\tau) R(\tau)] = E_{\pi_\theta}[\nabla_\theta \log \pi_\theta(a|s) Q_{\pi_\theta}(s,a)] \qquad (6.4)$$

The proof of the policy gradient theorem is beyond the scope of this book, and thus, isn't included. However, you can find it in the book by Sutton and Barto (http://incompleteideas.net/book/the-book-2nd.html or) or from other online resources.

Now that the derivative of the objective doesn't involve the derivative of the state distribution, the expectation can be estimated by sampling from the policy. Thus, the derivative of the objective can be approximated as follows:

$$\nabla_\theta J(\theta) \approx \frac{1}{N} \sum_{i=0}^{N} [\nabla_\theta \log \pi_\theta(a_i|s_i) Q_{\pi_\theta}(s_i, a_i)] \quad (6.5)$$

This can be used to produce a stochastic update with gradient ascent:

$$\theta = \theta + \alpha \nabla_\theta J(\theta) \quad (6.5a)$$

Note, that because the goal is to maximize the objective function, gradient ascent is used to move the parameters in the same direction as the gradient (contrary to gradient descent, which performs $\theta = \theta - \alpha \nabla_\theta J(\theta)$).

The idea behind equation (6.5) is to increase the probability that good actions will be re-proposed in the future, while reducing the probability of bad actions. The quality of the actions is carried on by the usual scalar value of $Q_{\pi_\theta}(s_i, a_i)$, which gives the quality of the state-action pair.

Computing the gradient

As long as the policy is differentiable, its gradient can be easily computed, taking advantage of modern automatic differentiation software.

To do that in TensorFlow, we can define the computational graph and call `tf.gradient(loss_function, variables)` to calculate the gradient of the loss function (`loss_function`) with respect to the `variables` trainable parameters. An alternative would be to directly maximize the `objective` function using the stochastic gradient descent optimizer, for example, by calling `tf.train.AdamOptimizer(lr).minimize(-objective_function)`.

Learning Stochastic and PG Optimization

The following snippet is an example of the steps that are required to compute the approximation in formula (6.5), with a policy of discrete action space of the `env.action_space.n` dimension:

```
pi = policy(states) # actions probability for each action
onehot_action = tf.one_hot(actions, depth=env.action_space.n)
pi_log = tf.reduce_sum(onehot_action * tf.math.log(pi), axis=1)

pi_loss = -tf.reduce_mean(pi_log * Q_function(states, actions))

# calculate the gradients of pi_loss with respect to the variables
gradients = tf.gradient(pi_loss, variables)

# or optimize directly pi_loss with Adam (or any other SGD optimizer)
# pi_opt = tf.train.AdamOptimizer(lr).minimize(pi_loss) #
```

`tf.one_hot` produces a one-hot encoding of the `actions` actions. That is, it produces a mask with 1, corresponding with the numerical value of the action, 0, in the others.

Then, in the third line of the code, the mask is multiplied by the logarithm of the action probability, in order to obtain the log probability of the `actions` actions. The fourth line computes the loss as follows:

$$\frac{1}{N} \sum_{i=0}^{N} [log\, \pi_\theta(a_i|s_i)\, Q_{\pi_\theta}(s_i, a_i)]$$

And finally, `tf.gradient` calculates the gradients of `pi_loss`, with respect to the `variables` parameter, as in formula (6.5).

The policy

In the case that the actions are discrete and limited in number, the most common approach is to create a parameterized policy that produces a numerical value for each action.

Note that, differently from the Deep Q-Network algorithm, here, the output values of the policy aren't the $Q(s,a)$ action values.

Then, each output value is converted to a probability. This operation is performed with the softmax function, which is given as follows:

$$\pi_\theta(a|s) = \frac{e^{z(s,a)}}{\sum_i e^{z(s,a_i)}}$$

The softmax values are normalized to have a sum of one, so as to produce a probability distribution where each value corresponds to the probability of selecting a given action.

The next two plots show an example of five action-value predictions before (the plot on the left) and after (the right plot) they are applied to the softmax function. Indeed, from the plot on the right, you can see that, after the softmax is computed, the sum of the new values is one, and that they all have values greater than zero:

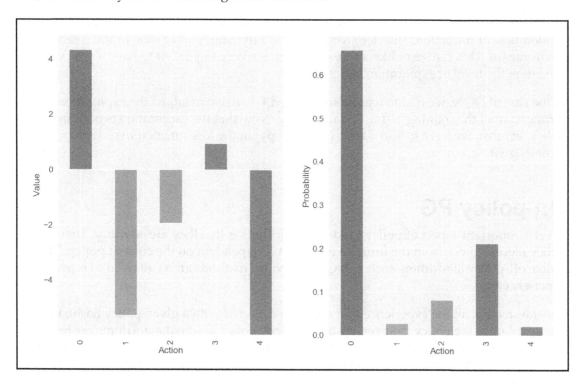

The right plot indicates that actions 0,1,2,3, and 4, will be selected approximately, with probabilities of 0.64, 0.02, 0.09, 0.21, and 0.02, correspondingly.

To use a softmax distribution on the action values that are returned by the parameterized policy, we can use the code that is given in the *Computing the gradient* section, with only one change, which has been highlighted in the following snippet:

```
pi = policy(states) # actions probability for each action
onehot_action = tf.one_hot(actions, depth=env.action_space.n)

pi_log = tf.reduce_sum(onehot_action * tf.nn.log_softmax(pi), axis=1) #
instead of tf.math.log(pi)

pi_loss = -tf.reduce_mean(pi_log * Q_function(states, actions))
gradients = tf.gradient(pi_loss, variables)
```

Here, we used `tf.nn.log_softmax`, because it's been designed to be more stable than first calling `tf.nn.softmax`, and then `tf.math.log`.

An advantage of having actions according to stochastic distribution, is in the intrinsic randomness of the actions selected, which enable a dynamic exploration of the environment. This can seem like a side effect, but it's very important to have a policy that can adapt the level of exploration by itself.

In the case of DQN, we had to use a hand-crafted ϵ variable to adjust the exploration throughout all the training, using linear ϵ decay. Now that the exploration is built into the policy, at most, we have to add a term (the entropy) in the loss function in order to incentivize it.

On-policy PG

A very important aspect of policy gradient algorithms is that they are *on-policy*. Their on-policy nature comes from the formula (6.4), as it is dependent on the current policy. Thus, unlike off-policy algorithms such as DQN, on-policy methods aren't allowed to reuse old experiences.

This means that all the experience that has been collected with a given policy has to be discarded once the policy changes. As a side effect, policy gradient algorithms are less sample efficient, meaning that they are required to gain more experience to reach the same performance as the off-policy counterpart. Moreover, they usually tend to generalize slightly worse.

Understanding the REINFORCE algorithm

The core of policy gradient algorithms has already been covered, but we have another important concept to explain. We are yet to look at how action values are computed.

We already saw with the formula (6.4):

$$\nabla_\theta J(\theta) = E_{\pi_\theta}[\nabla_\theta log\, \pi_\theta(a|s)\, Q_{\pi_\theta}(s,a)] \qquad (6.4)$$

that we are able to estimate the gradient of the objective function by sampling directly from the experience that is collected following the π_θ policy.

The only two terms that are involved are the values of $Q_{\pi_\theta}(s,a)$ and the derivative of the logarithm of the policy, which can be obtained through modern deep learning frameworks (such as TensorFlow and PyTorch). While we defined π_θ, we haven't explained how to estimate the action-value function, yet.

The simpler way, introduced for the first time in the REINFORCE algorithm by Williams, is to estimate the return is using **Monte Carlo (MC)** returns. For this reason, REINFORCE is considered an MC algorithm. If you remember, MC returns are the return values of sampled trajectories run with a given policy. Thus, we can rewrite equation (6.4), changing the action-value function, Q, with the MC return, G:

$$\begin{aligned}\nabla_\theta J(\theta) &= E_{\pi_\theta}[\nabla_\theta log\, \pi_\theta(a|s)\, Q_{\pi_\theta}(s,a)] \\ &= E_{\pi_\theta}[\nabla_\theta log\, \pi_\theta(a_t|s_t)\, G_t]\end{aligned} \qquad (6.6)$$

The G_t return is computed from a complete trajectory, implying that the PG update is available only after $T-t$ steps, where T is the total number of steps in a trajectory. Another consequence is that the MC return is well defined only in episodic problems, where there is an upper bound to the maximum number of steps (the same conclusions that we came up with in the other MC algorithms that we previously learned).

To get more practical, the discounted return at time t, which can also be called the *reward to go*, as it uses only future rewards, is as follows:

$$G_t = \sum_{t'=t}^{T} \gamma^{t'-t} r(s_{t'}, a_{t'})$$

Learning Stochastic and PG Optimization

This can be rewritten recursively, as follows:

$$G(s_t, a_t) = r(s_t, a_t) + \lambda G(s_{t+1}, a_{t+1})$$

This function can be implemented by proceeding in reverse order, starting from the last reward, as shown here:

```
def discounted_rewards(rews, gamma):
    rtg = np.zeros_like(rews, dtype=np.float32)
    rtg[-1] = rews[-1]
    for i in reversed(range(len(rews)-1)):
        rtg[i] = rews[i] + gamma*rtg[i+1]
    return rtg
```

Here, in the first place, a NumPy array is created, and the value of the last reward is assigned to the `rtg` variable. This is done because, at time T, $G(s_T, a_T) = r(s_T, a_T)$. Then, the algorithm computes `rtg[i]` backward, using the subsequent value.

The main cycle of the REINFORCE algorithm involves running a few epochs until it gathers enough experience, and optimizing the policy parameter. To be effective, the algorithm has to complete at least one epoch before performing the update step (it needs at least a full trajectory to compute the reward to go (G_t)). REINFORCE is summarized in the following pseudocode:

```
Initialize πθ with random weight
for episode 1..M do
        Initialize environment s ← env.reset()
        Initialize empty buffer

        > Generate a few episodes
        for step 1..MaxSteps do
                > Collect experience by acting on the environment
                a ← πθ(s)
                s',r,d ← env(a)
                s ← s'
                if d == True:
                    s ← env.reset()

                    > Compute the reward to go
                    G(st,at) = r(st,at) + λG(st+1,at+1)   # for each t
                    > Store the episode in the buffer
```

$D \leftarrow D \cup (s_{1..T}, a_{1..T}, G_{1..T})$ # where T is the length of the episode

> REINFORCE update step using all the experience in D following formula (6.5)

$$\theta \leftarrow \theta + \alpha \frac{1}{|D|} \sum_i [\nabla_\theta log\, \pi_\theta(a_i|s_i)\, G_i^{\pi_\theta}]$$

Implementing REINFORCE

It's time to implement REINFORCE. Here, we provide a mere implementation of the algorithm, without the procedures for its debugging and monitoring. The complete implementation is available in the GitHub repository. So, make sure that you check it out.

The code is divided into three main functions, and one class:

- `REINFORCE(env_name, hidden_sizes, lr, num_epochs, gamma, steps_per_epoch)`: This is the function that contains the main implementation of the algorithm.
- `Buffer`: This is a class that is used to temporarily store the trajectories.
- `mlp(x, hidden_layer, output_size, activation, last_activation)`: This is used to build a multi-layer perceptron in TensorFlow.
- `discounted_rewards(rews, gamma)`: This computes the discounted reward to go.

We'll first look at the main `REINFORCE` function, and then implement the supplementary functions and class.

The `REINFORCE` function is divided into two main parts. In the first part, the computational graph is created, while in the second, the environment is run and the policy is optimized cyclically until a convergence criterion is met.

The `REINFORCE` function takes the name of the `env_name` environment as the input, a list with the sizes of the hidden layers—`hidden_sizes`, the learning rate—`lr`, the number of training epochs—`num_epochs`, the discount value—`gamma`, and the minimum number of steps per epoch—`steps_per_epoch`. Formally, the heading of `REINFORCE` is as follows:

```
def REINFORCE(env_name, hidden_sizes=[32], lr=5e-3, num_epochs=50,
gamma=0.99, steps_per_epoch=100):
```

Learning Stochastic and PG Optimization

At the beginning of REINFORCE(..), the TensorFlow default graph is reset, an environment is created, the placeholder is initialized, and the policy is created. The policy is a fully connected multi-layer perceptron, with an output for each action, and tanh activation, on each hidden layer. The outputs of the multi-layer perceptron are the unnormalized values of the actions, called logits. All this is done in the following snippet:

```
def REINFORCE(env_name, hidden_sizes=[32], lr=5e-3, num_epochs=50,
gamma=0.99, steps_per_epoch=100):

    tf.reset_default_graph()

    env = gym.make(env_name)
    obs_dim = env.observation_space.shape
    act_dim = env.action_space.n

    obs_ph = tf.placeholder(shape=(None, obs_dim[0]), dtype=tf.float32, name='obs')
    act_ph = tf.placeholder(shape=(None,), dtype=tf.int32, name='act')
    ret_ph = tf.placeholder(shape=(None,), dtype=tf.float32, name='ret')
    p_logits = mlp(obs_ph, hidden_sizes, act_dim, activation=tf.tanh)
```

We can then create an operation that will compute the loss function, and one that will optimize the policy. The code is similar to the code that we saw earlier, in the *The policy* section. The only difference is that now the actions are sampled by tf.random.multinomial, which follows the action distribution that is returned by the policy. This function draws samples from a categorical distribution. In our case, it chooses a single action (depending on the environment, it could be more than one action).

The following snippet is the implementation of the REINFORCE update:

```
act_multn = tf.squeeze(tf.random.multinomial(p_logits, 1))
actions_mask = tf.one_hot(act_ph, depth=act_dim)
p_log = tf.reduce_sum(actions_mask * tf.nn.log_softmax(p_logits), axis=1)
p_loss = -tf.reduce_mean(p_log*ret_ph)
p_opt = tf.train.AdamOptimizer(lr).minimize(p_loss)
```

A mask is created over the actions that are chosen during the interaction with the environment and multiplied by log_softmax in order to obtain $log\ \pi_\theta(a|s)$. Then, the full loss function is computed. Be careful—there is a minus sign before tf.reduce_sum. We are interested in the maximization of the objective function. But because the optimizer needs a function to minimize, we have to pass a loss function. The last line optimizes the PG loss function using AdamOptimizer.

We are now ready to start a session, reset the global variables of the computational graph, and initialize some further variables that we'll use later:

```
sess = tf.Session()
sess.run(tf.global_variables_initializer())
step_count = 0
train_rewards = []
train_ep_len = []
```

Then, we create the two inner cycles that will interact with the environment to gather experience and optimize the policy, and print a few statistics:

```
for ep in range(num_epochs):
    obs = env.reset()
    buffer = Buffer(gamma)
    env_buf = []
    ep_rews = []

    while len(buffer) < steps_per_epoch:
        # run the policy
        act = sess.run(act_multn, feed_dict={obs_ph:[obs]})
        # take a step in the environment
        obs2, rew, done, _ = env.step(np.squeeze(act))

        env_buf.append([obs.copy(), rew, act])
        obs = obs2.copy()
        step_count += 1
        ep_rews.append(rew)

        if done:
            # add the full trajectory to the environment
            buffer.store(np.array(env_buf))
            env_buf = []
            train_rewards.append(np.sum(ep_rews))
            train_ep_len.append(len(ep_rews))
            obs = env.reset()
            ep_rews = []
    obs_batch, act_batch, ret_batch = buffer.get_batch()
    # Policy optimization
    sess.run(p_opt, feed_dict={obs_ph:obs_batch, act_ph:act_batch, ret_ph:ret_batch})

    # Print some statistics
    if ep % 10 == 0:
        print('Ep:%d MnRew:%.2f MxRew:%.1f EpLen:%.1f Buffer:%d -- Step:%d --' % (ep, np.mean(train_rewards), np.max(train_rewards), np.mean(train_ep_len), len(buffer), step_count))
```

Learning Stochastic and PG Optimization

```
            train_rewards = []
            train_ep_len = []
    env.close()
```

The two cycles follow the usual flow, with the exception that the interaction with the environment stops whenever the trajectory ends, and the temporary buffer has enough transitions.

We can now implement the `Buffer` class that contains the data of the trajectories:

```
class Buffer():
    def __init__(self, gamma=0.99):
        self.gamma = gamma
        self.obs = []
        self.act = []
        self.ret = []

    def store(self, temp_traj):
        if len(temp_traj) > 0:
            self.obs.extend(temp_traj[:,0])
            ret = discounted_rewards(temp_traj[:,1], self.gamma)
            self.ret.extend(ret)
            self.act.extend(temp_traj[:,2])

    def get_batch(self):
        return self.obs, self.act, self.ret
    def __len__(self):
        assert(len(self.obs) == len(self.act) == len(self.ret))
        return len(self.obs)
```

And finally, we can implement the function that creates the neural network with an arbitrary number of hidden layers:

```
def mlp(x, hidden_layers, output_size, activation=tf.nn.relu, last_activation=None):
    for l in hidden_layers:
        x = tf.layers.dense(x, units=l, activation=activation)
        return tf.layers.dense(x, units=output_size, activation=last_activation)
```

Here, `activation` is the non-linear function that is applied to the hidden layers, and `last_activation` is the non-linearity function that is applied to the output layer.

Landing a spacecraft using REINFORCE

The algorithm is complete however, the most interesting part has yet to be explained. In this section, we'll apply REINFORCE to LunarLander-v2, an episodic Gym environment with the aim of landing a lunar lander.

The following is a screenshot of the game in its initial position, and a hypothetical successful final position:

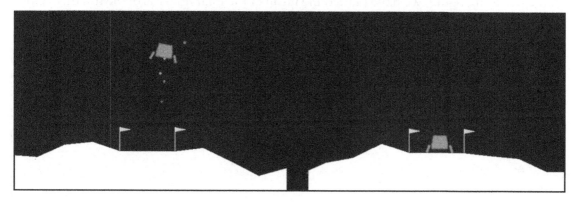

This is a discrete problem, and the lander has to land at coordinates (0,0), with a penalty if it lands far from that point. The lander has a positive reward when it moves from the top of the screen to the bottom, but when it fires the engine to slow down, it loses 0.3 points on each frame.

Moreover, depending on the conditions of the landing, it receives an additional -100 or +100 points. The game is considered solved with a total of 200 points. Each game is run for a maximum of 1,000 steps.

For that last reason, we'll gather at least 1,000 steps of experience, to be sure that at least one full episode has been completed (this value is set by the steps_per_epoch hyperparameter).

REINFORCE is run calling the function with the following hyperparameters:

```
REINFORCE('LunarLander-v2', hidden_sizes=[64], lr=8e-3, gamma=0.99,
num_epochs=1000, steps_per_epoch=1000)
```

Analyzing the results

Throughout the learning, we monitored many parameters, including `p_loss` (the loss of the policy), `old_p_loss` (the policy's loss before the optimization phase), the total rewards, and the length of the episodes, in order to get a better understanding of the algorithm, and to properly tune the hyperparameters. We also summarized some histograms. Look at the code in the book's repository to learn more about the TensorBoard summaries!

In the following figure, we have plotted the mean of the total rewards of the full trajectories that were obtained during training:

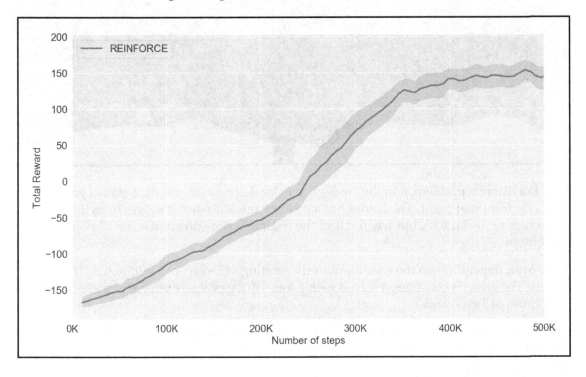

From this plot, we can see that it reaches a mean score of 200, or slightly less, in about 500,000 steps; therefore requiring about 1,000 full trajectories, before it is able to master the game.

When plotting the training performance, remember that it is likely that the algorithm is still exploring. To check whether this is true, monitor the entropy of the actions. If it's higher than 0, it means that the algorithm is uncertain about the actions selected, and it will keep exploring—choosing the other actions, and following their distribution. In this case, after 500,000 steps, the agent is also exploring the environment, as shown in the following plot:

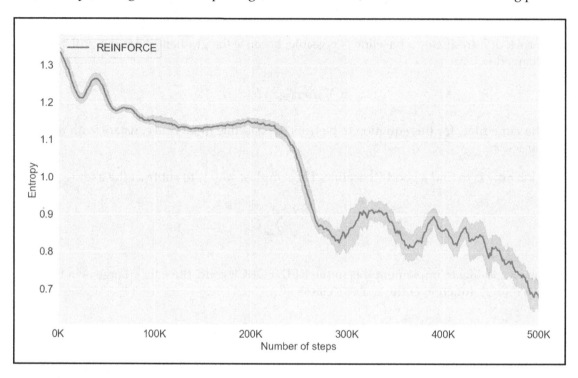

REINFORCE with baseline

REINFORCE has the nice property of being unbiased, due to the MC return, which provides the true return of a full trajectory. However, the unbiased estimate is to the detriment of the variance, which increases with the length of the trajectory. Why? This effect is due to the stochasticity of the policy. By executing a full trajectory, you would know its true reward. However, the value that is assigned to each state-action pair may not be correct, since the policy is stochastic, and executing it another time may lead to a new state, and consequently, a different reward. Moreover, you can see that the higher the number of actions in a trajectory, the more stochasticity you will have introduced into the system, therefore, ending up with higher variance.

Luckily, it is possible to introduce a baseline, b, in the estimation of the return, therefore decreasing the variance, and improving the stability and performance of the algorithm. The algorithms that adopt this strategy is called **REINFORCE** with baseline, and the gradient of its objective function is as follows:

$$\nabla_\theta J(\theta) = E_{\pi_\theta}[\nabla_\theta log\, \pi_\theta(a_t|s_t)\,(G_t - b)]$$

This trick of introducing a baseline is possible, because the gradient estimator still remains unchanged in bias:

$$E[\nabla_\theta log\pi_\theta(\tau)\,b] = 0$$

At the same time, for this equation to be true, the baseline must be a constant with respect to the actions.

Our job now is to find a good b baseline. The simplest way is to subtract the average return.

$$b = \frac{1}{N}\sum_{n=0}^{N} G_n$$

If you would like to implement this in the REINFORCE code, the only change is in the `get_batch()` function of the `Buffer` class:

```
def get_batch(self):
    b_ret = self.ret - np.mean(self.ret)
    return self.obs, self.act, b_ret
```

Although this baseline decreases the variance, it's not the best strategy. As the baseline can be conditioned on the state, a better idea is to use an estimate of the value function:

$$\nabla_\theta J(\theta) = E_{\pi_\theta}[\nabla_\theta log\, \pi_\theta(a_t|s_t)\,(G_t - V^{\pi_\theta}(s_t))]$$

Remember that the V^{π_θ} value function is, on average, the return that is obtained following the π_θ policy.

This variation introduces more complexity into the system, as we have to design an approximation of the value function, but it's very common to use, and it considerably increases the performance of the algorithm.

To learn $V^{\pi_\theta}(s)$, the best solution is to fit a neural network with MC estimates:

$$V_w^{\pi_\theta}(s) = \sum_{t'=t}^{T} \gamma^{t'-t} r(s_{t'}, a_{t'})$$

In the preceding equation, w is the parameters of the neural network to be learned.

In order to not overrun the notation, from now on, we'll neglect to specify the policy, so that $V_w^{\pi_\theta}(s)$ will become $V_w(s)$.

The neural network is trained on the same trajectories' data that is used for learning π_θ, without requiring additional interaction with the environment. Once computed, the MC estimates, for example, with `discounted_rewards(rews, gamma)`, will become the y target values, and the neural network will be optimized in order to minimize the mean square error (MSE) loss—just as you'd do in a supervised learning task:

$$\mathcal{L}(w) = \frac{1}{2} \sum_i (V_w(s_i) - y_i)^2$$

Here, w is the weights of the value function neural network, and each element of the dataset contains the s_i state, and the target value $y_i = \sum_{t'=t}^{T} \gamma^{t'-t} r(s_{t'}, a_{t'})$.

Implementing REINFORCE with baseline

The value function that baseline approximated with a neural network can be implemented by adding a few lines to our previous code:

1. Add the neural network, the operations for computing the MSE loss function, and the optimization procedure to the computational graph:

```
...
    # placeholder that will contain the reward to go values (i.e. the y values)
    rtg_ph = tf.placeholder(shape=(None,), dtype=tf.float32, name='rtg')
    # MLP value function
    s_values = tf.squeeze(mlp(obs_ph, hidden_sizes, 1, activation=tf.tanh))

    # MSE loss function
    v_loss = tf.reduce_mean((rtg_ph - s_values)**2)
```

Learning Stochastic and PG Optimization

```
# value function optimization
v_opt = tf.train.AdamOptimizer(vf_lr).minimize(v_loss)
...
```

2. Run `s_values`, and store the $V_w(s_i)$ predictions, as later we'll need to compute $(G_i - V_w(s_i))$. This operation can be done in the innermost cycle (the differences from the REINFORCE code are shown in bold):

```
    ...
    # besides act_multn, run also s_values
    act, val = sess.run([act_multn, s_values], feed_dict={obs_ph:[obs]})
    obs2, rew, done, _ = env.step(np.squeeze(act))

    # add the new transition, included the state value predictions
    env_buf.append([obs.copy(), rew, act, np.squeeze(val)])
    ...
```

3. Retrieve `rtg_batch`, which contains the "target" values from the buffer, and optimize the value function:

```
    obs_batch, act_batch, ret_batch, rtg_batch = buffer.get_batch()
    sess.run([p_opt, v_opt], feed_dict={obs_ph:obs_batch, act_ph:act_batch, ret_ph:ret_batch, rtg_ph:rtg_batch})
```

4. Compute the reward to go (G_i), and the target values $(G_i - V_w^\pi(s_i))$. This change is done in the `Buffer` class. We have to create a new empty `self.rtg` list in the initialization method of the class, and modify the `store` and `get_batch` functions, as follows:

```
def store(self, temp_traj):
    if len(temp_traj) > 0:
        self.obs.extend(temp_traj[:,0])
        rtg = discounted_rewards(temp_traj[:,1], self.gamma)
        # ret = G - V
        self.ret.extend(rtg - temp_traj[:,3])
        self.rtg.extend(rtg)
        self.act.extend(temp_traj[:,2])

def get_batch(self):
    return self.obs, self.act, self.ret, self.rtg
```

You can now test the REINFORCE with baseline algorithm on whatever environment you want, and compare the performance with the basic REINFORCE implementation.

Learning the AC algorithm

Simple REINFORCE has the notable property of being unbiased, but it exhibits high variance. Adding a baseline reduces the variance, while keeping it unbiased (asymptotically, the algorithm will converge to a local minimum). A major drawback of REINFORCE with baseline is that it'll converge very slowly, requiring a consistent number of interactions with the environment.

An approach to speed up training is called bootstrapping. This is a technique that we've already seen many times throughout the book. It allows the estimation of the return values from the subsequent state values. The policy gradient algorithms that use this techniques is called actor-critic (AC). In the AC algorithm, the actor is the policy, and the critic is the value function (typically, a state-value function) that "critiques" the behavior of the actor, to help him learn faster. The advantages of AC methods are multiple, but the most important is their ability to learn in non-episodic problems.

It's not possible to solve continuous tasks with REINFORCE, as to compute the reward to go, they need all the rewards until the end of the trajectory (if the trajectories are infinite, there is no end). Relying on the bootstrapping technique, AC methods are also able to learn action values from incomplete trajectories.

Using a critic to help an actor to learn

The action-value function that uses one-step bootstrapping is defined as follows:

$$Q(s,a) = r + \gamma V(s')$$

Here, s' is the notorious next state.

Thus, with an π_θ actor, and a V_w critic using bootstrapping, we obtain a one-step AC step:

$$\theta = \theta + \alpha \left(r_t + \gamma V_w(s'_t) - V_w(s)\right) \nabla_\theta log\, \pi_\theta(a_t|s_t)$$

This will replace the REINFORCE step with a baseline:

$$\theta = \theta + \alpha \left(G_t - V_w(s)\right) \nabla_\theta log\, \pi_\theta(a_t|s_t)$$

Note the difference between the use of the state-value function in REINFORCE and AC. In the former, it is used only as a baseline, to provide the state value of the current state. In the latter example, the state-value function is used to estimate the value of the next state, so as to only require the current reward to estimate $Q(s,a)$. Thus, we can say that the one-step AC model is a fully online, incremental algorithm.

The n-step AC model

In reality, as we already saw in TD learning, a fully online algorithm has low variance but high bias, the opposite of MC learning. However, usually, a middle-ground strategy, between fully online and MC methods, is preferred. To balance this trade-off, an n-step return can replace a one-step return of online algorithms.

If you remember, we already implemented n-step learning in the DQN algorithm. The only difference is that DQN is an off-policy algorithm, and in theory, n-step can be employed only on on-policy algorithms. Nevertheless, we showed that with a small n, the performance increased.

AC algorithms are on-policy, therefore, as far as the performance increase goes, it's possible to use arbitrary large n values. The integration of n-step in AC is pretty straightforward; the one-step return is replaced by $G_{t:t+n}$, and the value function is taken in the s_{t+n} state:

$$\theta = \theta + \alpha \left(G_{t:t+n} + \gamma^n V_w(s_{t+n}) - V_w(s_t) \right) \nabla_\theta \log \pi_\theta(a_t | s_t)$$

Here, $G_{t:t+n} = r_t + \gamma r_{t+1} + \ldots + \gamma^{n-1} r_{t+n-1}$. Pay attention here to how, if s_t is a final state, $V(s_{t+1}) = 0$.

Besides reducing the bias, the n-step return propagates the subsequent returns faster, making the learning much more efficient.

Interestingly, the $G_{t:t+n} + \gamma^n V_w(s_{t+n}) - V_w(s_t)$ quantity can be seen as an estimate of the advantage function. In fact, the advantage function is defined as follows:

$$A(a_t, s_t) = Q(a_t, s_t) - V(s_t)$$

Due to the fact that $G_{t:t+n} + \gamma^n V_w(s_{t+n})$ is an estimate of $Q_w(s_t, a_t)$, we obtain an estimate of the advantage function. Usually, this function is easier to learn, as it only denotes the preference of one particular action over the others in a particular state. It doesn't have to learn the value of that state.

Regarding the optimization of the weights of the critic, it is optimized using one of the well-known SGD optimization methods, minimizing the MSE loss:

$$\mathcal{L}(w) = \frac{1}{2} \sum_i (V_w(s_i) - y_i)^2$$

In the previous equation, the target values are computed as follows:
$y_i = G_{t:t+n} + \gamma^n V_w(s_{t+n})$.

The AC implementation

Overall, as we have seen so far, the AC algorithm is very similar to the REINFORCE algorithm, with the state function as a baseline. But, to provide a recap, the algorithm is summarized in the following code:

```
Initialize πθ with random weight
Initialize environment s ← env.reset()
for episode 1..M do
    Initialize empty buffer

    > Generate a few episodes
    for step 1..MaxSteps do
        > Collect experience by acting on the environment
        a ← πθ(s)
        s', r, d ← env(a)
        s ← s'
        if d == True:
            s ← env.reset()
        > Compute the n-step reward to go
        Gt = Gt:t+n + γⁿVw(st+n)   # for each t
        > Compute the advantage values
        At = Gt - Vw(st)   # for each t
        > Store the episode in the buffer
        D ← D ∪ (s1..T, a1..T, G1..T, A1..T)   # where T is the lenght of the
episode
```

Learning Stochastic and PG Optimization

> Actor update step using all the experience in D

$$\theta \leftarrow \theta + \alpha_\theta \frac{1}{|D|} \sum_i [\nabla_\theta log\, \pi_\theta(a_i|s_i)\, A_i]$$

> Critic update using all the experience in D

$$w \leftarrow w + \alpha_w \frac{1}{|D|} \sum_i (V_w(s_i) - G_i)^2$$

The only differences with REINFORCE are the calculation of the n-step reward to go, the advantage function calculation, and a few adjustments of the main function.

Let's first look at the new implementation of the discounted reward. Differently to before, the estimated value of the last `last_sv` state is now passed in the input and is used to bootstrap, as given in the following implementation:

```
def discounted_rewards(rews, last_sv, gamma):
    rtg = np.zeros_like(rews, dtype=np.float32)
    rtg[-1] = rews[-1] + gamma*last_sv    # Bootstrap with the estimate next state value

    for i in reversed(range(len(rews)-1)):
        rtg[i] = rews[i] + gamma*rtg[i+1]
    return rtg
```

The computational graph doesn't change, but in the main cycle, we have to take care of a few small, but very important, changes.

Obviously, the name of the function is changed to AC, and the learning rate of the `cr_lr` critic is added as an argument.

The first actual change involves the way in which the environment is reset. If, in REINFORCE, it was preferred to reset the environment on every iteration of the main cycle, in AC, we have to resume the environment from where we left off in the previous iteration, resetting it only when it reaches its final state.

The second change involves the way in which the action-value function is bootstrapped, and how the reward to go is calculated. Remember that $Q(s,a) = r + \gamma V(s')$ for every state-action pair, except in the case of when $V(s')$ is a final state. In this case, $Q(s,a) = r$. Thus, we have to bootstrap with a value of 0, whenever we are in the last state, and bootstrap with $V(s')$ in all the other cases. With these changes, the code is as follows:

```
obs = env.reset()
ep_rews = []

for ep in range(num_epochs):
```

```
        buffer = Buffer(gamma)
        env_buf = []

        for _ in range(steps_per_env):
            act, val = sess.run([act_multn, s_values],
feed_dict={obs_ph:[obs]})
            obs2, rew, done, _ = env.step(np.squeeze(act))

            env_buf.append([obs.copy(), rew, act, np.squeeze(val)])
            obs = obs2.copy()
            step_count += 1
            last_test_step += 1
            ep_rews.append(rew)

            if done:
                buffer.store(np.array(env_buf), 0)
                env_buf = []

                train_rewards.append(np.sum(ep_rews))
                train_ep_len.append(len(ep_rews))
                obs = env.reset()
                ep_rews = []

        if len(env_buf) > 0:
            last_sv = sess.run(s_values, feed_dict={obs_ph:[obs]})
            buffer.store(np.array(env_buf), last_sv)

        obs_batch, act_batch, ret_batch, rtg_batch = buffer.get_batch()
        sess.run([p_opt, v_opt], feed_dict={obs_ph:obs_batch,
act_ph:act_batch, ret_ph:ret_batch,          rtg_ph:rtg_batch})
        ...
```

The third change is in the `store` method of the `Buffer` class. In fact, now, we also have to deal with incomplete trajectories. In the previous snippet, we saw that the estimated $V(s')$ state values are passed as the third argument to the `store` function. Indeed, we use them to bootstrap and to compute the reward to go. In the new version of `store`, we call the variable that is associated with the state values, `last_sv`, and pass it as the input to the `discounted_reward` function, as follows:

```
    def store(self, temp_traj, last_sv):
        if len(temp_traj) > 0:
            self.obs.extend(temp_traj[:,0])
            rtg = discounted_rewards(temp_traj[:,1], last_sv, self.gamma)
            self.ret.extend(rtg - temp_traj[:,3])
            self.rtg.extend(rtg)
            self.act.extend(temp_traj[:,2])
```

Landing a spacecraft using AC

We applied AC to LunarLander-v2, the same environment used for testing REINFORCE. It is an episodic game, and as such, it doesn't fully emphasize the main qualities of the AC algorithm. Nonetheless, it provides a good testbed, and you can freely test it in another environment.

We call the AC function with the following hyperparameters:

```
AC('LunarLander-v2', hidden_sizes=[64], ac_lr=4e-3, cr_lr=1.5e-2,
gamma=0.99, steps_per_epoch=100, num_epochs=8000)
```

The resulting plot that shows the total reward accumulated in the training epochs is as follows:

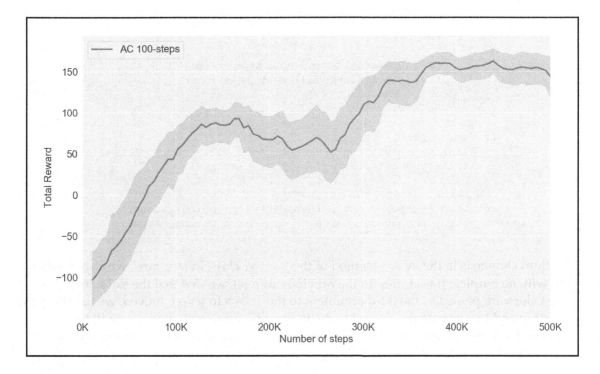

You can see that AC is faster than REINFORCE, as shown in the following plot. However, it is less stable, and after about 200,000 steps, the performance declines a little bit, fortunately continuing to increment afterward:

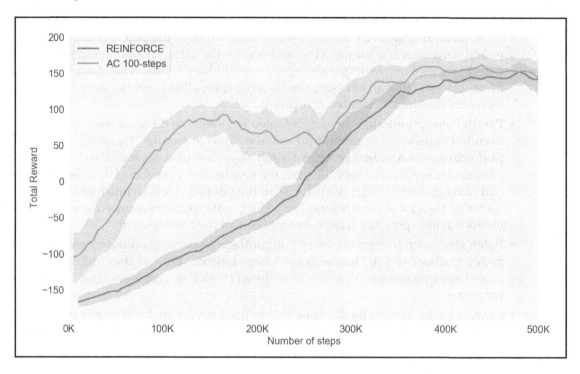

In this configuration, the AC algorithm updates the actor and critic every 100 steps. In theory, you could use a smaller `steps_per_epochs` but, usually, it makes the training more unstable. Using a longer epoch can stabilize the training, but the actor learns more slowly. It's all about finding a good trade-off and good learning rates.

 For all the color references mentioned in the chapter, please refer to the color images bundle at `http://www.packtpub.com/sites/default/files/downloads/9781789131116_ColorImages.pdf`.

Advanced AC, and tips and tricks

There are several further advancements of AC algorithms, and there are many tips and tricks to keep in mind, while designing such algorithms:

- **Architectural design**: In our implementation, we implemented two distinct neural networks, one for the critic, and one for the actor. It's also possible to design a neural network that shares the main hidden layers, while keeping the heads distinct. This architecture can be more difficult to tune, but overall, it increases the efficiency of the algorithms.
- **Parallel environments**: A widely adopted technique to decrease the variance is to collect experience from multiple environments in parallel. The **A3C** (**Asynchronous Advantage Actor-Critic**) algorithm updates the global parameters asynchronously. Instead, the synchronous version of it, called **A2C** (**Advantage Actor-Critic**) waits for all of the parallel actors to finish before updating the global parameters. The agent parallelization ensures more independent experience from different parts of the environment.
- **Batch size**: With respect to other RL algorithms (especially off-policy algorithms), policy gradient and AC methods need large batches. Thus, if after tuning the other hyperparameters, the algorithm doesn't stabilize, consider using a larger batch size.
- **Learning rate**: Tuning the learning rate in itself is very tricky, so make sure that you use a more advanced SGD optimization method, such as Adam or RMSprop.

Summary

In this chapter, we learned about a new class of reinforcement learning algorithms called policy gradients. They approach the RL problem in a different way, compared to the value function methods that were studied in the previous chapters.

The simpler version of PG methods is called REINFORCE, which was learned, implemented, and tested throughout the course of this chapter. We then proposed adding a baseline in REINFORCE in order to decrease the variance and increase the convergence property of the algorithm. AC algorithms are free from the need for a full trajectory using a critic, and thus, we then solved the same problem using the AC model.

With a solid foundation of the classic policy gradient algorithms, we can now go further. In the next chapter, we'll look at some more complex, state-of-the-art policy gradient algorithms; namely, **Trust Region Policy Optimization (TRPO)** and **Proximal Policy Optimization (PPO)**. These two algorithms are built on top of the material that we have covered in this chapter, but additionally, they propose a new objective function that improves the stability and efficiency of PG algorithms.

Questions

1. How do PG algorithms maximize the objective function?
2. What's the main idea behind policy gradient algorithms?
3. Why does the algorithm remain unbiased when introducing a baseline in REINFORCE?
4. What broader class of algorithms does REINFORCE belong to?
5. How does the critic in AC methods differ from a value function that is used as a baseline in REINFORCE?
6. If you had to develop an algorithm for an agent that has to learn to move, would you prefer REINFORCE or AC?
7. Could you use an n-step AC algorithm as a REINFORCE algorithm?

Further reading

To learn about an asynchronous version of the actor-critic algorithm, read `https://arxiv.org/pdf/1602.01783.pdf`.

7
TRPO and PPO Implementation

In the previous chapter, we looked at policy gradient algorithms. Their uniqueness lies in the order in which they solve a **reinforcement learning** (**RL**) problem—policy gradient algorithms take a step in the direction of the highest gain of the reward. The simpler version of this algorithm (**REINFORCE**) has a straightforward implementation that alone achieves good results. Nevertheless, it is slow and has a high variance. For this reason, we introduced a value function that has a double goal—to critique the actor and to provide a baseline. Despite their great potential, these actor-critic algorithms can suffer from unwanted rapid variations in the action distribution that may cause a drastic change in the states that are visited, followed by a rapid decline in the performance from which they could never recover from.

In this chapter, we will address this problem by showing you how introducing a trust-region, or a clipped objective, can mitigate it. We'll show two practical algorithms, namely TRPO and PPO. These have shown ability in controlling simulated walking, controlling hopping and swimming robots, and playing Atari games. We'll cover a new set of environments for continuous control and show how policy gradient algorithms can be adapted to work in a continuous action space. By applying TRPO and PPO to these new environments, you'll be able to train an agent to run, jump, and walk.

The following topics will be covered in this chapter:

- Roboschool
- Natural policy gradient
- Trust region policy optimization
- Proximal policy optimization

Roboschool

Up until this point, we have worked with discrete control tasks such as the Atari games in Chapter 5, *Deep Q-Network*, and LunarLander in Chapter 6, *Learning Stochastic and PG Optimization*. To play these games, only a few discrete actions have to be controlled, that is, approximately two to five actions. As we learned in Chapter 6, *Learning Stochastic and PG Optimization*, policy gradient algorithms can be easily adapted to continuous actions. To show these properties, we'll deploy the next few policy gradient algorithms in a new set of environments called Roboschool, in which the goal is to control a robot in different situations. Roboschool has been developed by OpenAI and uses the famous OpenAI Gym interface that we used in the previous chapters. These environments are based on the Bullet Physics Engine (a physics engine that simulates soft and rigid body dynamics) and are similar to the ones of the famous Mujoco physical engine. We opted for Roboschool as it is open source (Mujoco requires a license) and because it includes some more challenging environments.

Specifically, Roboschool incorporates 12 environments, from the simple Hopper (RoboschoolHopper), displayed on the left in the following figure and controlled by three continuous actions, to a more complex humanoid (RoboschoolHumanoidFlagrun) with 17 continuous actions, shown on the right:

Figure 7.1. Render of RoboschoolHopper-v1 on the left and RoboschoolHumanoidFlagrun-v1 on the right

In some of these environments, the goal is to run, jump, or walk as fast as possible to reach the 100 m endpoint while moving in a single direction. In others, the goal is to move in a three-dimensional field while being careful of possible external factors, such as objects that have been thrown. Also included in the set of 12 environments is a multiplayer Pong environment, as well as an interactive environment in which a 3D humanoid is free to move in all directions and has to move toward a flag in a continuous movement. In addition to this, there is a similar environment in which the robot is bombarded with cubes to destabilize the robot, who then has to build a more robust control to keep its balance.

The environments are fully observable, meaning that an agent has a complete view of its state that is encoded in a `Box` class of variable size, from about 10 to 40. As we mentioned previously, the action space is continuous and it is represented by a `Box` class of variable size, depending on the environment.

Control a continuous system

Policy gradient algorithms such as REINFORCE and AC, as well as PPO and TRPO, all of which will be implemented in this chapter, can work with a discrete and continuous action space. The migration from one type of action to the other is pretty simple. Instead of computing a probability for each action in a continuous control, the actions can be specified through the parameters of a probability distribution. The most common approach is to learn the parameters of a normal Gaussian distribution, which is a very important family of distributions that is parametrized by a mean, μ, and a standard deviation, σ. Examples of Gaussian distributions and the change of these parameters are shown in the following figure:

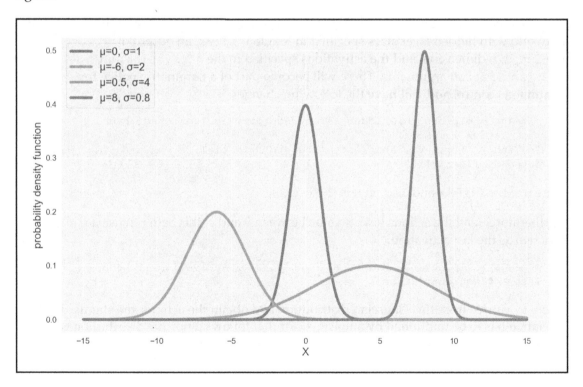

Figure 7.2. A plot of three Gaussian distributions with different means and standard deviations

For all the color references mentioned in the chapter, please refer to the color images bundle at http://www.packtpub.com/sites/default/files/downloads/9781789131116_ColorImages.pdf.

For example, a policy that's represented by a parametric function approximation (such as deep neural networks) can predict the mean and the standard deviation of a normal distribution in the functionality of a state. The mean can be approximated as a linear function and, usually, the standard deviation is independent of the state. In this case, we'll represent the parameterized mean as a function of a state denoted by $\mu_\theta(s)$ and the standard deviation as a fixed value denoted by σ. Moreover, instead of working with standard deviation, it is preferred to use the logarithm of the standard deviation.

Wrapping this up, a parametric policy for discrete control can be defined using the following line of code:

```
p_logits = mlp(obs_ph, hidden_sizes, act_dim, activation=tf.nn.relu, last_activation=None)
```

`mlp` is a function that builds a multi-layer perceptron (also called a fully connected neural network) with hidden layer sizes specified in `hidden_sizes`, an output of the `act_dim` dimension, and the activations specified in the `activation` and `last_activation` arguments. These will become part of a parametric policy for continuous control and will have the following changes:

```
p_means = mlp(obs_ph, hidden_sizes, act_dim, activation=tf.tanh, last_activation=None)
log_std = tf.get_variable(name='log_std', initializer=np.zeros(act_dim, dtype=np.float32))
```

Here `p_means` is $\mu_\theta(s)$ and `log_std` is $\log(\sigma)$.

Furthermore, if all the actions have a value between 0 and 1, it is better to use a `tanh` function as the last activation:

```
p_means = mlp(obs_ph, hidden_sizes, act_dim, activation=tf.tanh, last_activation=tf.tanh)
```

Then, to sample from this Gaussian distribution and obtain the actions, the standard deviation has to be multiplied by a noisy vector that follows a normal distribution with a mean of 0 and a standard deviation of 1 that have been summed to the predicted mean:

$$a = \mu_\theta(s) + \sigma * z$$

Here, z is the vector of Gaussian noise, $z \sim N(0,1)$, with the same shape as $\mu_\theta(s)$. This can be implemented in just one line of code:

```
p_noisy = p_means + tf.random_normal(tf.shape(p_means), 0, 1) * tf.exp(log_std)
```

Since we are introducing noise, we cannot be sure that the values still lie in the limit of the actions, so we have to clip p_noisy in such a way that the action values remain between the minimum and maximum allowed values. The clipping is done in the following line of code:

```
act_smp = tf.clip_by_value(p_noisy, envs.action_space.low, envs.action_space.high)
```

In the end, the log probability is computed as follows:

$$\log \pi_\theta(a|s) = -\frac{1}{2}\left(|a|\log 2\pi + \frac{(a-\mu_\theta(s))^2}{\sigma^2} + 2\log\sigma\right)$$

This formula is computed in the `gaussian_log_likelihood` function, which returns the log probability. Thus, we can retrieve the log probability as follows:

```
p_log = gaussian_log_likelihood(act_ph, p_means, log_std)
```

Here, `gaussian_log_likelihood` is defined in the following snippet:

```
def gaussian_log_likelihood(x, mean, log_std):
    log_p = -0.5 * (np.log(2*np.pi) + (x-mean)**2 / (tf.exp(log_std)**2 + 1e-9) + 2*log_std)
    return tf.reduce_sum(log_p, axis=-1)
```

That's it. Now, you can implement it in every PG algorithm and try all sorts of environments with continuous action space. As you may recall, in the previous chapter, we implemented REINFORCE and AC on LunarLander. The same game is also available with continuous control and is called `LunarLanderContinuous-v2`.

With the necessary knowledge to tackle problems with an inherent continuous action space, you are now able to address a broader variety of tasks. However, generally speaking, these are also more difficult to solve and the PG algorithms we've learned about so far are too weak and not best suited to solving hard problems. Thus, in the remaining chapters, we'll look at more advanced PG algorithms, starting with the natural policy gradient.

Natural policy gradient

REINFORCE and Actor-Critic are very intuitive methods that work well on small to medium-sized RL tasks. However, they present some problems that need to be addressed so that we can adapt policy gradient algorithms so that they work on much larger and complex tasks. The main problems are as follows:

- **Difficult to choose a correct step size**: This comes from the nature of RL being non-stationary, meaning that the distribution of the data changes continuously over time and as the agent learns new things, it explores a different state space. Finding an overall stable learning rate is very tricky.
- **Instability**: The algorithms aren't aware of the amount by which the policy will change. This is also related to the problem we stated previously. A single, not controlled update could induce a substantial shift of the policy that will drastically change the action distribution, and that consequently will move the agent toward a bad state space. Additionally, if the new state space is very different from the previous one, it could take a long time before recovering from it.
- **Bad sample efficiency**: This problem is common to almost all on-policy algorithms. The challenge here is to extract more information from the on-policy data before discarding it.

The algorithms that are proposed in this chapter, namely TRPO and PPO, try to address these three problems by taking different approaches, though they share a common background that will be explained soon. Also, both TRPO and PPO are on-policy policy gradient algorithms that belong to the model-free family, as shown in the following categorization RL map:

Chapter 7

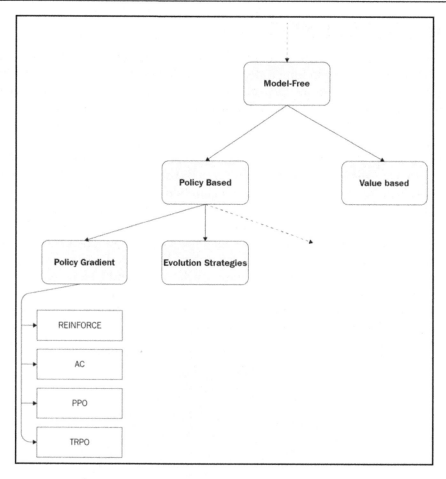

Figure 7.3. The collocation of TRPO and PPO inside the categorization map of the RL algorithms

Natural Policy Gradient (**NPG**) is one of the first algorithms that has been proposed to tackle the instability problem of the policy gradient methods. It does this by presenting a variation in the policy step that takes care of guiding the policy in a more controlled way. Unfortunately, it is designed for linear function approximations only, and it cannot be applied to deep neural networks. However, it's the base for more powerful algorithms such as TRPO and PPO.

Intuition behind NPG

Before looking at a potential solution to the instability of PG methods, let's understand why it appears. Imagine you are climbing a steep volcano with a crater on the top, similar to the function in the following diagram. Let's also imagine that the only sense you have is the inclination of your foot (the gradient) and that you cannot see the world around you—you are blind. Let's also set a fixed length of each step you can take (a learning rate), for example, one meter. You take the first step, perceive the inclination of your feet, and move 1 m toward the steepest ascent direction. After repeating this process many times, you arrive at a point near the top where the crater lies, but still, you are not aware of it since you are blind. At this point, you observe that the inclination is still pointing in the direction of the crater. However, if the volcano only gets higher for a length smaller than your step, with the next step, you'll fall down. At this point, the space around you is totally new. In the case outlined in the following diagram, you'll recover pretty soon as it is a simple function, but in general, it can be arbitrarily complex. As a remedy, you could use a much smaller step size but you'll climb the mountain much slower and still, there is no guarantee of reaching the maximum. This problem is not unique to RL, but here it is more serious as the data is not stationary and the damage could be way bigger than in other contexts, such as supervised learning. Let's take a look at the following diagram:

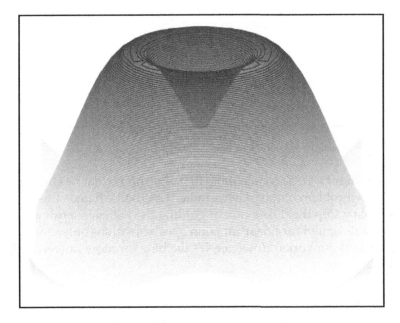

Figure 7.4. While trying to reach the maximum of this function, you may fall inside the crater

A solution that could come to mind, and one that has been proposed in NPG, is to use the curvature of the function in addition to the gradient. The information regarding the curvature is carried on by the second derivative. It is very useful because a high value indicates a drastic change in the gradient between two points and, as prevention, a smaller and more cautious step could be taken, thus avoiding possible cliffs. With this new approach, you can use the second derivative to gain more information about the action distribution space and make sure that, in the case of a drastic shift, the distribution of the action spaces don't vary too much. In the following section, we'll see how this is done in NPG.

A bit of math

The novelty of the NPG algorithm is in how it updates the parameters with a step update that combines the first and second derivatives. To understand the natural policy gradient step, we have to explain two key concepts: the **Fisher Information Matrix (FIM)** and the **Kullback-Leibler (KL)** divergence. But before explaining these two key concepts, let's look at the formula behind the update:

$$\theta \leftarrow \theta + \alpha F^{-1} \nabla_\theta J(\theta) \quad (7.1)$$

This update differentiates from the vanilla policy gradient, but only by the term F^{-1}, which is used to enhance the gradient term.

In this formula, F is the FIM and $J(\theta)$ is the objective function.

As we mentioned previously, we are interested in making all the steps of the same length in the distribution space, no matter what the gradient is. This is accomplished by the inverse of the FIM.

FIM and KL divergence

The FIM is defined as the covariance of an objective function. Let's look at how it can help us. To be able to limit the distance between the distributions of our model, we need to define a metric that provides the distance between the new and the old distributions. The most popular choice is to use the KL divergence. It measures how far apart two distributions are and is used in many places in RL and machine learning. The KL divergence is not a proper metric as it is not symmetric, but it is a good approximation of it. The more different two distributions, are the higher the KL divergence value. Consider the plot in the following diagram. In this example, the KL divergences are computed with respect to the green function. Indeed, because the orange function is similar to the green function, the KL divergence is 1.11, which is close to 0. Instead, it's easy to see that the blue and the green lines are quite different. This observation is confirmed by the high KL divergence between the two: 45.8. Note that the KL divergence between the same function will be always 0.

 For those of you who are interested, the KL divergence for discrete probability distribution is computed as $D_{KL}(P||Q) = -\sum_{x \in X} P(x) log\left(\frac{Q(x)}{P(x)}\right)$.

Let's take a look at the following diagram:

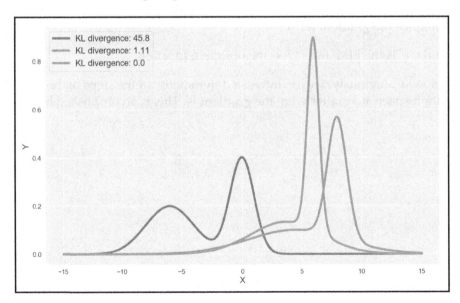

Figure 7.5. The KL divergence that's shown in the box is measured between each function and the function colored in green. The bigger the value, the farther the two functions are apart.

Thus, using the KL divergence, we are able to compare two distributions and get an indication of how they relate to each other. So, how can we use this metric in our problem and limit the divergence between two subsequent policies distribution?

It so happens that the FIM defines the local curvature in the distribution space by using the KL divergence as a metric. Thereby, we can obtain the direction and the length of the step that keeps the KL divergence distance constant by combining the curvature (second-order derivative) of the KL divergence with the gradient (first-order derivative) of the objective function (as in formula (7.1)). Thus, the update that follows from formula (7.1) will be more cautious by taking small steps along the steepest direction when the FIM is high (meaning that there is a big distance between the action distributions) and big steps when the FIM is low (meaning that there is a plateau and the distributions don't vary too much).

Natural gradient complications

Despite knowing the usefulness of the natural gradient in the RL framework, one of the major drawbacks of it is the computational cost that involves the calculation of FIM. While the computation of the gradient has a computational cost of $O(n)$, the natural gradient has a computational cost of $O(n^2)$, where n is the number of parameters. In fact, in the NPG paper that dates back to 2003, the algorithm has been applied to very small tasks with linear policies. The computation of F^{-1} is too expensive with modern deep neural networks that have hundreds of thousands of parameters. Nonetheless, by introducing some approximations and tricks, the natural gradient can be also used with deep neural networks.

In supervised learning, the use of the natural gradient is not needed as much as in reinforcement learning because the second-order gradient is somehow approximated in an empirical way by modern optimizers such as Adam and RMSProp.

Trust region policy optimization

Trust region policy optimization (TRPO) is the first successful algorithm that makes use of several approximations to compute the natural gradient with the goal of training a deep neural network policy in a more controlled and stable way. From NPG, we saw that it isn't possible to compute the inverse of the FIM for nonlinear functions with a lot of parameters. TRPO overcomes these difficulties by building on top of NPG. It does this by introducing a surrogate objective function and making a series of approximations, which means it succeeds in learning about complex policies for walking, hopping, or playing Atari games from raw pixels.

TRPO is one of the most complex model-free algorithms and though we already learned the underlying principles of the natural gradient, there are still difficult parts behind it. In this chapter, we'll only give an intuitive level of detail regarding the algorithm and provide the main equations. If you want to dig into the algorithm in more detail, check their paper (https://arxiv.org/abs/1502.05477) for a complete explanation and proof of the theorems.

We'll also implement the algorithm and apply it to a Roboschool environment. Nonetheless, we won't discuss every component of the implementation here. For the complete implementation, check the GitHub repository of this book.

The TRPO algorithm

From a broad perspective, TRPO can be seen as a continuation of the NPG algorithm for nonlinear function approximation. The biggest improvement that was introduced in TRPO is the use of a constraint on the KL divergence between the new and the old policy that forms a *trust region*. This allows the network to take larger steps, always within the trust region. The resulting constraint problem is formulated as follows:

$$maximize_\theta \; J_{\theta_{old}}(\theta)$$
$$subject \; to \; D_{KL}(\theta_{old}, \theta) \leq \delta \quad (7.2)$$

Here, $J_{\theta_{old}}$ is the objective surrogate function that we'll see soon, $D_{KL}(\theta_{old}, \theta)$ is the KL divergence between the old policy with the θ_{old} parameters, and the new policy with the θ and δ parameters is a coefficient of the constraint.

The objective surrogate function is designed in such a way that it is maximized with respect to the new policy parameters using the state distribution of the old policy. This is done using importance sampling, which estimates the distribution of the new policy (the desired one) while only having the distribution of the old policy (the known distribution). Importance sampling is required because the trajectory was sampled with the old policy, but what we actually care about is the distribution of the new one. Using importance sampling, the surrogate objective function is defined:

$$J_{\theta_{old}}(\theta) = E_{s \sim p_{old}, a \sim \pi_{old}} \left[\frac{\pi_\theta(a|s)}{\pi_{\theta_{old}}(a|s)} A_{\theta_{old}}(s, a) \right] \quad (7.3)$$

$A_{\theta_{old}}$ is the advantage function of the old policy. Thus, the constraint optimization problem is equivalent to the following:

$$maximize_\theta \ E_{s \sim p_{old}, a \sim \pi_{old}} \left[\frac{\pi_\theta(a|s)}{\pi_{\theta_{old}}(a|s)} A_{\theta_{old}}(s, a) \right]$$
$$subject \ to \ E_{s \sim p_{old}} [D_{KL}(\pi_{\theta_{old}}(\cdot|s) \ || \ \pi_\theta(\cdot|s))] \leq \delta \quad (7.4)$$

Here, $\pi(\cdot|s)$ indicates the actions distributions conditioned on the state, s.

What we are left to do is replace the expectation with an empirical average over a batch of samples and substitute $A_{\theta_{old}}$ with an empirical estimate.

Constraint problems are difficult to solve and in TRPO, the optimization problem in equation (7.4) is approximately solved by using a linear approximation of the objective function and a quadratic approximation to the constraint so that the solution becomes similar to the NPG update:

$$\theta \leftarrow \theta + \beta F^{-1} g$$

Here, $g = \nabla_\theta J(\theta)$.

The approximation of the original optimization problem can now be solved using the **Conjugate Gradient** (CG) method, an iterative method for solving linear systems. When we talked about NPG, we emphasize that computing F^{-1} is computationally very expensive with a large number of parameters. However, CG can approximately solve a linear problem without forming the full matrix, F. Thus, using CG, we can compute s as follows:

$$s \approx F^{-1} g \quad (7.5)$$

TRPO also gives us a way of estimating the step size:

$$\beta = \sqrt{\frac{2\delta}{s^T F s}} \quad (7.6)$$

Therefore, the update becomes as follows:

$$\theta \leftarrow \theta + \sqrt{\frac{2\delta}{s^T F s}} s \quad (7.7)$$

So far, we have created a special case of the natural policy gradient step, but to complete the TRPO update, we are missing a key ingredient. Remember that we approximated the problem with the solution of a linear objective function and quadratic constraint. Thus, we are solving only a local approximation to the expected return. With the introduction of these approximations, we cannot be certain that the KL divergence constraint is still satisfied. To ensure the nonlinear constraint while improving the nonlinear objective, TRPO performs a line search to find the higher value, α, that satisfies the constraint. The TRPO update with the line search becomes the following:

$$\theta \leftarrow \theta + \alpha \sqrt{\frac{2\delta}{s^T F s}} s \quad (7.8)$$

It may seem to you that the line search is a negligible part of the algorithm, but as demonstrated in the paper, it has a fundamental role. Without it, the algorithm may compute large steps, causing catastrophic degradation in the performance.

In terms of the TRPO algorithm, it computes a search direction with the conjugate gradient algorithm to find a solution for the approximated objective function and constraint. Then it uses a line search for the maximal step length, β, so that the constraint on the KL divergence is satisfied and the objective is improved. To further increase the speed of the algorithm, the conjugate gradient algorithm also makes use of an efficient Fisher-Vector product (to learn more about it, check out the paper that can be found at https://arxiv.org/abs/1502.05477paper).

TRPO can be integrated into an AC architecture where the critic is included in the algorithm to provide additional support to the policy (the actor) in the learning of the task. A high-level implementation of such an algorithm (that is, TRPO combined with a critic), when written in pseudocode, is as follows:

```
Initialize π_θ with random weight
Initialize environment  s ← env.reset()
```

```
for episode 1..M do
    Initialize empty buffer

    > Generate few trajectories
    for step 1..TimeHorizon do
        > Collect experience by acting on the environment
        a ← π_θ(s)
        s', r, d ← env(a)
        s ← s'
        if d == True:
            s ← env.reset()
            > Store the episode in the buffer
            D ← D ∪ (s_{1..T}, a_{1..T}, r_{1..T}, d_{1..T})  # where T is the length of the
episode
```

Compute the advantage values A_i and n-step reward to go G_i

> Estimate the gradient of the objective function

$$g = \nabla_\theta \widetilde{E}\left[\frac{\pi_\theta(a|s)}{\pi_{\theta_{old}}(a|s)} A_{\theta_{old}}(s,a)\right] \quad (1)$$

> Compute s using conjugate gradient

$$s \approx F^{-1} g \quad (2)$$

> Compute the step length

$$\beta = \sqrt{\frac{2\delta}{s^T F s}} \quad (3)$$

> Update the policy using all the experience in D

Backtracking line search to find the maximum α value that satisfy the constraint

$$\theta \leftarrow \theta + \alpha \beta s \quad (4)$$

> Critic update using all the experience in D

$$w \leftarrow w + \alpha_w \nabla_w \frac{1}{|D|} \sum_i (V_w(s_i) - G_i)^2$$

After this high-level overview of TRPO, we can finally start implementing it.

Implementation of the TRPO algorithm

In this implementation section of the TRPO algorithm, we'll concentrate our efforts on the computational graph and the steps that are required to optimize the policy. We'll leave out the implementation of other aspects that we looked at in the previous chapters (such as the cycle to gather trajectories from the environment, the conjugate gradient algorithm, and the line search algorithm). However, make sure to check out the full code in this book's GitHub repository. The implementation is for continuous control.

First, let's create all the placeholders and the two deep neural networks for the policy (the actor) and the value function (the critic):

```
act_ph = tf.placeholder(shape=(None,act_dim), dtype=tf.float32, name='act')
obs_ph = tf.placeholder(shape=(None, obs_dim[0]), dtype=tf.float32, name='obs')
ret_ph = tf.placeholder(shape=(None,), dtype=tf.float32, name='ret')
adv_ph = tf.placeholder(shape=(None,), dtype=tf.float32, name='adv')
old_p_log_ph = tf.placeholder(shape=(None,), dtype=tf.float32, name='old_p_log')
old_mu_ph = tf.placeholder(shape=(None, act_dim), dtype=tf.float32, name='old_mu')
old_log_std_ph = tf.placeholder(shape=(act_dim), dtype=tf.float32, name='old_log_std')
p_ph = tf.placeholder(shape=(None,), dtype=tf.float32, name='p_ph')
# result of the conjugate gradient algorithm
cg_ph = tf.placeholder(shape=(None,), dtype=tf.float32, name='cg')

# Actor neural network
with tf.variable_scope('actor_nn'):
    p_means = mlp(obs_ph, hidden_sizes, act_dim, tf.tanh, last_activation=tf.tanh)
    log_std = tf.get_variable(name='log_std', initializer=np.ones(act_dim, dtype=np.float32))

# Critic neural network
with tf.variable_scope('critic_nn'):
    s_values = mlp(obs_ph, hidden_sizes, 1, tf.nn.relu, last_activation=None)
    s_values = tf.squeeze(s_values)
```

There are a few things to note here:

1. The placeholder with the `old_` prefix refers to the tensors of the old policy.
2. The actor and the critic are defined in two separate variable scopes because we'll need to select the parameters separately later.

3. The action space is a Gaussian distribution with a covariance matrix that is diagonal and independent of the state. A diagonal matrix can then be resized as a vector with one element for each action. We also work with the logarithm of this vector.

Now, we can add normal noise to the predicted mean according to the standard deviation, clip the actions, and compute the Gaussian log likelihood, as follows:

```
p_noisy = p_means + tf.random_normal(tf.shape(p_means), 0, 1) *
tf.exp(log_std)

a_sampl = tf.clip_by_value(p_noisy, low_action_space, high_action_space)

p_log = gaussian_log_likelihood(act_ph, p_means, log_std)
```

We then have to compute the objective function, $\tilde{E}\left[\frac{\pi_\theta(a|s)}{\pi_{\theta_{old}}(a|s)} A_{\theta_{old}}(s,a)\right]$, the MSE loss function of the critic, and create the optimizer for the critic, as follows:

```
# TRPO loss function
ratio_new_old = tf.exp(p_log - old_p_log_ph)
p_loss = - tf.reduce_mean(ratio_new_old * adv_ph)

# MSE loss function
v_loss = tf.reduce_mean((ret_ph - s_values)**2)

# Critic optimization
v_opt = tf.train.AdamOptimizer(cr_lr).minimize(v_loss)
```

Then, the subsequent steps involve the creation of the graph for the points (2), (3), and (4), as given in the preceding pseudocode. Actually, (2) and (3) are not done in TensorFlow and so they aren't part of the computational graph. Nevertheless, in the computational graph, we have to take care of some related things. The steps for this are as follows:

1. Estimate the gradient of the policy loss function.
2. Define a procedure to restore the policy parameters. This is needed because in the line search algorithm, we'll optimize the policy and test the constraints, and if the new policy doesn't satisfy them, we'll have to restore the policy parameters and try with a smaller α coefficient.
3. Compute the Fisher-vector product. It is an efficient way to compute Fx without forming the full F.
4. Compute the TRPO step.
5. Update the policy.

TRPO and PPO Implementation

Let's start from step 1, that is, estimating the gradient of the policy loss function:

```
def variables_in_scope(scope):
    return tf.get_collection(tf.GraphKeys.TRAINABLE_VARIABLES, scope)

# Gather and flatten the actor parameters
p_variables = variables_in_scope('actor_nn')
p_var_flatten = flatten_list(p_variables)

# Gradient of the policy loss with respect to the actor parameters
p_grads = tf.gradients(p_loss, p_variables)
p_grads_flatten = flatten_list(p_grads)
```

Since we are working with vector parameters, we have to flatten them using `flatten_list`. `variable_in_scope` returns the trainable variables in `scope`. This function is used to get the variables of the actor since the gradients have to be computed with respect to these variables only.

Regarding step 2, the policy parameters are restored in this way:

```
p_old_variables = tf.placeholder(shape=(None,), dtype=tf.float32, name='p_old_variables')

# variable used as index for restoring the actor's parameters
it_v1 = tf.Variable(0, trainable=False)
restore_params = []

for p_v in p_variables:
    upd_rsh = tf.reshape(p_old_variables[it_v1 : it_v1+tf.reduce_prod(p_v.shape)], shape=p_v.shape)
    restore_params.append(p_v.assign(upd_rsh))
    it_v1 += tf.reduce_prod(p_v.shape)

restore_params = tf.group(*restore_params)
```

It iterates over each layer's variables and assigns the values of the old variables to the current one.

The Fisher-vector product of step 3 is done by calculating the second derivative of the KL divergence with respect to the policy variables:

```
# gaussian KL divergence of the two policies
dkl_diverg = gaussian_DKL(old_mu_ph, old_log_std_ph, p_means, log_std)

# Jacobian of the KL divergence (Needed for the Fisher matrix-vector product)
dkl_diverg_grad = tf.gradients(dkl_diverg, p_variables)
```

```
dkl_matrix_product = tf.reduce_sum(flatten_list(dkl_diverg_grad) * p_ph)

# Fisher vector product
Fx = flatten_list(tf.gradients(dkl_matrix_product, p_variables))
```

Steps 4 and 5 involve the application of the updates to the policy, where `beta_ph` is β, which is calculated using formula (7.6), and `alpha` is the rescaling factor found by line search:

```
# NPG update
beta_ph = tf.placeholder(shape=(), dtype=tf.float32, name='beta')
npg_update = beta_ph * cg_ph
alpha = tf.Variable(1., trainable=False)

# TRPO update
trpo_update = alpha * npg_update

# Apply the updates to the policy
it_v = tf.Variable(0, trainable=False)
p_opt = []
for p_v in p_variables:
    upd_rsh = tf.reshape(trpo_update[it_v : it_v+tf.reduce_prod(p_v.shape)], shape=p_v.shape)
    p_opt.append(p_v.assign_sub(upd_rsh))
    it_v += tf.reduce_prod(p_v.shape)

p_opt = tf.group(*p_opt)
```

Note how, without α, the update can be seen as the NPG update.

The update is applied to each variable of the policy. The work is done by `p_v.assign_sub(upd_rsh)`, which assigns the `p_v` - `upd_rsh` values to `p_v`, that i,: $\theta \leftarrow \theta - \alpha \beta s$. The subtraction is due to the fact that we converted the objective function into a loss function.

Now, let's briefly see how all the pieces we implemented come together when we update the policy at every iteration of the algorithm. The snippets of code we'll present here should be added after the innermost cycle where the trajectories are sampled. But before digging into the code, let's recap what we have to do:

1. Get the output, log probability, standard deviation, and parameters of the policy that we used to sample the trajectory. This policy is our old policy.
2. Get the conjugate gradient.
3. Compute the step length, β.

4. Execute the backtracking line search to get α.
5. Run the policy update.

The first point is achieved by running a few operations:

```
...
    old_p_log, old_p_means, old_log_std = sess.run([p_log, p_means,
log_std], feed_dict={obs_ph:obs_batch, act_ph:act_batch, adv_ph:adv_batch,
ret_ph:rtg_batch})
    old_actor_params = sess.run(p_var_flatten)
    old_p_loss = sess.run([p_loss], feed_dict={obs_ph:obs_batch,
act_ph:act_batch, adv_ph:adv_batch, ret_ph:rtg_batch,
old_p_log_ph:old_p_log})
```

The conjugate gradient algorithm requires an input function that returns the estimated Fisher Information Matrix, the gradient of the objective function, and the number of iterations (in TRPO, this is a value between 5 and 15):

```
def H_f(p):
    return sess.run(Fx, feed_dict={old_mu_ph:old_p_means,
old_log_std_ph:old_log_std, p_ph:p, obs_ph:obs_batch, act_ph:act_batch,
adv_ph:adv_batch, ret_ph:rtg_batch})

    g_f = sess.run(p_grads_flatten,
feed_dict={old_mu_ph:old_p_means,obs_ph:obs_batch, act_ph:act_batch,
adv_ph:adv_batch, ret_ph:rtg_batch, old_p_log_ph:old_p_log})
    conj_grad = conjugate_gradient(H_f, g_f, iters=conj_iters)
```

We can then compute the step length, β, beta_np, and the maximum coefficient, α, best_alpha, which satisfies the constraint using the backtracking line search algorithm, and run the optimization by feeding all the values to the computational graph:

```
    beta_np = np.sqrt(2*delta / np.sum(conj_grad * H_f(conj_grad)))

    def DKL(alpha_v):
        sess.run(p_opt, feed_dict={beta_ph:beta_np, alpha:alpha_v,
cg_ph:conj_grad, obs_ph:obs_batch, act_ph:act_batch, adv_ph:adv_batch,
old_p_log_ph:old_p_log})
        a_res = sess.run([dkl_diverg, p_loss],
feed_dict={old_mu_ph:old_p_means, old_log_std_ph:old_log_std,
obs_ph:obs_batch, act_ph:act_batch, adv_ph:adv_batch, ret_ph:rtg_batch,
old_p_log_ph:old_p_log})
        sess.run(restore_params, feed_dict={p_old_variables:
old_actor_params})
        return a_res

    best_alpha = backtracking_line_search(DKL, delta, old_p_loss, p=0.8)
```

```
        sess.run(p_opt, feed_dict={beta_ph:beta_np, alpha:best_alpha,
    cg_ph:conj_grad, obs_ph:obs_batch, act_ph:act_batch, adv_ph:adv_batch,
    old_p_log_ph:old_p_log})
```
        ...

As you can see, `backtracking_line_search` takes a function called `DKL` that returns the KL divergence between the old and the new policy, the δ coefficient (this is the constraint value), and the loss of the old policy. What `backtracking_line_search` does is, starting from $\alpha = 1$, incrementally decrease the value until it satisfies the following condition: the KL divergence is less than δ and the new loss function has decreased.

To this end, the hyperparameters that are unique to TRPO are as follows:

- `delta`, (δ), the maximum KL divergence between the old and new policy.
- The number of conjugate iterations, `conj_iters`. Usually, it is a number between 5 and 15.

Congratulations for coming this far! That was tough.

Application of TRPO

The efficiency and stability of TRPO allowed us to test it on new and more complex environments. We applied it on Roboschool. Roboschool and its Mujoco counterpart are often used as a testbed for algorithms that are able to control complex agents with continuous actions, such as TRPO. Specifically, we tested TRPO on RoboschoolWalker2d, where the task of the agent is to learn to walk as fast as possible. This environment is shown in the following figure. The environment terminates whenever the agent falls or when more than 1,000 timesteps have passed since the start. The state is encoded in a `Box` class of size 22 and the agent is controlled with 6 float values with a range of $[-1,1]$:

Figure 7.6. Render of the RoboschoolWalker2d environment

TRPO and PPO Implementation

In TRPO, the number of steps to collect from an environment on each episode is called the *time horizon*. This number will also determine the size of the batch. Moreover, it can be beneficial to run multiple agents in parallel so as to collect more representative data of the environment. In this case, the batch size will be equal to the time horizon, multiplied by the number of agents. Although our implementation is not predisposed to running multiple agents in parallel, the same objective can be achieved by using a time horizon longer than the maximum number of steps allowed on each episode. For example, knowing that, in RoboschoolWalker2d, an agent has a maximum of 1,000 time steps to reach the goal, by using a time horizon of 6,000, we are sure that at least six full trajectories are run.

We run TRPO with the hyperparameters that are reported in the following table. Its third column also shows the standard ranges for each hyperparameter:

Hyperparameter	For RoboschoolWalker2	Range
Conjugate iterations	10	[7-10]
Delta (δ)	0.01	[0.005-0.03]
Batch size (Time Horizon * Number of Agents)	6000	[500-20000]

The progress of TRPO (and PPO, as we'll see in the next section) can be monitored by specifically looking at the total reward accumulated in each game and the state values that were predicted by the critic.

We trained for 6 million steps and the result of the performance is shown in the following diagram. With 2 million steps, it is able to reach a good score of 1,300 and it is able to walk fluently and with a moderate speed. In the first phase of training, we can note a transition period where the score decreases a little bit, probably due to a local optimum. After that, the agent recovers and improves until reaching a score of 1,250:

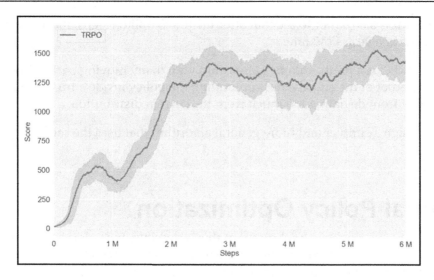

Figure 7.7. Learning curve of TRPO on RoboschoolWalker2d

Also, the predicted state value offers an important metric with which we can study the results. Generally, it is more stable than the total reward and is easier to analyze. The shown is provided in the following diagram. Indeed, it confirms our hypothesis since it is showing a smoother function in general, despite a few spikes around 4 million and 4.5 million steps:

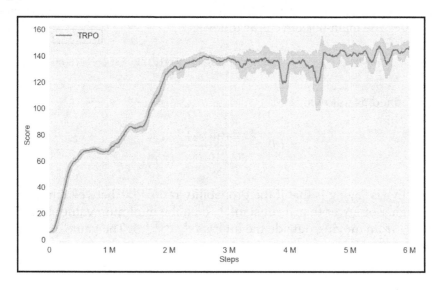

Figure 7.8. State values predicted by the critic of TRPO on RoboschoolWalker2d

From this plot, it is also easier to see that after the first 3 million steps, the agent continues to learn, if even at a very slow rate.

As you saw, TRPO is a pretty complex algorithm with many moving parts. Nonetheless, it constitutes as proof of the effectiveness of limiting the policy inside a trust region so as to keep the policy from deviating too much from the current distribution.

But can we design a simpler and more general algorithm that uses the same underlying approach?

Proximal Policy Optimization

A work by Schulman and others shows that this is possible. Indeed, it uses a similar idea to TRPO while reducing the complexity of the method. This method is called **Proximal Policy Optimization (PPO)** and its strength is in the use of the first-order optimization only, without degrading the reliability compared to TRPO. PPO is also more general and sample-efficient than TRPO and enables multi updates with mini-batches.

A quick overview

The main idea behind PPO is to clip the surrogate objective function when it moves away, instead of constraining it as it does in TRPO. This prevents the policy from making updates that are too large. The main objective is as follows:

$$\mathcal{L}^{CLIP}(\theta) = E_{s \sim p_{old}, a \sim \pi_{old}}[min(r_t(\theta)A_t, clip(r_t(\theta), 1-\epsilon, 1+\epsilon)A_t)] \quad (7.9)$$

Here, $r_t(\theta)$ is defined as follows:

$$r_t(\theta) = \frac{\pi_\theta(a_t|s_t)}{\pi_{\theta_{old}}(a_t|s_t)} \quad (7.10)$$

What the objective is saying is that if the probability ratio, $r_t(\theta)$, between the new and the old policy is higher or lower than a constant, ϵ, then the minimum value should be taken. This prevents r_t from moving outside the interval $[1-\epsilon, 1+\epsilon]$. The value of 1 is taken as the reference point, $r_t(\theta_{old}) = 1$.

The PPO algorithm

The practical algorithm that is introduced in the PPO paper uses a truncated version of **Generalized Advantage Estimation (GAE)**, an idea that was introduced for the first time in the paper `High-Dimensional Continuous Control using Generalized Advantage Estimation`. GAE calculates the advantage as follows:

$$A_t = \delta_t + (\gamma\lambda)\delta_{t+1} + \ldots + (\gamma\lambda)^{T-t+1}\delta_{t-1}$$
$$\text{where } \delta_t = r_t + \gamma V(s_{t+1}) - V(s_t) \quad (7.11)$$

It does this instead of using the common advantage estimator:

$$A_t = r_t + \gamma t_{t+1} + \ldots + \gamma^{T-t+1} r_{T-1} V(s_T) \quad (7.12)$$

Continuing with the PPO algorithm, on each iteration, N trajectories from multiple parallel actors are collected with time horizon T, and the policy is updated K times with mini-batches. Following this trend, the critic can also be updated multiple times using mini-batches. The following table contains standard values of every PPO hyperparameter and coefficient. Despite the fact that every problem needs ad hoc hyperparameters, it would be useful to get an idea of their ranges (reported in the third column of the table):

Hyperparameter	Symbol	Range
Policy learning rate	-	[$1e^{-5}$, $1e^{-3}$]
Number of policy iterations	K	[3, 15]
Number of trajectories (equivalent to the number of parallel actors)	N	[1, 20]
Time horizon	T	[64, 5120]
Mini-batch size	-	[64, 5120]
Clipping coefficient	ϵ	0.1 or 0.2
Delta (for GAE)	δ	[0.9, 0.97]
Gamma (for GAE)	γ	[0.8, 0.995]

Implementation of PPO

Now that we have the basic ingredients of PPO, we can implement it using Python and TensorFlow.

TRPO and PPO Implementation

The structure and implementation of PPO is very similar to the actor-critic algorithms but with only a few additional parts, all of which we'll explain here.

One such addition is the generalized advantage estimation (7.11) that takes just a few lines of code using the already implemented `discounted_rewards` function, which computes (7.12):

```python
def GAE(rews, v, v_last, gamma=0.99, lam=0.95):
    vs = np.append(v, v_last)
    delta = np.array(rews) + gamma*vs[1:] - vs[:-1]
    gae_advantage = discounted_rewards(delta, 0, gamma*lam)
    return gae_advantage
```

The `GAE` function is used in the `store` method of the `Buffer` class when a trajectory is stored:

```python
class Buffer():
    def __init__(self, gamma, lam):
        ...

    def store(self, temp_traj, last_sv):
        if len(temp_traj) > 0:
            self.ob.extend(temp_traj[:,0])
            rtg = discounted_rewards(temp_traj[:,1], last_sv, self.gamma)
            self.adv.extend(GAE(temp_traj[:,1], temp_traj[:,3], last_sv, self.gamma, self.lam))
            self.rtg.extend(rtg)
            self.ac.extend(temp_traj[:,2])

    def get_batch(self):
        return np.array(self.ob), np.array(self.ac), np.array(self.adv), np.array(self.rtg)

    def __len__(self):
        ...
```

Here, ... stands for the lines of code that we didn't report.

We can now define the clipped surrogate loss function (7.9):

```python
def clipped_surrogate_obj(new_p, old_p, adv, eps):
    rt = tf.exp(new_p - old_p) # i.e. pi / old_pi
    return -tf.reduce_mean(tf.minimum(rt*adv, tf.clip_by_value(rt, 1-eps, 1+eps)*adv))
```

It is quite intuitive and it doesn't need further explanation.

The computational graph holds nothing new, but let's go through it quickly:

```
# Placeholders
act_ph = tf.placeholder(shape=(None,act_dim), dtype=tf.float32, name='act')
obs_ph = tf.placeholder(shape=(None, obs_dim[0]), dtype=tf.float32,
name='obs')
ret_ph = tf.placeholder(shape=(None,), dtype=tf.float32, name='ret')
adv_ph = tf.placeholder(shape=(None,), dtype=tf.float32, name='adv')
old_p_log_ph = tf.placeholder(shape=(None,), dtype=tf.float32,
name='old_p_log')

# Actor
with tf.variable_scope('actor_nn'):
    p_means = mlp(obs_ph, hidden_sizes, act_dim, tf.tanh,
last_activation=tf.tanh)
    log_std = tf.get_variable(name='log_std', initializer=np.ones(act_dim,
dtype=np.float32))
    p_noisy = p_means + tf.random_normal(tf.shape(p_means), 0, 1) *
tf.exp(log_std)
    act_smp = tf.clip_by_value(p_noisy, low_action_space,
high_action_space)
    # Compute the gaussian log likelihood
    p_log = gaussian_log_likelihood(act_ph, p_means, log_std)

# Critic
with tf.variable_scope('critic_nn'):
    s_values = tf.squeeze(mlp(obs_ph, hidden_sizes, 1, tf.tanh,
last_activation=None))

# PPO loss function
p_loss = clipped_surrogate_obj(p_log, old_p_log_ph, adv_ph, eps)
# MSE loss function
v_loss = tf.reduce_mean((ret_ph - s_values)**2)

# Optimizers
p_opt = tf.train.AdamOptimizer(ac_lr).minimize(p_loss)
v_opt = tf.train.AdamOptimizer(cr_lr).minimize(v_loss)
```

The code for interaction with the environment and the collection of the experience is equal to AC and TRPO. However, in the PPO implementation in this book's GitHub repository, you can find a simple implementation that uses multiple agents.

TRPO and PPO Implementation

Once $N * T$ transitions (where N is the number of trajectories to run and T is the time horizon of each trajectory) are collected, we are ready to update the policy and the critic. In both cases, the optimization is run multiple times and done on mini-batches. But before it, we have to run `p_log` on the full batch because the clipped objective needs the action log probabilities of the old policy:

```
            ...
            obs_batch, act_batch, adv_batch, rtg_batch = buffer.get_batch()
            old_p_log = sess.run(p_log, feed_dict={obs_ph:obs_batch,
act_ph:act_batch, adv_ph:adv_batch, ret_ph:rtg_batch})
            old_p_batch = np.array(old_p_log)
lb = len(buffer)
            lb = len(buffer)
            shuffled_batch = np.arange(lb)

            # Policy optimization steps
            for _ in range(actor_iter):
                # shuffle the batch on every iteration
                np.random.shuffle(shuffled_batch)

                for idx in range(0, lb, minibatch_size):
                    minib = shuffled_batch[idx:min(idx+batch_size,lb)]
                    sess.run(p_opt, feed_dict={obs_ph:obs_batch[minib],
act_ph:act_batch[minib], adv_ph:adv_batch[minib],
old_p_log_ph:old_p_batch[minib]})

            # Value function optimization steps
            for _ in range(critic_iter):
                # shuffle the batch on every iteration
                np.random.shuffle(shuffled_batch)

                for idx in range(0, lb, minibatch_size):
                    minib = shuffled_batch[idx:min(idx+minibatch_size,lb)]
                    sess.run(v_opt, feed_dict={obs_ph:obs_batch[minib],
ret_ph:rtg_batch[minib]})
            ...
```

On each optimization iteration, we shuffle the batch so that every mini-batch is different from the others.

That's everything for the PPO implementation, but keep in mind that before and after every iteration, we are also running the summaries that we will later use with TensorBoard to analyze the results and debug the algorithm. Again, we don't show the code here as it is always the same and is quite long, but you can go through it in the full form in this book's repository. It is fundamental for you to understand what each plot displays if you want to master these RL algorithms.

PPO application

PPO and TRPO are very similar algorithms and we choose to compare them by testing PPO in the same environment as TRPO, namely RoboschoolWalker2d. We devoted the same computational resources for tuning both of the algorithms so that we have a fairer comparison. The hyperparameters for TRPO are the same as those we listed in the previous section but instead, the hyperparameters of PPO are shown in the following table:

Hyperparameter	Value
Neural network	64, tanh, 64, tanh
Policy learning rate	3e-4
Number of actor iterations	10
Number of agents	1
Time horizon	5,000
Mini-batch size	256
Clipping coefficient	0.2
Delta (for GAE)	0.95
Gamma (for GAE)	0.99

A comparison between PPO and TRPO is shown in the following diagram. PPO needs more experience to take off, but once it reaches this state, it has a rapid improvement that outpaces TRPO. In these specific settings, PPO also outperforms TRPO in terms of its final performance. Keep in mind that further tuning of the hyperparameters could bring better and slightly different results:

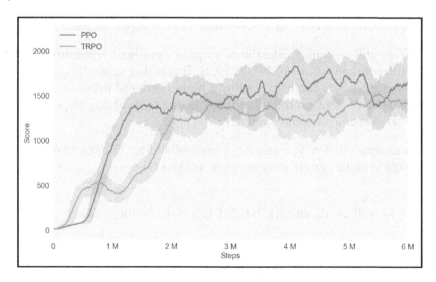

Figure 7.9. Comparison of performance between PPO and TRPO

TRPO and PPO Implementation

 A few personal observations: we found PPO more difficult to tune compared to TRPO. One reason for that is the higher number of hyperparameters in PPO. Moreover, the actor learning rate is one of the most important coefficients to tune, and if not properly tuned, it can greatly affect the final results. A great point in favor of TRPO is that it doesn't have a learning rate and that the policy is conditioned on a few hyperparameters that are easy to tune. Instead, an advantage of PPO is that it's faster and has been shown to work with a bigger variety of environments.

Summary

In this chapter, you learned how policy gradient algorithms can be adapted to control agents with continuous actions and then used a new set of environments called Roboschool.

You also learned aboutand developed two advanced policy gradient algorithms: trust region policy optimization and proximal policy optimization. These algorithms make better use of the data sampled from the environment and both use techniques to limit the difference in the distribution of two subsequent policies. In particular, TRPO (as the name suggests) builds a trust region around the objective function using a second-order derivative and some constraints based on the KL divergence between the old and the new policy. PPO, on the other hand, optimizes an objective function similar to TRPO but using only a first-order optimization method. PPO prevents the policy from taking steps that are too large by clipping the objective function when it becomes too large.

PPO and TRPO are still on-policy (like the other policy gradient algorithms) but they are more sample-efficient than AC and REINFORCE. This is due to the fact that TRPO, using a second-order derivative, is actually extracting a higher order of information from the data. The sample efficiency of PPO, on the other hand, is due to its ability to perform multiple policy updates on the same on-policy data.

Thanks to their sample efficiency, robustness, and reliability, TRPO and especially PPO are used in many very complex environments such as Dota (`https://openai.com/blog/openai-five/`).

PPO and TRPO, as well as AC and REINFORCE, are stochastic gradient algorithms.

In the next chapter, we'll look at two policy gradient algorithms that are deterministic. Deterministic algorithms are an interesting alternative because they have some useful properties that cannot be replicated in the algorithms we have seen so far.

Questions

1. How can a policy neural network control a continuous agent?
2. What's the KL divergence?
3. What's the main idea behind TRPO?
4. How is the KL divergence used in TRPO?
5. What's the main benefit of PPO?
6. How does PPO achieve good sample efficiency?

Further reading

- If you are interested in the original paper of the NPG, read **A Natural Policy Gradient**: https://papers.nips.cc/paper/2073-a-natural-policy-gradient.pdf.
- For the paper that introduced the Generalized Advantage Function, please read *High-Dimensional Continuous Control Using Generalized Advantage Estimation*: https://arxiv.org/pdf/1506.02438.pdf.
- If you are interested in the original Trust Region Policy Optimization paper, then please read **Trust Region Policy Optimization**: https://arxiv.org/pdf/1502.05477.pdf.
- If you are interested in the original paper that introduced the Proximal Policy Optimization algorithm, then please read *Proximal Policy Optimization Algorithms*: https://arxiv.org/pdf/1707.06347.pdf.
- For a further explanation of Proximal Policy Optimization, read the following blog post: https://openai.com/blog/openai-baselines-ppo/.
- If you are interested in knowing how PPO has been applied on Dota 2, check the following blog post regarding OpenAI: https://openai.com/blog/openai-five/.

8
DDPG and TD3 Applications

In the previous chapter, we concluded a comprehensive overview of all the major policy gradient algorithms. Due to their capacity to deal with continuous action spaces, they are applied to very complex and sophisticated control systems. Policy gradient methods can also use a second-order derivative, as is done in TRPO, or use other strategies, in order to limit the policy update by preventing unexpected bad behaviors. However, the main concern when dealing with this type of algorithm is their poor efficiency, in terms of the quantity of experience needed to hopefully master a task. This drawback comes from the on-policy nature of these algorithms, which makes them require new experiences each time the policy is updated. In this chapter, we will introduce a new type of off-policy actor-critic algorithm that learns a target deterministic policy, while exploring the environment with a stochastic policy. We call these methods deterministic policy gradient methods, due to their characteristic of learning a deterministic policy. We'll first show how these algorithms work, and we will also show their close relationship with Q-learning methods. Then, we'll present two deterministic policy gradient algorithms: **deep deterministic policy gradient (DDPG)**, and a successive version of it, known as **twin delayed deep deterministic policy gradient (TD3)**. You'll get a sense of their capabilities by implementing and applying them to a new environment.

The following topics will be covered in this chapter:

- Combining policy gradient optimization with Q-learning
- Deep deterministic policy gradient
- Twin delayed deep deterministic policy gradient (TD3)

Combining policy gradient optimization with Q-learning

Throughout this book, we approach two main types of model-free algorithms: the ones based on the gradient of the policy, and the ones based on the value function. From the first family, we saw REINFORCE, actor-critic, PPO, and TRPO. From the second, we saw Q-learning, SARSA, and DQN. As well as the way in which the two families learn a policy (that is, policy gradient algorithms use stochastic gradient ascent toward the steepest increment on the estimated return, and value-based algorithms learn an action value for each state-action to then build a policy), there are key differences that let us prefer one family over the other. These are the on-policy or off-policy nature of the algorithms, and their predisposition to manage large action spaces. We already discussed the differences between on-policy and off-policy in the previous chapters, but it is important to understand them well, in order to actually appreciate the algorithms that will be introduced in this chapter.

Off-policy learning is able to use previous experiences in order to refine the current policy, despite the fact that that experience comes from a different distribution. DQN benefits from this by storing all the memories that the agent had throughout its life in a replay buffer, and by sampling mini-batches from the buffer to update the target policy. At the opposite end of the spectrum, there is on-policy learning, which requires experience to be gained from the current policy. This means that old experiences cannot be used, and every time the policy is updated, the old data has to be discarded. As a result, because off-policy learning can reuse data multiple times, it requires fewer interactions with the environment in order to learn a task. In cases where the acquisition of new samples is expensive or very difficult to do, this difference matters a lot, and choosing off-policy algorithms could be vital.

The second factor is a matter of action spaces. As we saw in `Chapter 7`, *TRPO and PPO Implementation*, policy gradient algorithms have the ability to deal with very large and continuous action spaces. Unfortunately, the same does not hold true for Q-learning algorithms. To choose an action, they have to perform maximization across all the action space, and whenever this is very large or continuous, it is intractable. Thus, Q-learning algorithms can be applied to arbitrarily complex problems (with a very large state space) but their action space has to be limited.

In conclusion, none of the previous algorithms are always preferred over others, and the choice is mostly task dependent. Nevertheless, their advantages and disadvantages are quite complementary, and thus the question arises: Is it possible to combine the benefits of both families into a single algorithm?

Deterministic policy gradient

Designing an algorithm that is both off-policy and able to learn stable policies in high-dimensional action spaces is challenging. DQN already solves the problem of learning a stable deep neural network policy in off-policy settings. An approach to making DQN also suitable for continuous actions is to discretize the action space. For example, if an action has values between 0 and 1, a solution could be to discretize it in 11 values (0, 0.1, 0.2,..., 0.9, 1.0), and predict their probabilities using DQN. However, this solution is not manageable with a lot of actions, because the number of possible discrete actions increases exponentially with the degree of freedom of the agent. Moreover, this technique isn't applicable in tasks that need more fine-grained control. Thus, we need to find an alternative.

A valuable idea is to learn a deterministic actor-critic. It has a close relationship with Q-learning. If you remember, in Q-learning, the best action is chosen in order to maximize the approximated Q-function among all of the possible actions:

$$max_a Q_\phi(s,a) = Q_\phi(s, argmax_a\ Q_\phi(s,a))$$

DDPG and TD3 Applications

The idea is to learn a deterministic $\mu_\theta(s)$ policy that approximates $argmax_a\, Q_\phi(s,a)$. This overcomes the problem of computing a global maximization at every step, and opens up the possibility of extending it to very high-dimensional and continuous actions.

Deterministic policy gradient (**DPG**) applies this concept successfully to some simple problems such as Mountain Car, Pendulum, and an octopus arm. After DPG, DDPG expands the ideas of DPG, using deep neural networks as policies and adopting some more careful design choices in order to make the algorithm more stable. A further algorithm, TD3, addresses the problems of high variance, and the overestimation bias that is common in DPG and DDPG. Both DDPG and TD3 will be explained and developed in the following sections. When we construct a map that categorizes RL algorithms, we place DPG, DDPG, and TD3 in the intersection between policy gradient and Q-learning algorithms, as in the following diagram. For now, let's focus on the foundation of DPGs and how they work:

Categorization of the model-free RL algorithms developed so far

Chapter 8

The new DPG algorithms combine both Q-learning and policy gradient methods. A parametrized deterministic policy only outputs deterministic values. In continuous contexts, these can be the mean of the actions. The parameters of the policy can then be updated by solving the following equation:

$$\theta \leftarrow argmax_\theta \ Q_\phi(s, \mu_\theta(s)) \qquad (8.1)$$

Q_ϕ is the parametrized action-value function. Note that deterministic approaches differ from stochastic approaches in the absence of additional noise added to the actions. In PPO and TRPO, we were sampling from a normal distribution, with a mean and a standard deviation. Here, the policy has only a deterministic mean. Going back to the update (8.1), as always, maximization is done with stochastic gradient ascent, which will incrementally improve the policy with small updates. Then, the gradient of the objective function can be computed as follows:

$$\nabla_\theta J(\mu_\theta) = E_{s \sim p^\mu} [\nabla_\theta \mu_\theta(s) \ \nabla_a Q_\phi(s, a)|_{a=\mu_\theta}] \qquad (8.2)$$

p^μ is the state distribution following the μ policy. This formulation comes from the deterministic policy gradient theorem. It says that the gradient of the objective function is obtained in expectation by following the chain rule that is applied to the Q-function, which is taken with respect to the θ policy parameters. Using automated differentiable software such as TensorFlow, it's very easy to compute. In fact, the gradient is estimated just by computing the gradient, starting from the Q-values, all the way through the policy, but updating only the parameters of the latter, as shown here:

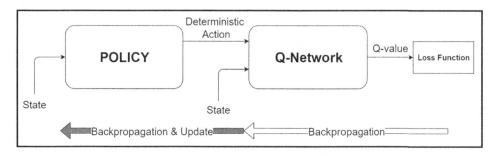

An illustration of the DPG theorem

The gradient is computed starting from the Q-values, but only the policy is updated.

This is a more theoretical result. As we know, deterministic policies don't explore the environment, and thus, they won't find a good solution. To make the DPG off-policy, we need to take a step further, and define the gradient of the objective function in such a way that the expectation follows the distribution of a stochastic exploratory policy:

$$\nabla_\theta J_\beta(\mu_\theta) \approx E_{s \sim p^\beta}[\nabla_\theta \mu_\theta(s) \nabla_a Q_\phi(s,a)|_{a=\mu_\theta}] \quad (8.3)$$

β is an exploratory policy, also called a behavior policy. This equation gives the *off-policy deterministic policy gradient* and gives the estimated gradient with respect to a deterministic policy (μ), while generating trajectories that follow a behavior policy (β). Note that, in practice, the behavior policy is just the deterministic policy with additional noise.

Though we have talked about deterministic actor-critic previously, until now, we have only shown how the policy learning takes place. Instead, we are learning both the actor that is represented by the deterministic policy (μ_θ), and the critic that is represented by the Q-function (Q_ϕ). The differentiable action-value function (Q_ϕ) can easily be learned with the Bellman updates that minimize the Bellman error
($\delta_t = r_t + \gamma Q_\phi(s_{t+1}, a_{t+1}) - Q_\phi(s_t, a_t)$), as done in Q-learning algorithms.

Deep deterministic policy gradient

If you implemented DPG with the deep neural networks that were presented in the previous section, the algorithm would be very unstable and it wouldn't be capable of learning anything. We encountered a similar problem when we extended Q-learning with deep neural networks. Indeed, to combine DNN and Q-learning in the DQN algorithm, we had to employ some other tricks to stabilize learning. The same holds true for DPG algorithms. These methods are off-policy, just like Q-learning, and as we'll soon see, some ingredients that make deterministic policies work with DNN are similar to the ones used in DQN.

DDPG (*Continuous Control with Deep Reinforcement Learning* by Lillicrap, and others: https://arxiv.org/pdf/1509.02971.pdf) is the first deterministic actor-critic that employs deep neural networks, for learning both the actor and the critic. This model-free, off-policy, actor-critic algorithm extends both DQN and DPG, in that it uses some insight from DQN, such as the replay buffer and the target network, to make DPG work with deep neural networks.

The DDPG algorithm

DDPG uses two key ideas, both borrowed from DQN but adapted for the actor-critic case:

- **Replay buffer**: All the transitions acquired during the lifetime of the agent are stored in a replay buffer, also called experienced replay. Then, this is used for training the actor and the critic by sampling mini-batches from it.
- **Target network**: Q-learning is unstable, since the network that is updated is also the one that is used for computing the target values. If you remember, DQN mitigates this problem by employing a target network that is updated every N iterations (copying the parameters of the online network in the target network). In the DDQN paper, they show that a soft target update works better in this context. With a soft update, the parameters of the target network, θ', are partially updated on each step with the parameters of the online network, θ:
$\theta' \leftarrow \tau\theta + (1-\tau)\theta'$ with $\tau \ll 1$. Yes, it may slow the learning, as the target network is changed only partially, but it outweighs the benefit that is derived from the increased instability. The trick of using a target network is used for both the actor and the critic, thereby the parameters of the target critic will also be updated following the soft update: $\phi' \leftarrow \tau\phi + (1-\tau)\phi'$.

Note that, from now on, we'll refer to θ and ϕ as the parameters of the online actor and the online critic, and to θ' and ϕ' as the parameters of the target actor and the target critic.

A characteristic that DDPG inherits from DQN is the ability to update the actor and the critic for each step taken in the environment. This follows on from the fact that DDPG is off-policy, and learns from the mini-batches that were sampled from the replay buffer. DDPG doesn't have to wait until a sufficiently large batch is gathered from the environment, as would be the case in on-policy stochastic policy gradient methods.

Previously, we saw how DPG acts according to an exploratory behavior policy, despite that fact that it is still learning a deterministic policy. But, how is this exploratory policy built? In DDPG, the β_θ policy is constructed by adding noise that is sampled from a noise process (N):

$$\beta_\theta(s_t) = \mu_\theta(s_t) + N$$

The N process will make sure that the environment is sufficiently explored.

DDPG and TD3 Applications

Wrapping up, DDPG learns by cyclically repeating these three steps until convergence occurs:

- The β_θ behavior policy interacts with the environment, collecting observations and rewards from it by storing them in a buffer.
- At each step, the actor and the critic are updated, based on the information held in the mini-batch that was sampled from the buffer. Specifically, the critic is updated by minimizing the mean squared error (MSE) loss between the values that were predicted by the online critic (Q_ϕ), and the target values that were computed using the target policy ($\mu_{\theta'}$) and the target critic ($Q_{\phi'}$). Instead, the actor is updated following formula (8.3).
- The target network parameters are updated following the soft update.

The whole algorithm is summarized in this pseudocode:

```
----------------------------------------------------------------------
DDPG Algorithm
----------------------------------------------------------------------

Initialize online networks Q_φ and μ_θ
Initialize target networks Q_φ' and μ_θ' with the same weights as the online networks
Initialize empty replay buffer D
Initialize environment s ← env.reset()

for episode = 1..M do
    > Run an episode
    while not d:
        a ← μ_β(s)
        s', r, d ← env(a)
        > Store the transition in the buffer
        D ← D ∪ (s, a, r, s', d)
        s ← s'

        > Sample a minibatch
        b ~ D
        > Calculate the target value for every i in b
        y_i ← r_i + γ(1 − d_i)Q_φ'(s'_i, μ_θ'(s'_i))      (8.4)

        > Update the critic
```

$$\phi \leftarrow \phi - \alpha_\phi \nabla_\phi \frac{1}{|b|} \sum_i (Q_\phi(s_i, a_i) - y_i)^2 \quad (8.5)$$

> Update the policy

$$\theta \leftarrow \theta - \alpha_\theta \frac{1}{|b|} \sum_i \nabla_\theta \mu_\theta(s_i) \nabla_a Q_\phi(s_i, a_i)|_{a=\mu(s_i)} \quad (8.6)$$

> Targets update
$$\theta' \leftarrow \tau\theta + (1-\tau)\theta'$$
$$\phi' \leftarrow \tau\phi + (1-\tau)\phi'$$

if $d == True$:
    $s \leftarrow env.reset()$

With a more clear understanding of the algorithm, we can now start implementing it.

DDPG implementation

The pseudocode that was given in the preceding section already provides a comprehensive view of the algorithm, but from an implementation standpoint, there are a few things that are worth looking at in more depth. Here, we'll show the more interesting features that could also recur in other algorithms. The full code is available in the GitHub repository of the book: https://github.com/PacktPublishing/Reinforcement-Learning-Algorithms-with-Python.

Specifically, we'll focus on a few main parts:

- How to build a deterministic actor-critic
- How to do soft updates
- How to optimize a loss function, with respect to only some parameters
- How to calculate the target values

We defined a deterministic actor and a critic inside a function called `deterministic_actor_critic`. This function will be called twice, as we need to create both an online and a target actor-critic. The code is as follows:

```
def deterministic_actor_critic(x, a, hidden_sizes, act_dim, max_act):
    with tf.variable_scope('p_mlp'):
        p_means = max_act * mlp(x, hidden_sizes, act_dim, last_activation=tf.tanh)
    with tf.variable_scope('q_mlp'):
```

DDPG and TD3 Applications

```
        q_d = mlp(tf.concat([x,p_means], axis=-1), hidden_sizes, 1,
last_activation=None)
    with tf.variable_scope('q_mlp', reuse=True): # reuse the weights
        q_a = mlp(tf.concat([x,a], axis=-1), hidden_sizes, 1,
last_activation=None)
    return p_means, tf.squeeze(q_d), tf.squeeze(q_a)
```

There are three interesting things happening inside this function. The first is that we are distinguishing between two types of input for the same critic. One that takes a state as the input, and a `p_means` deterministic action is returned by the policy; and the other that takes a state and an arbitrary action as the input. This distinction is needed, because one critic will be used for optimizing the actor, while the other is used for optimizing the critic. Nevertheless, despite these two critics having two different inputs, they are the same neural network, meaning that they share the same parameters. This different use case is accomplished by defining the same variable scope for both instances of the critic, and setting `reuse=True` on the second one. This will make sure that the parameters are the same for both definitions, in practice creating only one critic.

The second observation is that we are defining the actor inside a variable scope called `p_mlp`. This is because, later on, we'll need to retrieve only these parameters, and not those of the critic.

The third observation is that, because the policy has a `tanh` function as its final activation layer (to constrain the values to be between -1 and 1) but our actor may need values out of this range, we have to multiply the output by a `max_act` factor (this assumes that the minimum and maximum values are opposite, that is, if the maximum allowed value is 3, the minimum is -3).

Nice! Let's now have a look through the remaining of the computational graph, where we define the placeholders; create the online and target actors, as well as the online and target critics; define the losses; implement the optimizers; and update the target networks.

We'll start from the creation of the placeholders that we'll need for the observations, the actions, and the target values:

```
obs_dim = env.observation_space.shape
act_dim = env.action_space.shape

obs_ph = tf.placeholder(shape=(None, obs_dim[0]), dtype=tf.float32,
name='obs')
act_ph = tf.placeholder(shape=(None, act_dim[0]), dtype=tf.float32,
name='act')
y_ph = tf.placeholder(shape=(None,), dtype=tf.float32, name='y')
```

In the preceding code, `y_ph` is the placeholder for the target Q-values, `obs_ph` for the observations, and `act_ph` for the actions.

We then call the previously defined `deterministic_actor_critic` function inside an `online` and `target` variable scope, so as to differentiate the four neural networks:

```
with tf.variable_scope('online'):
    p_onl, qd_onl, qa_onl = deterministic_actor_critic(obs_ph, act_ph,
hidden_sizes, act_dim[0], np.max(env.action_space.high))

with tf.variable_scope('target'):
    _, qd_tar, _ = deterministic_actor_critic(obs_ph, act_ph, hidden_sizes,
act_dim[0], np.max(env.action_space.high))
```

The loss of the critic is the MSE loss between the Q-values of the `qa_onl` online network, and the `y_ph` target action value:

```
q_loss = tf.reduce_mean((qa_onl - y_ph)**2)
```

This will be minimized with the Adam optimizer:

```
q_opt = tf.train.AdamOptimizer(cr_lr).minimize(q_loss)
```

With regard to the actor's loss function, it is the opposite sign of the online Q-network. In this case, the online Q-network has the actions chosen by the online deterministic actor as the input (as from formula (8.6), which was defined in the pseudocode of *The DDPG algorithm* section). Thus, the Q-values are represented by `qd_onl`, and the policy loss function is written as follows:

```
p_loss = -tf.reduce_mean(qd_onl)
```

We took the opposite sign of the objective function, because we have to convert it to a loss function, considering that the optimizers need to minimize a loss function.

Now, the most important thing to remember here is that, despite computing the gradient from the `p_loss` loss function that depends on both the critic and the actor, we only need to update the actor. Indeed, from DPG we know that
$\nabla_\theta J_\beta(\mu_\theta) \approx E_{s \sim p^\beta}[\nabla_\theta \mu_\theta(s) \nabla_a Q_\phi(s,a)|_{a=\mu_\theta}]$.

This is accomplished by passing `p_loss` to the `minimize` method of the optimizer, which specifies the variables that need updating. In this case, we need to update only the variables of the online actor that was defined in the `online/m_mlp` variable scope:

```
p_opt = tf.train.AdamOptimizer(ac_lr).minimize(p_loss,
    var_list=variables_in_scope('online/p_mlp'))
```

In this way, the computation of the gradient will start from `p_loss`, go through the critic's network, and then the actor's network. By the end, only the parameters of the actor will be optimized.

Now, we have to define the `variable_in_scope(scope)` function that returns the variables in the scope named `scope`:

```
def variables_in_scope(scope):
    return tf.get_collection(tf.GraphKeys.GLOBAL_VARIABLES, scope)
```

It's now time to look at how the target networks are updated. We can use `variable_in_scope` to get the target and online variables of both the actors and the critics, and use the TensorFlow `assign` function on the target variables to update them, following the soft update formula:

$$\theta' \leftarrow \tau\theta + (1 - \tau)\theta'$$

This is done in the following snippet of code:

```
update_target = [target_var.assign(tau*online_var + (1-tau)*target_var) for
target_var, online_var in zip(variables_in_scope('target'),
variables_in_scope('online'))]
update_target_op = tf.group(*update_target)
```

That's it! For the computational graph, that's everything. Pretty straightforward, right? Now we can take a quick look at the main cycle, where the parameters are updated, following the estimated gradient on a finite batch of samples. The interaction of the policy with the environment is standard, with the exception that now the actions that are returned by the policy are deterministic, and we have to add a certain amount of noise in order to adequately explore the environment. Here, we don't provide this part of the code, but you can find the full implementation on GitHub.

When a minimum amount of experience has been acquired, and the buffer has reached a certain threshold, the optimization of the policy and the critic starts. The steps that follow are those that are summarized in the DDPG pseudocode that was provided in *The DDPG algorithm* section. These are as follows:

1. Sample a mini-batch from the buffer
2. Calculate the target action values
3. Optimize the critic
4. Optimize the actor
5. Update the target networks

All these operations are executed in just a few lines of code:

```
    ...
    mb_obs, mb_rew, mb_act, mb_obs2, mb_done = buffer.sample_minibatch(batch_size)

    q_target_mb = sess.run(qd_tar, feed_dict={obs_ph:mb_obs2})
    y_r = np.array(mb_rew) + discount*(1-np.array(mb_done))*q_target_mb

    _, q_train_loss = sess.run([q_opt, q_loss], feed_dict={obs_ph:mb_obs, y_ph:y_r, act_ph: mb_act})

    _, p_train_loss = sess.run([p_opt, p_loss], feed_dict={obs_ph:mb_obs})

    sess.run(update_target_op)

    ...
```

The first line of code samples a mini-batch of size `batch_size`, the second and third lines compute the target action values, as defined in equation (8.4), by running the critic and actor target networks on `mb_obs2`, which contains the next states. The fourth line optimizes the critic by feeding the dictionary with the target action values that were just computed, as well as the observations and actions. The fifth line optimizes the actor, and the last one updates the target networks by running `update_target_op`.

Appling DDPG to BipedalWalker-v2

Let's now apply DDPG to a continuous task called BipedalWalker-v2, that is, one of the environments provided by Gym that uses Box2D, a 2D physical engine. A screenshot of this environment follows. The goal is to make the agent walk as fast as possible in rough terrains. A score of 300+ is given for moving until the end, but every application of the motors costs a small amount. The more optimally the agent moves, the less it costs. Furthermore, if the agent falls, it receives a reward of -100. The state consists of 24 float numbers that represent the speeds and the positions of the joints and the hull, and LiDar rangefinder measurements. The agent is controlled by four continuous actions, with the range [-1,1]. The following is a screenshot of BipedalWalker 2D environment:

Screenshot of BipedalWalker2d environment

We run DDPG with the hyperparameters that are given in the following table. In the first row, the hyperparameters that are needed to run DDPG are listed, while the corresponding values that are used in this particular case are listed in the second row. Let's refer to the following table:

Hyperparameter	Actor Learning Rate	Critic Learning Rate	DNN architecture	Buffer Size	Batch Size	Tau
Value	3e-4	4e-4	[64,relu,64,relu]	200000	64	0.003

Chapter 8

During training, we added extra noise in the actions that were predicted by the policy, however, to measure the performance of the algorithm, we run 10 games on a pure deterministic policy (without extra noise) every 10 episodes. The cumulative rewards that is averaged across the 10 games in the function of the timesteps is plotted in the following diagram:

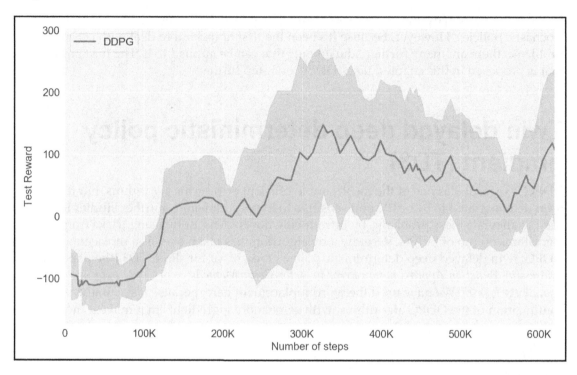

Performance of the DDPG algorithm on BipedalWalker2d-v2

From the results, we can see that the performance is quite unstable, ranging from 250 to less than -100, after only a few thousand steps. It is known that DDPG is unstable and very sensitive to the hyperparameters, but with more careful fine-tuning, the results may be smoother. Nonetheless, we can see that the performance increases in the first 300k steps, reaching an average score of about 100, with peaks of up to 300.

Additionally, BipedalWalker-v2 is a notoriously difficult environment to solve. Indeed, it is considered solved when the agent obtains an average reward of at least 300 points, on 100 consecutive episodes. With DDPG, we aren't able to reach those performances, but still, we obtained a good policy that is able to make the agent run fairly fast.

In our implementation, we used a constant exploratory factor. By using a more sophisticated function, you could probably reach a higher performance in fewer iterations. For example, in the DDPG paper, they use an Ornstein-Uhlenbeck process. You can start from this process, if you wish to.

DDPG is a beautiful example of how deterministic policy can be used in contraposition to stochastic policies. However, because it's been the first of its kind to deal with complex problems, there are many further adjustments that can be applied to it. The next algorithm that is proposed in this chapter, takes DDPG one step further.

Twin delayed deep deterministic policy gradient (TD3)

DDPG is regarded as one of the most sample-efficient actor-critic algorithms, but it has been demonstrated to be brittle and sensitive to hyperparameters. Further studies have tried to alleviate these problems, by introducing novel ideas, or by using tricks from other algorithms on top of DDPG. Recently, one algorithm has taken over as a replacement of DDPG: twin delayed deep deterministic policy gradient, or for short, TD3 (the paper is *Addressing Function Approximation Error in Actor-Critic Methods*: https://arxiv.org/pdf/1802.09477.pdf). We have used the word replacement here, because it's actually a continuation of the DDPG algorithms, with some more ingredients that make it more stable, and more performant.

TD3 focuses on some of the problems that are also common in other off-policy algorithms. These problems are the overestimation of the value estimate, and high-variance estimates of the gradient. For the former problem, they employ a solution similar to the one used in DQN, and for the latter, they employ two novel solutions. Let's first consider the overestimation bias problem.

Addressing overestimation bias

Overestimation bias means that the action values that are predicted by the approximated Q-function are higher than what they should be. Having been widely studied in Q-learning algorithms with discrete actions, this often leads to bad predictions that affect the end performance. Despite being less affected, this problem is also present in DDPG.

If you remember, the DQN variant that reduces the overestimation of the action values is called double DQN and it proposes two neural networks; one for choosing the action, and one for calculating the Q-value. In particular, the work of the second neural network is done by a frozen target network. This is a sound idea, but as explained in the TD3 paper, it isn't effective on actor-critic methods, as in these methods, the policy changes too slowly. So, they propose a variation called clipped double Q-learning that takes the minimum between the estimates of two different critics (Q_{ϕ_1}, Q_{ϕ_2}). Thus, the target value is computed as follows:

$$y = r + \gamma \, min_{i=1,2} Q_{\phi'_i}(s', \mu_{\theta'}(s')) \qquad (8.7)$$

On the opposite side, this doesn't prevent an underestimation bias, but it is way less harmful than its overestimation. Clipped double Q-learning can be used in any actor-critic method, and it works following the assumption that the two critics will have different biases.

Implementation of TD3

To put this strategy into code, we have to create two critics with different initializations, compute the target action value as in (8.7), and optimize both critics.

TD3 is applied on the DDPG implementation that we discussed in the previous section. The following snippets are only a portion of the additional code that is needed to implement TD3. The complete implementation is available in the GitHub repository of the book: https://github.com/PacktPublishing/Hands-On-Reinforcement-Learning-Algorithms-with-Python.

With regard to the double critic, you have just to create them by calling `deterministic_actor_double_critic` twice, once for the target and once for the online networks, as done in DDPG. The code will be similar to this:

```
def deterministic_actor_double_critic(x, a, hidden_sizes, act_dim, max_act):
    with tf.variable_scope('p_mlp'):
        p_means = max_act * mlp(x, hidden_sizes, act_dim, last_activation=tf.tanh)
    # First critic
    with tf.variable_scope('q1_mlp'):
        q1_d = mlp(tf.concat([x,p_means], axis=-1), hidden_sizes, 1, last_activation=None)
    with tf.variable_scope('q1_mlp', reuse=True): # Use the weights of the
```

DDPG and TD3 Applications

```
mlp just defined
        q1_a = mlp(tf.concat([x,a], axis=-1), hidden_sizes, 1,
last_activation=None)

    # Second critic
    with tf.variable_scope('q2_mlp'):
        q2_d = mlp(tf.concat([x,p_means], axis=-1), hidden_sizes, 1,
last_activation=None)
    with tf.variable_scope('q2_mlp', reuse=True):
        q2_a = mlp(tf.concat([x,a], axis=-1), hidden_sizes, 1,
last_activation=None)

    return p_means, tf.squeeze(q1_d), tf.squeeze(q1_a), tf.squeeze(q2_d),
tf.squeeze(q2_a)
```

The clipped target value ($y = r + \gamma\, min_{i=1,2} Q_{\phi'_i}(s', \mu_\theta(s'))$ (8.7)) is implemented by first running the two target critics that we called `qa1_tar` and `qa2_tar`, and then calculating the minimum between the estimated values, and finally, using it to estimate the target values:

```
        ...
        double_actions = sess.run(p_tar, feed_dict={obs_ph:mb_obs2})

        q1_target_mb, q2_target_mb = sess.run([qa1_tar,qa2_tar],
feed_dict={obs_ph:mb_obs2, act_ph:double_actions})
        q_target_mb = np.min([q1_target_mb, q2_target_mb], axis=0)
        y_r = np.array(mb_rew) + discount*(1-
np.array(mb_done))*q_target_mb
        ..
```

Next, the critics can be optimized as usual:

```
        ...
        q1_train_loss, q2_train_loss = sess.run([q1_opt, q2_opt],
feed_dict={obs_ph:mb_obs, y_ph:y_r, act_ph: mb_act})
        ...
```

An important observation to make is that the policy is optimized with respect to only one approximated Q-function, in our case, Q_{ϕ_1}. In fact, if you look at the full code, you'll see that `p_loss` is defined as `p_loss = -tf.reduce_mean(qd1_onl)`.

Addressing variance reduction

The second, and last, contribution by TD3, is the reduction of the variance. Why is high variance a problem? Well, it provides a noisy gradient, which involves a wrong policy update impacting the performance of the algorithm. The complication of high variance arises in the TD error, which estimates the action values from subsequent states.

To mitigate this problem, TD3 introduces a delayed policy update, and a target regularization technique. Let's see what they are, and why they work so well.

Delayed policy updates

Since high variance is attributed to an inaccurate critic, TD3 proposes to delay the update of the policy until the critic error is small enough. TD3 delays the update in an empirical way, by updating the policy only after a fixed number of iterations. In this manner, the critic has time to learn and stabilize itself, before the policy's optimization takes place. In practice, the policy remains fixed only for a few iterations, typically between 1 and 6. If set to 1, then it is the same as in DDPG. The delayed policy updates can be implemented as follows:

```
        ...
        q1_train_loss, q2_train_loss = sess.run([q1_opt, q2_opt],
feed_dict={obs_ph:mb_obs, y_ph:y_r, act_ph: mb_act})
        if step_count % policy_update_freq == 0:
            sess.run(p_opt, feed_dict={obs_ph:mb_obs})
            sess.run(update_target_op)
        ...
```

Target regularization

Critics that update from deterministic actions tend to overfit in narrow peaks. The consequence is an increase in variance. TD3 presents a smoothing regularization technique that adds a clipped noise to a small area near the target action:

$$y = r + \gamma \, min_{i=1,2} Q_{\phi'_i}(s', \mu_{\theta'}(s') + \epsilon)$$

$$\epsilon \sim clip(N(0, \sigma), -c, c)$$

The regularization can be implemented in a function that takes a vector and a scale as arguments:

```
def add_normal_noise(x, noise_scale):
    return x + np.clip(np.random.normal(loc=0.0, scale=noise_scale,
size=x.shape), -0.5, 0.5)
```

Then, `add_normal_noise` is called after running the target policy, as shown in the following lines of code (the changes with respect to the DDPG implementation are written in bold):

```
...
        double_actions = sess.run(p_tar, feed_dict={obs_ph:mb_obs2})
        double_noisy_actions = np.clip(add_normal_noise(double_actions,
target_noise), env.action_space.low, env.action_space.high)

        q1_target_mb, q2_target_mb = sess.run([qa1_tar,qa2_tar],
feed_dict={obs_ph:mb_obs2, act_ph:double_noisy_actions})
        q_target_mb = np.min([q1_target_mb, q2_target_mb], axis=0)
        y_r = np.array(mb_rew) + discount*(1-
np.array(mb_done))*q_target_mb
...
```

We clipped the actions, after having added the extra noise, to make sure that they don't exceed the ranges that were set by the environment.

Putting everything together, we obtain the algorithm that is shown in the following pseudocode:

```
TD 3 Algorithm
```

Initialize online networks Q_{ϕ_1}, Q_{ϕ_2} and μ_θ
Initialize target networks $Q_{\phi'_1}, Q_{\phi'_2}$ and $\mu_{\theta'}$ with the same weights as the online networks
Initialize empty replay buffer D
Initialize environment $s \leftarrow env.reset()$

    for $episode = 1..M$ do
        > Run an episode
        while not d:
            $a \leftarrow \mu_\beta(s)$
            $s', r, d \leftarrow env(a)$
            > Store the transition in the buffer
            $D \leftarrow D \cup (s,a,r,s',d)$
            $s \leftarrow s'$

            > Sample a minibatch
            $b \sim D$

> Calculate the target value for every i in b
$$y \leftarrow r + \gamma \min_{i=1,2} Q_{\phi'_i}(s', \mu_{\theta'}(s') + \epsilon)$$
$$\epsilon \sim clip(N(0,\sigma), -c, c)$$

> Update the critics
$$\phi_1 \leftarrow \phi_1 - \alpha_\phi \nabla_{\phi_1} \frac{1}{|b|} \sum_i (Q_{\phi_1}(s_i, a_i) - y_i)^2$$
$$\phi_2 \leftarrow \phi_2 - \alpha_\phi \nabla_{\phi_2} \frac{1}{|b|} \sum_i (Q_{\phi_2}(s_i, a_i) - y_i)^2$$

if iter % policy_update_frequency == 0:
> Update the policy
$$\theta \leftarrow \theta - \alpha_\theta \frac{1}{|b|} \sum_i \nabla_\theta \mu_\theta(s_i) \nabla_a Q_{\phi_1}(s_i, a_i)|_{a=\mu(s_i)}$$

> Targets update
$$\theta' \leftarrow \tau\theta + (1-\tau)\theta'$$
$$\phi'_1 \leftarrow \tau\phi_1 + (1-\tau)\phi'_1$$
$$\phi'_2 \leftarrow \tau\phi_2 + (1-\tau)\phi'_2$$

if $d == True$:
$$s \leftarrow env.reset()$$

That's everything for the TD3 algorithm. Now, you have a clear understanding of all the deterministic and non-deterministic policy gradient methods. Almost all of the model-free algorithms are based on the principles that we explained in these chapters, and if you master them, you will be able to understand and implement all of them.

Applying TD3 to BipedalWalker

For a direct comparison of TD3 and DDPG, we tested TD3 in the same environment that we used for DDPG: BipedalWalker-v2.

The best hyperparameters for TD3 for this environment are listed in this table:

Hyperparameter	Actor l.r.	Critic l.r.	DNN Architecture	Buffer Size	Batch Size	Tau	Policy Update Freq	Sigma
Value	4e-4	4e-4	[64,relu,64,relu]	200000	64	0.005	2	0.2

The result is plotted in the following diagram. The curve has a smooth trend, and reaches good results after about 300K steps, with top peaks at 450K steps of training. It arrives very close to the goal of 300 points, but it does not actually gain them:

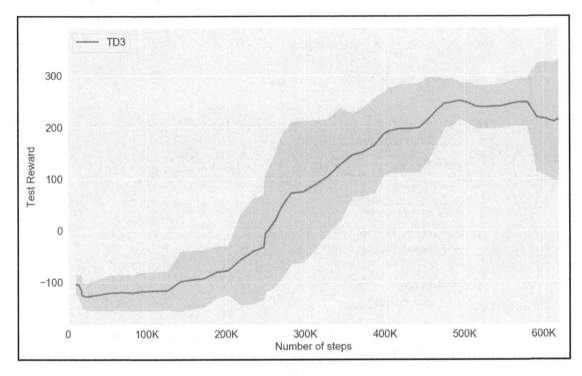

Performance of the TD3 algorithm on BipedalWalker-v2

The time spent finding a good set of hyperparameters for TD3 was less compared to DDPG. And, despite the fact that we are comparing the two algorithms on only one game, we think that it is a good first insight into their differences, in terms of stability and performance. The performance of both DDPG and TD3 on BipedalWalker-v2 are shown here:

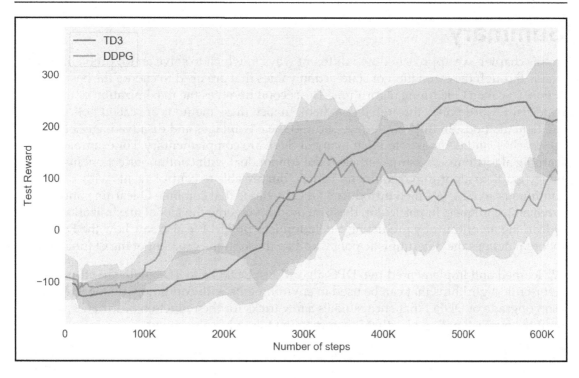

DDPG versus TD3 performance comparison

If you want to train the algorithms in a harder environment, you can try BipedalWalkerHardcore-v2. It is very similar to BipedalWalker-v2, with the exception that it has ladders, stumps, and pitfalls. Very few algorithms are able to finish and solve this environment. It's also funny to see how the agent fails to pass the obstacles!

The superiority of TD3 compared to DDPG is immediately clear, both in terms of the end performance, the rate of improvement, and the stability of the algorithm.

For all the color references mentioned in the chapter, please refer to the color images bundle at http://www.packtpub.com/sites/default/files/downloads/9781789131116_ColorImages.pdf.

Summary

In this chapter, we approached two different ways in which to solve an RL problem. The first is through the estimation of state-action values that are used to choose the best next action, so-called Q-learning algorithms. The second involves the maximization of the expected reward policy through its gradient. In fact, these methods are called policy gradient methods. In this chapter, we showed the advantages and disadvantages of such approaches, and demonstrated that many of these are complementary. For example, Q-learning algorithms are sample efficient but cannot deal with continuous action. Instead, policy gradient algorithms require more data, but are able to control agents with continuous actions. We then introduced DPG methods that combine Q-learning and policy gradient techniques. In particular, these methods overcome the global maximization of the Q-learning algorithms by predicting a deterministic policy. We also saw how the DPG theorem defines the deterministic policy update through the gradient of the Q-function.

We learned and implemented two DPG algorithms: DDPG and TD3. Both are off-policy, actor-critic algorithms that can be used in environments with continuous action spaces. TD3 is an upgrade of DDPG that encapsulates a few tricks for the reduction of variance, and to limit the overestimation bias that is common in Q-learning algorithms.

This chapter concludes the overview of the model-free reinforcement learning algorithms. We took a look at all the best, and most influential algorithms known so far, from SARSA to DQN, and from REINFORCE to PPO, and combined them in algorithms such as DDPG and TD3. These algorithms alone are capable of amazing things, with the right fine-tuning and a large amount of data (see OpenAI Five and AlphaStar). However, this isn't all there is to know about RL. In the next chapter, we move away from model-free algorithms, showing a model-based algorithm whose intent is to reduce the amount of data that is required for learning a task, by learning a model of the environment. In subsequent chapters, we'll also show more advanced techniques, such as imitation learning, new useful RL algorithms such as ESBAS, and non-RL algorithms such as evolutional strategies.

Questions

1. What is the primary limitation of Q-learning algorithms?
2. Why are stochastic gradient algorithms sample inefficient?
3. How does DPG overcome the maximization problem?
4. How does DPG guarantee enough exploration?
5. What does DDPG stand for? And what is its main contribution?
6. What problems does TD3 propose to minimize?
7. What new mechanisms does TD3 employ?

Further reading

You can use the following links to learn more:

- If you are interested in the paper that introduced the **Deterministic Policy Gradient (DPG)** algorithm, read: http://proceedings.mlr.press/v32/silver14.pdf.
- If you are interested in the paper that introduced the **Deep Deterministic Policy Gradient (DDPG)** algorithm, read: https://arxiv.org/pdf/1509.02971.pdf.
- The paper that presented **Twin Delayed Deep Deterministic** Policy Gradient **(TD3)** can be found here: https://arxiv.org/pdf/1802.09477.pdf
- For a brief overview of all the main policy gradient algorithms, checkout this article by Lilian Weng: https://lilianweng.github.io/lil-log/2018/04/08/policy-gradient-algorithms.html.

Section 3: Beyond Model-Free Algorithms and Improvements

In this section, you will implement model-based algorithms, imitation learning, evolutionary strategies, and learn about some ideas that could further improve RL algorithms.

This section includes the following chapters:

- `Chapter 9`, *Model-Based RL*
- `Chapter 10`, *Imitation Learning with the DAgger Algorithm*
- `Chapter 11`, *Understanding Black-box Optimization Algorithms*
- `Chapter 12`, *Developing the ESBAS Algorithm*
- `Chapter 13`, *Practical Implementation to Resolve RL Challenges*

9
Model-Based RL

Reinforcement learning algorithms are divided into two classes—model-free methods and model-based methods. These two classes differ by the assumption made about the model of the environment. Model-free algorithms learn a policy from mere interactions with the environment without knowing anything about it, whereas model-based algorithms already have a deep understanding of the environment and use this knowledge to take the next actions according to the dynamics of the model.

In this chapter, we'll give you a comprehensive overview of model-based approaches, highlighting their advantages and disadvantages vis-à-vis model-free approaches, and the differences that arise when the model is known or has to be learned. This latter division is important because it influences how problems are approached and the tools used to solve them. After this introduction, we'll talk about more advanced cases where model-based algorithms have to deal with high-dimensional observation spaces such as images.

Furthermore, we'll look at a class of algorithms that combine both model-based and model-free methods to learn both a model and a policy in high dimensional spaces. We'll learn their inner workings and give the reasons for using such methods. Then, to deepen our understanding of model-based algorithms, and especially of algorithms that combine both model-based and model-free approaches, we'll develop a state-of-the-art algorithm called **model-ensemble trust region policy optimization** (**ME-TRPO**) and apply it to a continuous inverted pendulum.

The following topics will be covered in this chapter:

- Model-based methods
- Combining model-based with model-free learning
- ME-TRPO applied to an inverted pendulum

Model-based methods

Model-free algorithms are a formidable kind of algorithm that have the ability to learn very complex policies and accomplish objectives in complicated and composite environments. As demonstrated in the latest works by OpenAI (`https://openai.com/five/`) and DeepMind (`https://deepmind.com/blog/article/alphastar-mastering-real-time-strategy-game-starcraft-ii`), these algorithms can actually show long-term planning, teamwork, and adaptation to unexpected situations in challenge games such as StarCraft and Dota 2.

Trained agents have been able to beat top professional players. However, the biggest downside is in the huge number of games that need to be played in order to train agents to master these games. In fact, to achieve these results, the algorithms have been scaled massively to let the agents play hundreds of years' worth of games against themselves. But, what's the problem with this approach?

Well, until you are training an agent for a simulator, you can gather as much experience as you want. The problem arises when you are running the agents in an environment as slow and complex as the world you live in. In this case, you cannot wait hundreds of years before seeing some interesting capabilities. So, can we develop an algorithm that uses fewer interactions with the real environment? Yes. And, as you probably remember, we already tackled this question in model-free algorithms.

The solution was to use off-policy algorithms. However, the gains were relatively marginal and not substantial enough for many real-world problems.

As you might expect, the answer (or at least one possible answer) is in model-based reinforcement learning algorithms. You have already developed a model-based algorithm. Do you remember which one? In `Chapter 3`, *Solving Problems with Dynamic Programming*, we used a model of the environment in conjunction with dynamic programming to train an agent to navigate a map with pitfalls. And because DP uses a model of the environment, it is considered a model-based algorithm.

Unfortunately, DP isn't usable in moderate or complex problems. So, we need to explore other types of model-based algorithms that can scale up and be useful in more challenging environments.

A broad perspective on model-based learning

Let's first remember what a model is. A model consists of the transition dynamics and rewards of an environment. Transition dynamics are a mapping from a state, s, and an action, a, to the next state, s'.

Having this information, the environment is fully represented by the model that can be used in its place. And if an agent has access to it, then the agent has the ability to predict its own future.

In the following sections, we'll see that a model can be either known or unknown. In the former case, the model is used as it is to exploit the dynamics of the environment; that is, the model provides a representation that is used in place of the environment. In the latter case, where the model of the environment is unknown, it can be learned by direct interaction with the environment. But since, in most cases, only an approximation of the environment is learned, additional factors have to be taken into account when using it.

Now that we have explained what a model is, we can see how can we use one and how it can help us to reduce the number of interactions with the environment. The way in which a model is used depends on two very important factors—the model itself and the way in which actions are chosen.

Indeed, as we just noted, the model can be known or unknown, and actions can be planned or chosen by a learned policy. The algorithms vary a lot depending on each case, so let's first elaborate on the approaches used when the model is known (meaning that we already have the transition dynamics and rewards of the environment).

A known model

When a model is known, it can be used to simulate complete trajectories and compute the return for each of them. Then, the actions that yield the highest reward are chosen. This process is called **planning**, and the model of the environment is indispensable as it provides the information required to produce the next state (given a state and an action) and reward.

Planning algorithms are used everywhere, but the ones we are interested in differ from the type of action space on which they operate. Some of them work with discrete actions, others with continuous actions.

Model-Based RL

Planning algorithms for discrete actions are usually search algorithms that build a decision tree, such as the one illustrated in the following diagram:

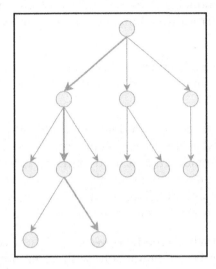

The current state is the root, the possible actions are represented by the arrows, and the other nodes are the states that are reached following a sequence of actions.

You can see that by trying every possible sequence of actions, you'll eventually find the optimal one. Unfortunately, in most problems, this procedure is intractable as the number of possible actions increases exponentially. Planning algorithms used for complex problems adopt strategies that allow planning by relying on a limited number of trajectories.

An algorithm of these, adopted also in AlphaGo, is called Monte Carlo Tree Search (MCTS). MCTS iteratively builds a decision tree by generating a finite series of simulated games, while sufficiently exploring parts of the tree that haven't been visited yet. Once a simulated game or trajectory reaches a leaf (that is, it ends the game), it backpropagates the results on the states visited and updates the information of win/loss or reward held by the nodes. Then, the action that yields to the next state with the higher win/loss ratio or reward is taken.

On the opposite side, planning algorithms that operate with continuous actions involve trajectory optimization techniques. These are much more difficult to solve than their counterpart with discrete actions, as they deal with an infinite-dimensional optimization problem.

Furthermore, many of them require the gradient of the model. An example is Model Predictive Control (MPC), which optimizes for a finite time horizon, but instead of executing the trajectory found, it only executes the first action. Doing so, MPC has a faster response compared to other methods with infinite time horizon planning.

Unknown model

What should you do when the model of the environment is unknown? Learn it! Almost everything we have seen so far involves learning. So, is it the best approach? Well, if you actually want to use a model-based approach, the answer is yes, and soon we'll see how to do it. However, this isn't always the best way to proceed.

In reinforcement learning, the end goal is to learn an optimal policy for a given task. Previously in this chapter, we said that the model-based approach is primarily used to reduce the number of interactions with the environment, but is this always true? Imagine your goal is to prepare an omelet. Knowing the exact breaking point of the egg isn't useful at all; you just need to know approximately how to break it. Thus, in this situation, a model-free algorithm that doesn't deal with the exact structure of the egg is more appropriate.

However, this shouldn't lead you to think that model-based algorithms are not worth it. For example, model-based approaches outweigh model-free approaches in situations where the model is much easier to learn than the policy.

The only way to learn a model is (unfortunately) through interactions with the environment. This is an obligatory step, as it allows us to acquire and create a dataset about the environment. Usually, the learning process takes place in a supervised fashion, where a function approximator (such as a deep neural network) is trained to minimize a loss function, such as the mean squared error loss between the transitions obtained from the environment and the prediction. An example of this is shown in the following diagram, where a deep neural network is trained to model the environment by predicting the next state, s', and the reward, r, from a state, s and an action, a:

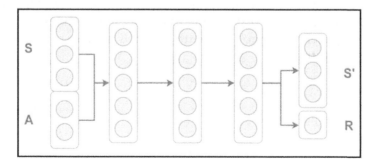

Model-Based RL

There are other options besides neural networks, such as Gaussian processes, and Gaussian mixture models. In particular, Gaussian processes have the particularity of taking into account the uncertainty of the model and are regarded as being very data efficient. In fact, until the advent of deep neural networks, they were the most popular choice.

However, the main drawback of Gaussian processes is that they are slow with large datasets. Indeed, to learn more complex environments (thereby requiring bigger datasets), deep neural networks are preferred. Furthermore, deep neural networks can learn models of environments that have images as observations.

There are two main ways to learn a model of the environment; one in which the model is learned once and then kept fixed, and one in which the model is learned at the beginning but retrained once the plan or policy has changed. The two options are illustrated in the following diagram:

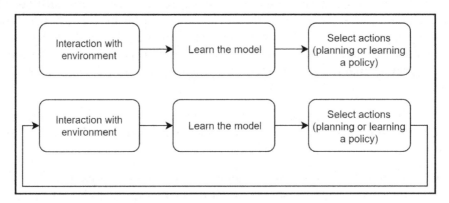

In the top half of the diagram, a sequential model-based algorithm is shown, where the agent interacts with the environment only before learning the model. In the bottom half, a cyclic approach to model-based learning is shown, where the model is refined with additional data from a different policy.

To understand how an algorithm can benefit from the second option, we have to define a key concept. In order to collect the dataset for learning the dynamics of the environment, you need a policy that lets you navigate it. But in the beginning, the policy may be deterministic or completely random. Thus, with a limited number of interactions, the space explored will be very restricted.

This precludes the model from learning those parts of the environment that are needed to plan or learn optimal trajectories. But if the model is retrained with new interactions coming from a newer and better policy, it will iteratively adapt to the new policy and capture all the parts of the environment (from a policy perspective) that haven't been visited yet. This is called data aggregation.

In practice, in most cases, the model is unknown and is learned using data aggregation methods to adapt to the new policy produced. However, learning a model can be challenging, and the potential problems are the following:

- **Overfitting the model**: The learned model overfits on a local region of the environment, missing its global structure.
- **Inaccurate model**: Planning or learning a policy on top of an imperfect model may induce a cascade of errors with potentially catastrophic conclusions.

Good model-based algorithms that learn a model have to deal with those problems. A potential solution may be to use algorithms that estimate the uncertainty, such as Bayesian neural networks, or by using an ensemble of models.

Advantages and disadvantages

When developing a reinforcement learning algorithm (all kinds of RL algorithms), there are three basic aspects to consider:

- **Asymptotical performance**: This is the maximum performance that an algorithm can achieve if it has infinite resources available in terms of both time and hardware.
- **Wall clock time**: This is the learning time required for an algorithm to reach a given performance with a given computational power.
- **Sample efficiency**: This is the number of interactions with the environment to reach a given performance.

We already explored sample efficiency in both model-free and model-based RL, and we saw how the latter is much more sample efficient. But what about wall clock time and performance? Well, model-based algorithms usually have lower asymptotic performance and are slower to train than model-free algorithms. Generally, higher data efficiency occurs to the detriment of performance and speed.

One of the reasons behind the lower performance of model-based learning can be attributed to model inaccuracies (if it's learned) that introduce additional errors into the policies. The higher learning wall clock time is due to the slowness of the planning algorithm or to the higher number of interactions needed to learn the policy in an inaccurate learned environment. Furthermore, planning model-based algorithms experience slower inference time due to the high computational cost of planning, which still has to be done on each step.

In conclusion, you have to take into account the extra time required to train a model-based algorithm and recognize the lower asymptotical performance of these approaches. However, model-based learning is extremely useful when the model is easier to learn than the policy itself and when interactions with the environment are costly or slow.

From the two sides, we have model-free learning and model-based learning, both with compelling characteristics but distinct disadvantages. Can we take the best from both worlds?

Combining model-based with model-free learning

We just saw how planning can be computationally expensive both during training and runtime, and how, in more complex environments, planning algorithms aren't able to achieve good performances. The other strategy that we briefly hinted at is to learn a policy. A policy is certainly much faster in inference as it doesn't have to plan at each step.

A simple, yet effective, way to learn a policy is to combine model-based with model-free learning. With the latest innovations in model-free algorithms, this combination has gained in popularity and is the most common approach to date. The algorithm we'll develop in the next section, ME-TRPO, is one such method. Let's dive further into these algorithms.

A useful combination

As you know, model-free learning has good asymptotic performance but poor sample complexity. On the other side, model-based learning is efficient from a data standpoint, but struggles when it comes to more complex tasks. By combining model-based and model-free approaches, it is possible to reach a smooth spot where sample complexity decreases consistently, while achieving the high performance of model-free algorithms.

There are many ways to integrate both worlds, and the algorithms that propose to do it are very different from one another. For example, when the model is given (as they are in the games of Go and Chess), search tree and value-based algorithms can help each other to produce a better action value estimate.

Another example is to combine the learning of the environment and the policy directly in a deep neural network architecture so that the learned dynamics can contribute to the planning of a policy. Another strategy used by a fair number of algorithms is to use a learned model of the environment to generate additional samples to optimize the policy.

To put it in another way, the policy is trained by playing simulated games inside the learned model. This can be done in multiple ways, but the main recipe is shown in the pseudocode that follows:

```
while not done:
    > collect transitions {(s, a, s', r)_i} from the real environment using a policy π
    > add the transitions to the buffer D
    > learn a model f(s, a) that minimizes ∑(f(s, a) − s')² in a supervised way using data in D
    > (optionally learn r(s, a))

    repeat K times:
        > sample an initial state s_0
        > simulate transitions {(s_s, a, s'_s, r_s)_i} from the model s'_s = f(s_s, a) using a policy π
        > update the policy π using a model-free RL
```

This blueprint involves two cycles. The outermost cycle collects data from the real environment to train the model, while, in the innermost cycle, the model generates simulated samples that are used to optimize the policy using model-free algorithms. Usually, the dynamics model is trained to minimize the MSE loss in a supervised fashion. The more precise the predictions made by the model, the more accurate the policy can be.

In the innermost cycle, either full or fixed-length trajectories can be simulated. In practice, the latter option can be adopted to mitigate the imperfections of the model. Furthermore, the trajectories can start from a random state sampled from the buffer that contains real transitions or from an initial state. The former option is preferred in situations where the model is inaccurate, because that prevents the trajectory from diverging too much from the real one. To illustrate this situation, take the following diagram. The trajectories that have been collected in the real environment are colored black, while those simulated are colored blue:

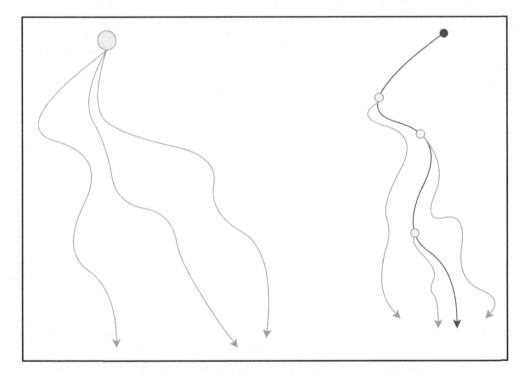

You can see that the trajectories that start from an initial state are longer, and thus will diverge more rapidly as the errors of the inaccurate model propagate in all the subsequent predictions.

 Note that you could do only a single iteration of the main cycle and gather all the data required to learn a decent approximated model of the environment. However, for the reasons outlined previously, it's better to use iterative data aggregation methods to cyclically retrain the model with transitions that come from the newer policy.

Building a model from images

The methods seen so far that combine model-based and model-free learning have been designed especially to work with low-dimensional state spaces. So, how do we deal with high-dimensional observation spaces as images?

One choice is to learn in latent space. Latent space is a low-dimensional representation, also called embedding, $g(s)$, of a high-dimensional input, s, such as an image. It can be produced by neural networks such as autoencoders. An example of an autoencoder is shown in the following diagram:

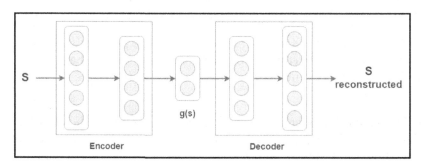

It comprises an encoder that maps the image to a small latent space, $g(s)$, and the decoder that maps the latent space to the reconstructed image. As a result of the autoencoder, the latent space should represent the main features of an image in a constrained space so that two similar images are also similar in latent space.

In RL, the autoencoder may be trained to reconstruct the input, S, or trained to predict the next frame observation, S', (along with the reward, if needed). Then, we can use the latent space to learn both the dynamic model and the policy. The main benefit arising from this approach is the big gain in speed due to the smaller representation of the image. However, the policy learned in the latent space may suffer from severe deficits when the autoencoder isn't able to recover the right representation.

Model-based learning on high-dimensional spaces is still a very active area of research.

 If you are interested in model-based algorithms that learn from image observation, you may find the paper entitled *Model-Based Reinforcement Learning for Atari*, by Kaiser, quite interesting (https://arxiv.org/pdf/1903.00374.pdf).

Model-Based RL

So far, we have covered model-based learning and its combination with model-free learning in a more figurative and theoretical way. Although it's indispensable in terms of understanding these paradigms, we want to put them into practice. So, without further ado, let's focus on the details and implementation of our first model-based algorithm.

ME-TRPO applied to an inverted pendulum

Many variants exist of the vanilla model-based and model-free algorithms introduced in the pseudocode in the *A useful combination* section. Pretty much all of them propose different ways to deal with the imperfections of the model of the environment.

This is a key problem to address in order to reach the same performance as model-free methods. Models learned from complex environments will always have some inaccuracies. So, the main challenge is to estimate or control the uncertainty of the model to stabilize and accelerate the learning process.

ME-TRPO proposes the use of an ensemble of models to maintain the model uncertainty and regularize the learning process. The models are deep neural networks with different weight initialization and training data. Together, they provide a more robust general model of the environment that is less prone to exploit regions where insufficient data is available.

Then, the policy is learned from trajectories simulated with the ensemble. In particular, the algorithm chosen to learn the policy is **trust region policy optimization** (TRPO), which was explained in Chapter 7, *TRPO and PPO Implementation*.

Understanding ME-TRPO

In the first part of ME-TRPO, the dynamics of the environment (that is, the ensemble of models) are learned. The algorithm starts by interacting with the environment with a random policy, π, to collect a dataset of transitions, $(s, a, s', r)_i$. This dataset is then used to train all the dynamic models, f_{θ_i}, in a supervised fashion. The models, f_{θ_i}, are initialized with different random weights and are trained with different mini-batches. To avoid overfitting issues, a validation set is created from the dataset. Also, a mechanism of *early stopping* (a regularization technique widely used in machine learning) interrupts the training process whenever the loss on the validation set stops improving.

In the second part of the algorithm, the policy is learned with TRPO. Specifically, the policy is trained on the data gathered from the learned models, which we'll also call the *simulated environment*, instead of the real environment. To avoid the policy exploiting inaccurate regions of a single learned model, the policy, π, is trained using the predicted transitions from the whole ensemble of models, f_{θ_i}. In particular, the policy is trained on the simulated dataset composed of transitions acquired from the models, f_{θ_i}, randomly chosen among the ensemble. During training, the policy is monitored constantly, and the process stops as soon as the performance stops improving.

Finally, the cycle constituted by the two parts is repeated until convergence. However, at each new iteration, the data from the real environment is collected by running the newly learned policy, π, and the data collected is aggregated with the dataset of the previous iterations. The ME-TRPO algorithm is briefly summarized in the following pseudocode:

```
Initialize randomly policy π and models f_θ₁..f_θ_N
Initialize empty buffer D

while not done:
    > populate buffer D with transitions (s,a,s',r)_i from the real
    environment using policy π (or random)
    > learn models f_θ₁(s,a)..f_θ_N(s,a) that minimize Σ(f_θᵢ(s,a) − s')² in a
    supervised way using data in D
    
    until convergence:
        > sample an initial state s₀
        > simulate transitions (s_s, a, s'_s, r_s)_i using models {f_θᵢ}ᵢ₌₁ᴷ and the
policy π
        > take a TRPO update to optimize policy π
```

An important note to make here is that, unlike most model-based algorithms, the reward is not embedded in the model of the environment. Therefore, ME-TRPO assumes that the reward function is known.

Implementing ME-TRPO

The code of ME-TRPO is quite long and, in this section, we won't give you the full code. Also, many parts are not interesting, and all the code concerning TRPO has already been discussed in Chapter 7, *TRPO and PPO Implementation*. However, if you are interested in the complete implementation, or if you want to play with the algorithm, the full code is available in the GitHub repository of this chapter.

Here, we'll provide an explanation and the implementation of the following:

- The inner cycle, where the games are simulated and the policy is optimized
- The function that trains the models

The remaining code is very similar to that of TRPO.

The following steps will guide us through the process of building and implementing the core of ME-TRPO:

1. **Changing the policy**: The only change in the interaction procedure with the real environment is the policy. In particular, the policy will act randomly on the first episode but, on the others, it will sample the actions from a Gaussian distribution with a random standard deviation fixed at the start of the algorithm. This change is done by replacing the line, `act, val = sess.run([a_sampl, s_values], feed_dict={obs_ph:[env.n_obs]})`, in the TRPO implementation with the following lines of code:

    ```
    ...
    if ep == 0:
        act = env.action_space.sample()
    else:
        act = sess.run(a_sampl, feed_dict={obs_ph:[env.n_obs],
    log_std:init_log_std})
    ...
    ```

2. **Fitting the deep neural networks**, f_{θ_i}: The neural networks learn the model of the environment with the dataset acquired in the preceding step. The dataset is divided into a training and a validation set, wherein the validation set is used by the early stopping technique to determine whether it is worth continuing with the training:

    ```
    ...
    model_buffer.generate_random_dataset()
    train_obs, train_act, _, train_nxt_obs, _ = 
    model_buffer.get_training_batch()
    valid_obs, valid_act, _, valid_nxt_obs, _ = 
    model_buffer.get_valid_batch()
    print('Log Std policy:', sess.run(log_std))
    for i in range(num_ensemble_models):
    train_model(train_obs, train_act, train_nxt_obs, valid_obs,
    valid_act, valid_nxt_obs, step_count, i)
    ```

`model_buffer` is an instance of the `FullBuffer` class that contains the samples generated by the environment, and `generate_random_dataset` creates two partitions for training and validation, which are then returned by calling `get_training_batch` and `get_valid_batch`.

In the next lines, each model is trained with the `train_model` function by passing the datasets, the current number of steps, and the index of the model that has to be trained. `num_ensemble_models` is the total number of models that populate the ensemble. In the ME-TRPO paper, it is shown that 5 to 10 models are sufficient. The argument, `i`, establishes which model of the ensemble has to be optimized.

3. **Generating fictitious trajectories in the simulated environments and fitting the policy**:

```
best_sim_test = np.zeros(num_ensemble_models)
for it in range(80):
    obs_batch, act_batch, adv_batch, rtg_batch = simulate_environment(sim_env, action_op_noise, simulated_steps)

    policy_update(obs_batch, act_batch, adv_batch, rtg_batch)
```

This is repeated 80 times or at least until the policy continues improving. `simulate_environment` collects a dataset (constituted by observations, actions, advantages, values, and return values) by rolling the policy in the simulated environment (represented by the learned models). In our case, the policy is represented by the function, `action_op_noise`, which, when given a state, returns an action following the learned policy. Instead, the environment, `sim_env`, is a model of the environment, f_{θ_i}, chosen randomly at each step among those in the ensemble. The last argument passed to the `simulated_environment` function is `simulated_steps`, which establishes the number of steps to take in the fictitious environments.

Ultimately, the `policy_update` function does a TRPO step to update the policy with the data collected in the fictitious environments.

4. **Implementing the early step mechanism and evaluating the policy**: The early stopping mechanism prevents the policy from overfitting on the models of the environment. It works by monitoring the performance of the policy on each separate model. If the percentage of models on which the policy improved exceeds a certain threshold, then the cycle is terminated. This should be a good indication of whether the policy has started to overfit. Note that, unlike the training, during testing, the policy is tested on one model at a time. During training, each trajectory is produced by all the learned models of the environment:

```
if (it+1) % 5 == 0:
    sim_rewards = []

    for i in range(num_ensemble_models):
        sim_m_env = NetworkEnv(gym.make(env_name), model_op, pendulum_reward, pendulum_done, i+1)
        mn_sim_rew, _ = test_agent(sim_m_env, action_op, num_games=5)
        sim_rewards.append(mn_sim_rew)

    sim_rewards = np.array(sim_rewards)
    if (np.sum(best_sim_test >= sim_rewards) > int(num_ensemble_models*0.7)) \
        or (len(sim_rewards[sim_rewards >= 990]) > int(num_ensemble_models*0.7)):
        break
    else:
        best_sim_test = sim_rewards
```

The evaluation of the policy is done every five training iterations. For each model of the ensemble, a new object of the `NetworkEnv` class is instantiated. It provides the same functionalities of a real environment but, under the hood, it returns transitions from a learned model of the environment. `NetworkEnv` does this by inheriting `Gym.wrapper` and overriding the `reset` and `step` functions. The first parameter of the constructor is a real environment that is used merely to get a real initial state, while `model_os` is a function that, when given a state and action, produces the next state. Lastly, `pendulum_reward` and `pendulum_done` are functions that return the reward and the done flag. These two functions are built around the particular functionalities of the environment.

5. **Training the dynamic model**: The `train_model` function optimizes a model to predict the future state. It is very simple to understand. We used this function in step 2, when we were training the ensemble of models. `train_model` is an inner function and takes the arguments that we saw earlier. On each ME-TRPO iteration of the outer loop, we retrain all the models, that is, we train the models starting from their random initial weights; we don't resume from the preceding optimization. Hence, every time `train_model` is called and before the training takes place, we restore the initial random weights of the model. The following code snippet restores the weights and computes the loss before and after this operation:

```
def train_model(tr_obs, tr_act, tr_nxt_obs, v_obs, v_act, v_nxt_obs,
step_count, model_idx):
    mb_valid_loss1 = run_model_loss(model_idx, v_obs, v_act, v_nxt_obs)
    model_assign(model_idx, initial_variables_models[model_idx])
    mb_valid_loss = run_model_loss(model_idx, v_obs, v_act, v_nxt_obs)
```

`run_model_loss` returns the loss of the current model, and `model_assign` restores the parameters that are in `initial_variables_models[model_idx]`.

We then train the model, as long as the loss on the validation set improved in the last `model_iter` iterations. But because the best model may not be the last one, we keep track of the best one and restore its parameters at the end of the training. We also randomly shuffle the dataset and divide it into mini-batches. The code is as follows:

```
acc_m_losses = []
last_m_losses = []
md_params = sess.run(models_variables[model_idx])
best_mb = {'iter':0, 'loss':mb_valid_loss, 'params':md_params}
it = 0

lb = len(tr_obs)
shuffled_batch = np.arange(lb)
np.random.shuffle(shuffled_batch)

while best_mb['iter'] > it - model_iter:
    # update the model on each mini-batch
    last_m_losses = []
    for idx in range(0, lb, model_batch_size):
        minib = shuffled_batch[idx:min(idx+minibatch_size,lb)]
        if len(minib) != minibatch_size:
            _, ml = run_model_opt_loss(model_idx, tr_obs[minib],
```

```
            tr_act[minib], tr_nxt_obs[minib])
                    acc_m_losses.append(ml)
                    last_m_losses.append(ml)

                # Check if the loss on the validation set has improved
                mb_valid_loss = run_model_loss(model_idx, v_obs, v_act,
v_nxt_obs)
                if mb_valid_loss < best_mb['loss']:
                    best_mb['loss'] = mb_valid_loss
                    best_mb['iter'] = it
                    best_mb['params'] = sess.run(models_variables[model_idx])

                it += 1

            # Restore the model with the lower validation loss
            model_assign(model_idx, best_mb['params'])

            print('Model:{}, iter:{} -- Old Val loss:{:.6f} New Val loss:{:.6f}
 -- New Train loss:{:.6f}'.format(model_idx, it, mb_valid_loss1,
best_mb['loss'], np.mean(last_m_losses)))
```

`run_model_opt_loss` is a function that executes the optimizer of the model with the `model_idx` index.

This concludes the implementation of ME-TRPO. In the next section, we'll see how it performs.

Experimenting with RoboSchool

Let's test ME-TRPO on **RoboSchoolInvertedPendulum**, a continuous inverted pendulum environment similar to the well-known discrete control counterpart, CartPole. A screenshot of **RoboSchoolInvertedPendulum-v1** is shown here:

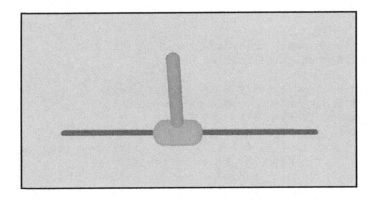

The goal is to keep the pole upright by moving the cart. A reward of +1 is obtained for every step that the pole points upward.

Considering that ME-TRPO needs the reward function and, consequently, a done function, we have to define both for this task. To this end, we defined `pendulum_reward`, which returns 1 no matter what the observation and actions are:

```
def pendulum_reward(ob, ac):
    return 1
```

`pendulum_done` returns `True` if the absolute value of the angle of the pole is higher than a fixed threshold. We can retrieve the angle directly from the state. In fact, the third and fourth elements of the state are the cosine and sine of the angle, respectively. We can then arbitrarily choose one of the two to compute the angle. Hence, `pendulum_done` is as follows:

```
def pendulum_done(ob):
    return np.abs(np.arcsin(np.squeeze(ob[3]))) > .2
```

Besides the usual hyperparameters of TRPO that remain almost unchanged compared to the ones used in Chapter 7, *TRPO and PPO Implementation*, ME-TRPO asks for the following:

- The learning rate of the dynamic models' optimizer, `mb_lr`
- The mini-batch size, `model_batch_size`, which is used to train the dynamic models
- The number of simulated steps to execute on each iteration, `simulated_steps` (this is also the batch size used to train the policy)
- The number of models that constitute the ensemble, `num_ensemble_models`
- The number of iterations to wait before interrupting the `model_iter` training of the model if the validation hasn't decreased

The values of these hyperparameters used in this environment are as follows:

Hyperparameters	Values
Learning rate (`mb_lr`)	1e-5
Model batch size (`model_batch_size`)	50
Number of simulated steps (`simulated_steps`)	50000
Number of models (`num_ensemble_models`)	10
Early stopping iterations (`model_iter`)	15

Results on RoboSchoolInvertedPendulum

The performance graph is shown in the following diagram:

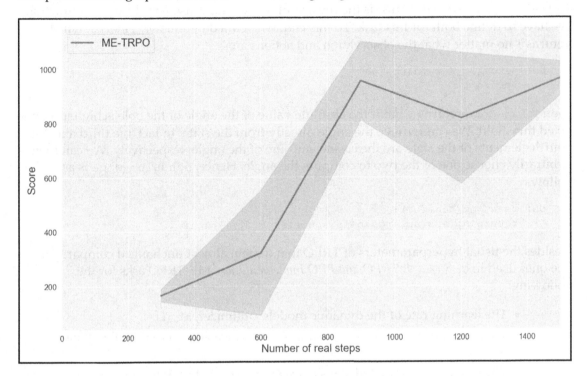

The reward is plotted as a function of the number of interactions with the real environment. After 900 steps and about 15 games, the agent achieves the top performance of 1,000. The policy updated itself 15 times and learned from 750,000 simulated steps. From a computational point of view, the algorithm trained for about 2 hours on a mid-range computer.

We noted that the results have very high variability and, if trained with different random seeds, you can obtain very different performance curves. This is also true for model-free algorithms, but here, the differences are more acute. One reason for this may be the different data collected in the real environment.

Summary

In this chapter, we took a break from model-free algorithms and started discussing and exploring algorithms that learn from a model of the environment. We looked at the key reasons behind the change of paradigm that inspired us to develop this kind of algorithm. We then distinguished two main cases that can be found when dealing with a model, the first in which the model is already known, and the second in which the model has to be learned.

Moreover, we learned how the model can either be used to plan the next actions or to learn a policy. There's no fixed rule to choose one over the other, but generally, it is related to the complexity of the action and observation space and the inference speed. We then investigated the advantages and disadvantages of model-free algorithms and deepened our understanding of how to learn a policy with model-free algorithms by combining them with model-based learning. This revealed a new way to use models in very high-dimensional observation spaces such as images.

Finally, to better grasp all the material related to model-based algorithms, we developed ME-TRPO. This proposed dealing with the uncertainty of the model by using an ensemble of models and trust region policy optimization to learn the policy. All the models are used to predict the next states and thus create simulated trajectories on which the policy is learned. As a consequence, the policy is trained entirely on the learned model of the environment.

This chapter concludes the arguments about model-based learning and, in the next one, we'll introduce new genera of learning. We'll talk about algorithms that learn by imitation. Moreover, we'll develop and train an agent that, by following the behavior of an expert, will be able to play FlappyBird.

Questions

1. Would you use a model-based or a model-free algorithm if you had only 10 games in which to train your agent to play checkers?
2. What are the disadvantages of model-based algorithms?
3. If a model of the environment is unknown, how can it be learned?
4. Why are data aggregation methods used?
5. How does ME-TRPO stabilize training?
6. How does using an ensemble of models improve policy learning?

Further reading

- To expand your knowledge of model-based algorithms that learn policies from image observations, read the paper *Model-Based Reinforcement Learning for Atari*: https://arxiv.org/pdf/1903.00374.pdf.
- To read the original paper relating to ME-TRPO, follow this link: https://arxiv.org/pdf/1802.10592.pdf.

10
Imitation Learning with the DAgger Algorithm

The ability of an algorithm to learn only from rewards is a very important characteristic that led us to develop reinforcement learning algorithms. This enables an agent to learn and improve its policy from scratch without additional supervision. Despite this, there are situations where other expert agents are already employed in a given environment. **Imitation learning** (IL) algorithms leverage the expert by imitating their actions and learning the policy from them.

This chapter focuses on imitation learning. Although different to reinforcement learning, imitation learning offers great opportunities and capabilities, especially in environments with very large state spaces and sparse rewards. Obviously, imitation learning is possible only when a more expert agent to imitate is available.

The chapter will focus on the main concepts and features of imitation learning methods. We'll implement an imitation learning algorithm called DAgger, and teach an agent to play Flappy Bird. This will help you to master this new family of algorithms and appreciate their basic principles.

In the last section of this chapter, we'll introduce **inverse reinforcement learning** (IRL). IRL is a method that extracts and learns the behaviors of another agent in terms of values and rewards; that is, IRL learns the reward function.

The following topics will be covered in this chapter:

- The imitation approach
- Playing with Flappy Bird
- Understanding the dataset aggregation algorithm
- IRL

Technical requirements

After a brief theoretical introduction to grasp the core concepts behind the imitation learning algorithms, we'll implement a real IL algorithm. However, we'll provide only the main and most interesting parts. Thus, if you are interested in the full implementation, you can find it in the GitHub repository of this book: `https://github.com/PacktPublishing/Reinforcement-Learning-Algorithms-with-Python`.

Installation of Flappy Bird

Later, we'll run our IL algorithm on a revisited version of a famous game called Flappy Bird (`https://en.wikipedia.org/wiki/Flappy_Bird`). In this section, we'll give you all the commands needed to install it.

But before installing the environment of the game, we need to take care of a few additional libraries:

- In Ubuntu, the procedure is as follows:

  ```
  $ sudo apt-get install git python3-dev python3-numpy libsdl-image1.2-dev libsdl-mixer1.2-dev libsdl-ttf2.0-dev libsmpeg-dev libsdl1.2-dev libportmidi-dev libswscale-dev libavformat-dev libavcodec-dev libfreetype6-dev
  $ sudo pip install pygame
  ```

- If you are a Mac user, you can install the libraries with the following commands:

  ```
  $ brew install sdl sdl_ttf sdl_image sdl_mixer portmidi
  $ pip install -c https://conda.binstar.org/quasiben pygame
  ```

- Then, for both Ubuntu and Mac users, the procedure is the following:

1. First, you have to clone PLE. The cloning is done with the following line of code:

   ```
   git clone https://github.com/ntasfi/PyGame-Learning-Environment
   ```

   PLE is a set of environments that also includes Flappy Bird. Thus, by installing PLE, you'll obtain Flappy Bird.

2. Then, you have to enter the `PyGame-Learning-Environment` folder:

   ```
   cd PyGame-Learning-Environment
   ```

Chapter 10

3. And finally, run the installation with the following command:

   ```
   sudo pip install -e .
   ```

   Now, you should be able to use Flappy Bird.

The imitation approach

IL is the art of acquiring a new skill by emulating an expert. This property of learning from imitation is not strictly necessary for learning sequential decision-making policies but nowadays, it is essential in plenty of problems. Some tasks cannot be solved through mere reinforcement learning, and bootstrapping a policy from the enormous spaces of complex environments is a key factor. The following diagram represents a high-level view of the core components involved in the imitation learning process:

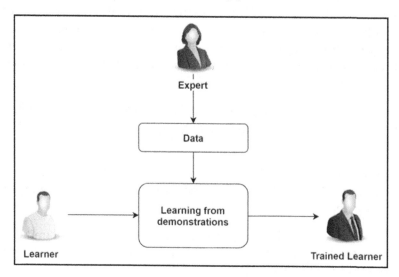

If intelligent agents (the experts) already exist in an environment, they can be used to provide a huge amount of information to a new agent (the learner) about the behaviors needed to accomplish the task and navigate the environment. In this situation, the newer agent can learn much faster without the need to learn from scratch. The expert agent can also be used as a teacher to instruct and feed back to the new agent on its performing. Note the difference here. The expert can be used both as a guide to follow and as a supervisor to correct the mistakes of the student.

If either the model of the guide, or the supervisor, is available, an imitation learning algorithm can leverage them. You can now understand why imitation learning plays such an important role and why we cannot leave it out of this book.

The driving assistant example

To grasp these key concepts better, we can use the example of a teenager learning to drive. Let's assume that they have never been in a car, that this is the first time they are seeing one, and that they don't have any knowledge of how it works. There are three approaches to learning:

1. They are given the keys and have to learn all by themselves, with no supervision at all.
2. Before being given the keys, they sit in the passenger seat for 100 hours and look at the expert driving in different weather conditions and on different roads.
3. They observe the expert driving but, most importantly, they have sessions where the expert provides feedback while driving. For example, the expert can give real-time instructions on how to park the car, and give direct feedback on how to stay in a lane.

As you may have guessed, the first case is a reinforcement learning approach where the agent has only sparse rewards from not breaking the car, pedestrians not yelling at them, and so on.

Regarding the second case, this is a passive IL approach with the competence that is acquired from the pure reproduction of the expert's actions. Overall, it's very close to a supervised learning approach.

The third and final case is an active IL approach that gives rise to a *real* imitation learning approach. In this case, it is required that, during the training phase, the expert instructs the learner on every move the learner makes.

Comparing IL and RL

Let's go more in-depth with the IL approach by highlighting the differences vis-à-vis RL. This contrast is very important. In imitation learning, the learner is not aware of any reward. This constraint can have very big implications.

Chapter 10

Going back to our example, the apprentice can only replicate the expert's moves as closely as possible, be it in a passive or an active way. Not having objective rewards from the environment, they are constrained to the subjective supervision of the expert. Thus, even if they wanted to, they aren't able to improve and understand the teacher's reasoning.

So, IL should be seen as a way to copy the moves of the expert but without knowing its main goal. In our example, it's as if the young driver assimilates the trajectories of the teacher very well but, still, they don't know the motivations that made the teacher choose them. Without being aware of the reward, an agent trained with imitation learning cannot maximize the total reward as executed in RL.

This highlights the main differences between IL and RL. The former lacks the understanding of the main objective, and thus cannot surpass the teacher. The latter instead lacks a direct supervision signal and, in most cases, has access only to a sparse reward. This situation is clearly depicted in the following diagram:

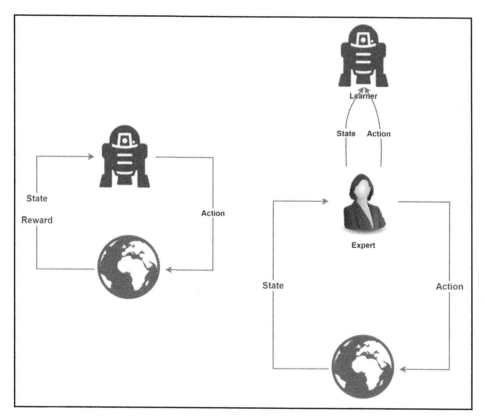

The diagram on the left represents the usual RL cycle, while on the right, the imitation learning cycle is represented. Here, the learner doesn't receive any reward; just the state and action given by the expert.

The role of the expert in imitation learning

The terms *expert*, *teacher*, and *supervisor* refer to the same concept when speaking of imitation learning algorithms. They express a figure from which the new agent (the learner) can learn.

Fundamentally, the expert can be of any form, from a real human expert to an expert system. The first case is more obvious and adopted. What you are doing is teaching an algorithm to perform a task that a human is already able to do. The advantages are evident and it can be employed in a vast number of tasks.

The second case may not be so common. One of the valid motivations behind choosing a new algorithm trained with IL can be attributed to a slow expert system that, due to technical limitations, cannot be improved. For example, the teacher could be an accurate, but slow, tree search algorithm that is not able to perform at a decent speed at inference time. A deep neural network could be employed in its place. The training of the neural network under the supervision of the tree search algorithm could take some time but, once trained, it could perform much faster during runtime.

By now, it should be clear that the quality of the policy coming from the learner is largely due to the quality of the information provided by the expert. The performance of the teacher is an upper limit to the final performances of the scholar. A poor teacher will always provide bad data to the learner. Thus, the expert is a key component that sets the bar for the quality of the final agent. With a weak teacher, we cannot pretend to obtain good policies.

The IL structure

Now that all the ingredients of imitation learning have been tackled, we can elaborate on the algorithms and approaches that can be used in order to design a full imitation learning algorithm.

The most straightforward way to tackle the imitation problem is shown in the following diagram:

Chapter 10

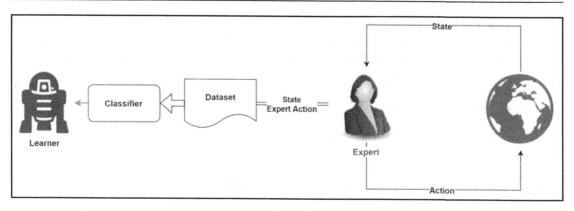

The preceding diagram can be summarized in two main steps:

- An expert collects data from the environment.
- A policy is learned through supervised learning on the dataset.

Unfortunately, despite supervised learning being the imitation algorithm for excellence, most of the time, it doesn't work.

To understand why the supervised learning approach isn't a good alternative, we have to recall the foundations of supervised learning. We are mostly interested in two basic principles: the training and test set should belong to the same distribution, and the data should be independent and identically distributed (i.i.d). However, a policy should be tolerant of different trajectories and be robust to eventual distribution shifts.

If an agent is trained using only a supervised learning approach to drive a car, whenever it shifts a little bit from the expert trajectories, it will be in a new state never seen before, and that will create a distribution mismatch. In this new state, the agent will be uncertain about the next action to take. In a usual supervised learning problem, it doesn't matter too much. If a prediction is missed, this will not have an influence on the next prediction. However, in an imitation learning problem, the algorithm is learning a policy and the i.i.d property is no longer valid because subsequent actions are strictly correlated to each other. Thus, they will have consequences and a compounding effect on all the others.

In our example of the self-driving car, once the distribution has changed from that of the expert, the correct path will be very difficult to recover, since bad actions will accumulate and lead to dramatic consequences. The longer the trajectory, the worse the effect of imitation learning. To clarify, supervised learning problems with i.i.d. data can be seen as having a trajectory of length 1. No consequences on the next actions are found. The paradigm we have just presented is what we referred to previously as *passive* learning.

To overcome the distributional shift that can have catastrophic effects on policies learned using *passive* imitation, different techniques can be adopted. Some are hacks, while others are more algorithmic variations. Two of these strategies that work well are the following:

- Learning a model that generalizes very well on the data without overfitting
- Using an active imitation in addition to the passive one

Because the first is more of a broad challenge, we will concentrate on the second strategy.

Comparing active with passive imitation

We introduced the term *active imitation* in the previous example, with the teenager learning to drive a car. Specifically, we referred to it in the situation in which the learner was driving with additional feedback from the expert. In general, for active imitation, we mean learning from on-policy data with the actions assigned by the expert.

Speaking in terms of input s (the state or observation) and output a (the action), in passive learning, s and a both come from the expert. In active learning, s is sampled from the learner, and a is the action that the expert would have taken in state s. The objective of the newbie agent is to learn a mapping, $\pi(a|s)$.

Active learning with on-policy data allows the learner to fix small deviations from the expert trajectory that the learner wouldn't know how to correct with only passive imitation.

Playing Flappy Bird

Later in this chapter, we'll develop and test an IL algorithm called DAgger on a new environment. The environment named Flappy Bird emulates the famous Flappy Bird game. Here, our mission is to give you the tools needed to implement code using this environment, starting from the explanation of the interface.

Flappy Bird belongs to the **PyGame Learning Environment** (**PLE**), a set of environments that mimic the **Arcade Learning Environment** (**ALE**) interface. This is similar to the **Gym** interface, and later we'll see the differences, although it's simple to use.

The goal of Flappy Bird is to make the bird fly through vertical pipes without hitting them. It is controlled by only one action that makes it flap its wings. If it doesn't fly, it progresses in a decreasing trajectory determined by gravity. A screenshot of the environment is shown here:

Chapter 10

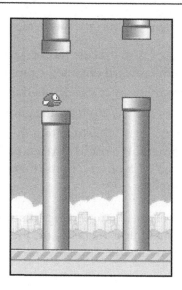

How to use the environment

In the following steps, we will see how to use the environment.

1. In order to use Flappy Bird in our Python scripts, firstly, we need to import PLE and Flappy Bird:

   ```
   from ple.games.flappybird import FlappyBird
   from ple import PLE
   ```

2. Then, we instance a `FlappyBird` object and pass it to `PLE` with a few parameters:

   ```
   game = FlappyBird()
   p = PLE(game, fps=30, display_screen=False)
   ```

   Here, with `display_screen`, you can choose whether to display the screen.

3. The environment is initialized by calling the `init()` method:

   ```
   p.init()
   ```

Imitation Learning with the DAgger Algorithm

To interact and get the state of the environment, we primarily use four functions:

- `p.act(act)`, to execute the `act` action in the game. `act(act)` returns the reward obtained from the action performed.
- `p.game_over()`, to check whether the game reached a final state.
- `p.reset_game()`, to reset the game to the initial conditions.
- `p.getGameState()`, to obtain the current state of the environment. We could also use `p.getScreenRGB()` if we want to obtain the RGB observations (that is, the full screen) of the environment.

4. Putting everything together, a simple script that plays Flappy Bird for five games can be designed as in the following code snippet. Note that in order to make it work, you still have to define the `get_action(state)` function that returns an action given a state:

```
from ple.games.flappybird import FlappyBird
from ple import PLE

game = FlappyBird()
p = PLE(game, fps=30, display_screen=False)
p.init()

reward = 0

for _ in range(5):
    reward += p.act(get_action(p.getGameState()))

    if p.game_over():
        p.reset_game()
```

A couple of things to point out here are as follows:

- `getGameState()` returns a dictionary with the position, velocity, and the distance of the player, as well as the position of the next pipe and the following one. Before giving the state to the policymaker that we represented here with the `get_action` function, the dictionary is converted to a NumPy array and normalized.
- `act(action)` expects `None` as input if no action has to be performed, or `119` if the bird has to flap its wings in order to fly higher.

Understanding the dataset aggregation algorithm

One of the most successful algorithms that learns from demonstrations is **Dataset Aggregation (DAgger)**. This is an iterative policy meta-algorithm that performs well under the distribution of states induced. The most notable feature of DAgger is that it addresses the distribution mismatch by proposing an active method in which the expert teaches the learner how to recover from the learner's mistakes.

A classic IL algorithm learns a classifier that predicts expert behaviors. This means that the model fits a dataset consisting of training examples, observed by an expert. The inputs are the observations, and the actions are the desired output values. However, following the previous reasoning, the predictions of the learner affect the future state or observation visited, violating the i.i.d assumption.

DAgger deals with the change in distribution by iterating a pipeline of aggregation of new data sampled from the learner multiple times, and training with the aggregated dataset. A simple diagram of the algorithm is shown here:

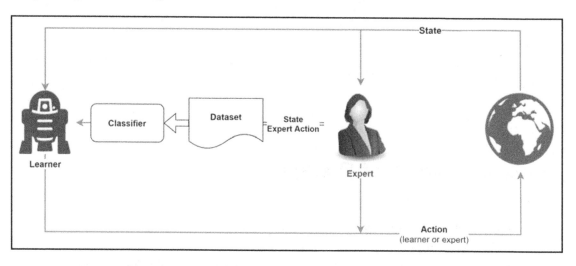

The expert populates the dataset used by the classifier, but, depending on the iteration, the action performed in the environment may come from the expert or the learner.

The DAgger algorithm

Specifically, DAgger proceeds by iterating the following procedure. At the first iteration, a dataset D of trajectories is created from the expert policy and used to train a first policy π_1 that best fits those trajectories without overfitting them. Then, during iteration i, new trajectories are collected with the learned policy π_i and added to the dataset D. After that, the aggregated dataset D with the new and old trajectories is used to train a new policy, π_{i+1}.

As per the report in the Dagger paper (https://arxiv.org/pdf/1011.0686.pdf), there is an active on-policy learning that outperforms many other imitation learning algorithms, and it's also able to learn very complex policies with the help of deep neural networks.

Additionally, at iteration i, the policy can be modified so that the expert takes control of a number of actions. This technique better leverages the expert and lets the learner gradually assume control over the environment.

The pseudocode of the algorithm can clarify this further:

```
Initialize D = ∅
Initialize π₀ = π*  (π* is the expert policy)

for i 0..n:
    > Populate dataset Dᵢ with (s, π*(s)). States are given by πᵢ (sometimes
    the expert could take the control over it) and actions are given by the
    expert π*

    > Train a classifier πᵢ₊₁ on the aggregate dataset D = D ∪ Dᵢ
```

Implementation of DAgger

The code is divided into three main parts:

- Load the expert inference function to predict an action given a state.
- Create a computational graph for the learner.
- Create the DAgger iterations to build the dataset and train the new policy.

Here, we'll explain the most interesting parts, leaving the others for your personal interest. You can check the remaining code and the complete version in the book's GitHub repository.

Loading the expert inference model

The expert should be a policy that takes a state as input and returns the best action. Despite this, it can be anything. In particular, for these experiments, we used an agent trained with Proximal Policy Optimization (PPO) as the expert. In principle, this doesn't make any sense, but we adopted this solution for academic purposes, to facilitate integration with the imitation learning algorithms.

The expert's model trained with PPO has been saved on file so that we can easily restore it with its trained weights. Three steps are required to restore the graph and make it usable:

1. Import the meta graph. The computational graph can be restored with `tf.train.import_meta_graph`.
2. Restore the weights. Now, we have to load the pretrained weights on the computational graph we have just imported. The weights have been saved in the latest checkpoint and they can be restored with `tf.train.latest_checkpoint(session, checkpoint)`.
3. Access the output tensors. The tensors of the restored graph are accessed with `graph.get_tensor_by_name(tensor_name)`, where `tensor_name` is the tensor's name in the graph.

The following lines of code summarize the entire process:

```
def expert():
    graph = tf.get_default_graph()
    sess_expert = tf.Session(graph=graph)

    saver = tf.train.import_meta_graph('expert/model.ckpt.meta')
    saver.restore(sess_expert,tf.train.latest_checkpoint('expert/'))

    p_argmax = graph.get_tensor_by_name('actor_nn/max_act:0')
    obs_ph = graph.get_tensor_by_name('obs:0')
```

Then, because we are only interested in a simple function that returns an expert action given a state, we can design the `expert` function in such a way that it returns that function. Thus, inside `expert()`, we define an inner function called `expert_policy(state)` and return it as output of `expert()`:

```
    def expert_policy(state):
        act = sess_expert.run(p_argmax, feed_dict={obs_ph:[state]})
        return np.squeeze(act)

    return expert_policy
```

Creating the learner's computational graph

All the following code is located inside a function called `DAgger`, which takes some hyperparameters that we'll see throughout the code as arguments.

The learner's computational graph is simple as its only goal is to build a classifier. In our case, there are only two actions to predict, one for doing nothing, and the other to make the bird flap its wings. We can instantiate two placeholders, one for the input state, and one for the *ground-truth* actions that are those of the expert. The actions are an integer corresponding to the action taken. In the case of two possible actions, they are just 0 (do nothing) or 1 (fly).

The steps to build such a computational graph are the following:

1. Create a deep neural network, specifically, a fully connected multilayer perceptron with a ReLu activations function in the hidden layers and a linear function on the final layer.
2. For every input state, take the action with the highest value. This is done using the `tf.math.argmax(tensor,axis)` function with `axis=1`.
3. Convert the action's placeholders in a one-hot tensor. This is needed because the logits and labels that we'll use in the loss function should have dimensions, `[batch_size, num_classes]`. However, our labels named `act_ph` have shapes, `[batch_size]`. Therefore, we convert them to the desired shape with one-hot encoding. `tf.one_hot` is the TensorFlow function that does just that.
4. Create the loss function. We use the softmax cross-entropy loss function. This is a standard loss function used for discrete classification with mutually exclusive classes, just like in our case. The loss function is computed using `softmax_cross_entropy_with_logits_v2(labels, logits)` between the logits and the labels.
5. Lastly, the mean of the softmax cross-entropy is computed across the batch and minimized using Adam.

These five steps are implemented in the following lines:

```
    obs_ph = tf.placeholder(shape=(None, obs_dim), dtype=tf.float32, name='obs')
    act_ph = tf.placeholder(shape=(None,), dtype=tf.int32, name='act')
    p_logits = mlp(obs_ph, hidden_sizes, act_dim, tf.nn.relu, last_activation=None)
    act_max = tf.math.argmax(p_logits, axis=1)
    act_onehot = tf.one_hot(act_ph, depth=act_dim)
    p_loss =
```

```
    tf.reduce_mean(tf.nn.softmax_cross_entropy_with_logits_v2(labels=act_onehot
, logits=p_logits))
        p_opt = tf.train.AdamOptimizer(p_lr).minimize(p_loss)
```

We can then initialize a session, the global variables, and define a function, `learner_policy(state)`. This function, given a state, returns the action with a higher probability chosen by the learner (this is the same thing we did for the expert):

```
sess = tf.Session()
sess.run(tf.global_variables_initializer())

def learner_policy(state):
    action = sess.run(act_max, feed_dict={obs_ph:[state]})
    return np.squeeze(action)
```

Creating a DAgger loop

It's now time to set up the core of the DAgger algorithm. The outline has already been defined in the pseudocode in *The DAgger algorithm* section, but let's take a more in-depth look at how it works:

1. Initialize the dataset composed of two lists, X and y, where we'll put the states visited and the expert target actions. We also initialize the environment:

```
X = []
y = []

env = FlappyBird()
env = PLE(env, fps=30, display_screen=False)
env.init()
```

2. Iterate across all the DAgger iterations. At the beginning of every DAgger iteration, we have to reinitialize the learner computational graph (because we retrain the learner on every iteration on the new dataset), reset the environment, and run a number of random actions. At the start of each game, we run a few random actions to add a stochastic component to the deterministic environment. The result will be a more robust policy:

```
for it in range(dagger_iterations):
    sess.run(tf.global_variables_initializer())
    env.reset_game()
    no_op(env)

    game_rew = 0
    rewards = []
```

3. Collect new data by interacting with the environment. As we said previously, the first iteration contains the expert that has to choose the actions by calling `expert_policy`, but, in the following iterations, the learner progressively takes control. The learned policy is executed by the `learner_policy` function. The dataset is collected by appending to `X` (the input variable) the current state of the game, and by appending to `y` (the output variable) the actions that the expert would have taken in that state. When the game is over, the game is reset and `game_rew` is set to 0. The code is as follows:

```python
for _ in range(step_iterations):
    state = flappy_game_state(env)

    if np.random.rand() < (1 - it/5):
        action = expert_policy(state)
    else:
        action = learner_policy(state)

    action = 119 if action == 1 else None

    rew = env.act(action)
    rew += env.act(action)

    X.append(state)
    y.append(expert_policy(state))
    game_rew += rew

    if env.game_over():
        env.reset_game()
        np_op(env)

        rewards.append(game_rew)
        game_rew = 0
```

Note that the actions are performed twice. This is done to reduce the number of actions every second to 15 instead of 30, as required by the environment.

4. Train the new policy on the aggregated dataset. The pipeline is standard. The dataset is shuffled and divided into mini-batches of length `batch_size`. Then, the optimization is repeated by running `p_opt` for a number of epochs equals to `train_epochs` on each mini-batch. This is done with the following code:

```python
n_batches = int(np.floor(len(X)/batch_size))
shuffle = np.arange(len(X))
np.random.shuffle(shuffle)
shuffled_X = np.array(X)[shuffle]
shuffled_y = np.array(y)[shuffle]
```

```
            ep_loss = []
         for _ in range(train_epochs):

             for b in range(n_batches):
                 p_start = b*batch_size
                 tr_loss, _ = sess.run([p_loss, p_opt], feed_dict=
                         obs_ph:shuffled_X[p_start:p_start+batch_size],
                         act_ph:shuffled_y[p_start:p_start+batch_size]})

                 ep_loss.append(tr_loss)
         print('Ep:', it, np.mean(ep_loss), 'Test:',
np.mean(test_agent(learner_policy)))
```

`test_agent` tests `learner_policy` on a few games to understand how well the learner is performing.

Analyzing the results on Flappy Bird

Before showing the results of the imitation learning approach, we want to provide some numbers so that you can compare these with those of a reinforcement learning algorithm. We know that this is not a fair comparison (the two algorithms work on very different conditions), but nevertheless, they underline why imitation learning can be rewarding when an expert is available.

The expert has been trained with proximal policy optimization for about 2 million steps and, after about 400,000 steps, reached a plateau score of about 138.

We tested DAgger on Flappy Bird with the following hyperparameters:

Hyperparameter	Variable name	Value
Learner hidden layers	hidden_sizes	16,16
DAgger iterations	dagger_iterations	8
Learning rate	p_lr	1e-4
Number of steps for every DAgger iteration	step_iterations	100
Mini-batch size	batch_size	50
Training epochs	train_epochs	2000

The plot in the following screenshot shows the trend of the performance of DAgger with respect to the number of steps taken:

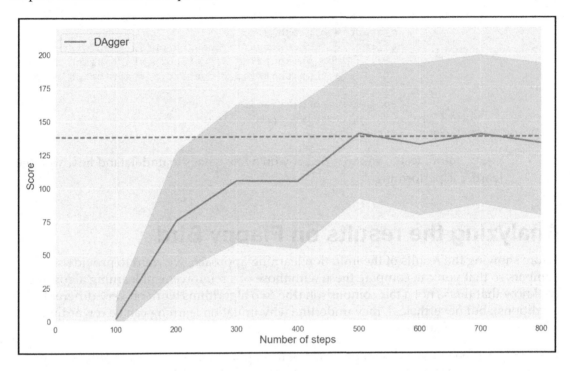

The horizontal line represents the average performance reached by the expert. From the results, we can see that a few hundred steps are sufficient to reach the performance of the expert. However, compared with the experience required by PPO to train the expert, this represents about a 100-fold increase in sample efficiency.

Again, this is not a fair comparison as the methods are in different contexts, but it highlights that whenever an expert is available, it is suggested that you use an imitation learning approach (perhaps at least to learn a starting policy).

IRL

One of the biggest limitations of IL lies in its inability to learn other trajectories to reach a goal, except those learned from the expert. By imitating an expert, the learner is constrained to the range of behaviors of its teacher. They are not aware of the end goal that the expert is trying to reach. Thus, these methods are only useful when there's no intention to perform better than the teacher.

IRL is an RL algorithm, such as IL, that uses an expert to learn. The difference is that IRL uses the expert to learn its reward function. Therefore, instead of copying the demonstrations, as is done in imitation learning, IRL figures out the goal of the expert. Once the reward function is learned, the agent uses it to learn the policy.

With the demonstrations used only to understand the goal of the expert, the agent is not bound to the actions of the teacher and can finally learn better strategies. For example, a self-driving car that learns by IRL would understand that the goal is to go from point A to point B in the minimum amount of time, while reducing the damage to things and people. The car would then learn a policy by itself (for example, with an RL algorithm) that maximizes this reward function.

However, IRL also has a number of challenges that limit its applicability. The expert's demonstration may not be optimal, and, as a result, the learner may not be able to achieve its full potential and may remain stuck in the wrong reward function. The other challenge lies in the evaluation of the learned reward function.

Summary

In this chapter, we took a break from reinforcement learning algorithms and explored a new type of learning called imitation learning. The novelty of this new paradigm lies in the way in which the learning takes place; that is, the resulting policy imitates the behavior of an expert. This paradigm differentiates from reinforcement learning in the absence of a reward signal and in its ability to leverage the incredible source of information brought by the expert entity.

We saw that the dataset from which the learner learns can be expanded with additional state action pairs to increase the confidence of the learner in new situations. This process is called data aggregation. Moreover, new data could come from the new learned policy and, in this case, we talked about on-policy data (as it comes from the same policy learned). This integration of on-policy states with expert feedback is a very valuable approach that increases the quality of the learner.

We then explored and developed one of the most successful imitation learning algorithms, called DAgger, and applied it to learn the Flappy Bird game.

However, because imitation learning algorithms only copy the behavior of an expert, these systems cannot do better than the expert. Therefore, we introduced inverse reinforcement learning, which overcomes this problem by inferring the reward function from the expert. In this way, the policy can be learned independently of the teacher.

In the next chapter, we'll take a look at another set of algorithms for solving sequential tasks; namely, evolutionary algorithms. You'll learn the mechanisms and advantages of these black-box optimization algorithms so that you'll be able to adopt them in challenging environments. Furthermore, we'll delve into an evolutionary algorithm called evolution strategy in greater depth and implement it.

Questions

1. Is imitation learning considered a reinforcement learning technique?
2. Would you use imitation learning to build an unbitable agent in Go?
3. What's the full name of DAgger?
4. What's the main strength of DAgger?
5. Where would you use IRL instead of IL?

Further reading

- To read the original paper that introduced DAgger, checkout the following paper, *A Reduction of Imitation Learning and Structured Prediction to No-Regret Online Learning*: `https://arxiv.org/pdf/1011.0686.pdf`.
- To learn more about imitation learning algorithms, checkout the following paper, *Global Overview of Imitation Learning*: `https://arxiv.org/pdf/1801.06503.pdf`.
- To learn more about inverse reinforcement learning, checkout the following survey, *A Survey of Inverse Reinforcement Learning: Challenges, Methods and Progress*: `https://arxiv.org/pdf/1806.06877.pdf`.

11
Understanding Black-Box Optimization Algorithms

In the previous chapters, we looked at reinforcement learning algorithms, ranging from value-based to policy-based methods and from model-free to model-based methods. In this chapter, we'll provide another solution for solving sequential tasks, that is, with a class of black-box algorithms **evolutionary algorithms** (EA). EAs are driven by evolutionary mechanisms and are sometimes preferred to **reinforcement learning** (RL) as they don't require backpropagation. They also offer other complementary benefits to RL. We'll start this chapter by giving you a brief recap of RL algorithms so that you'll better understand how EA fits into these sets of problems. Then, you'll learn about the basic building blocks of EA and how those algorithms work. We'll also take advantage of this introduction and look at one of the most well-known EAs, namely **evolution strategies** (ES), in more depth.

A recent algorithm that was developed by OpenAI caused a great boost in the adoption of ES for solving sequential tasks. They showed how ES algorithms can be massively parallelized and scaled linearly on a number of CPUs while achieving high performance. After an explanation of evolution strategies, we'll take a deeper look at this algorithm and develop it in TensorFlow so that you'll be able to apply it to the tasks you care about.

The following topics will be covered in this chapter:

- Beyond RL
- The core of EAs
- Scalable evolution strategies
- Scalable ES applied to LunarLander

Beyond RL

RL algorithms are the usual choice when we're faced with sequential decision problems. Usually, it's difficult to find other ways to solve these tasks other than using RL. Despite the hundreds of different optimization methods that are out there, so far, only RL has worked well on problems for sequential decision-making. But this doesn't mean it's the only option.

We'll start this chapter by recapping on the inner workings of RL algorithms and questioning the usefulness of their components for solving sequential tasks. This brief summary will help us introduce a new type of algorithm that offers many advantages (as well as some disadvantages) that could be used as a replacement for RL.

A brief recap of RL

In the beginning, a policy is initialized randomly and used to interact with the environment for either a given number of steps, or entire trajectories, to collect data. On each interaction, the state visited, the action taken, and the reward obtained are recorded. This information provides a full description of the influence of the agent in the environment. Then, in order to improve the policy, the backpropagation algorithm (based on the loss function, in order to move the predictions to a better estimate) computes the gradient of each weight of the network. These gradients are then applied with a stochastic gradient descent optimizer. This process (gathering data from the environment and optimizing the neural network with **stochastic gradient descent (SGD)**) is repeated until a convergence criterion is met.

There are two important things to note here that will be useful in the following discussion:

- **Temporal credit assignment**: Because RL algorithms optimize the policy on each step, allocating the quality of each action and state is required. This is done by assigning a value to each state-action pair. Moreover, a discount factor is used to minimize the influence of distant actions and to give more weight to the last actions. This will help us solve the problem of assigning the credit to the actions, but will also introduce inaccuracies in the system.

- **Exploration**: In order to maintain a degree of exploration in the actions, additional noise is injected into the policy of RL algorithms. The way in which the noise is injected depends on the algorithm, but usually, the actions are sampled from a stochastic distribution. By doing so, if the agent is in the same situation twice, it may take different actions that would lead to two different paths. This strategy also encourages exploration in deterministic environments. By deviating the path each time, the agent may discover different – and potentially better – solutions. With this additional noise that asymptotically tends to 0, the agent is then able to converge to a better and final deterministic policy.

But are backpropagation, temporal credit assignment, and stochastic actions actually a prerequisite for learning and building complex policies?

The alternative

The answer to this question is no.

As we learned in `Chapter 10`, *Imitation Learning with the DAgger Algorithm*, by reducing policy learning to an imitation problem using backpropagation and SGD, we can learn about a discriminative model from an expert in order to predict which actions to take next. Still, this involves backpropagation and requires an expert that may not always be available.

Another general subset of algorithms for global optimization does exist. They are called EAs, and they aren't based on backpropagation and don't require any of the other two principles, namely temporal credit assignment and noisy actions. Furthermore, as we said in the introduction to this chapter, these evolutionary algorithms are very general and can be used in a large variety of problems, including sequential decision tasks.

EAs

As you may have guessed, EAs differ in many aspects from RL algorithms and are principally inspired by biological evolution. EAs include many similar methods such as, genetic algorithms, evolution strategies, and genetic programming, which vary in their implementation details and in the nature of their representation. However, they are all mainly based on four basic mechanisms – reproductions, mutation, crossover, and selection – that are cycled in a guess-and-check process. We'll see what this means as we progress through this chapter.

Evolutionary algorithms are defined as black-box algorithms. These are algorithms that optimize a function, $f(w)$, with respect to w without making any assumption about f. Hence, f can be anything you want. We only care about the output of f. This has many advantages, as well as some disadvantages. The primary advantage is that we don't have to care about the structure of f and we are free to use what is best for us and for the problem at hand. On the other hand, the main disadvantage is that these optimization methods cannot be explained and thus their mechanism cannot be interpreted. In problems where interpretability is of great importance, these methods are not appealing.

Reinforcement learning has almost always been preferred for solving sequential tasks, especially for medium to difficult tasks. However, a recent paper from OpenAI highlights that the evolution strategy, which is an evolutionary algorithm, can be used as an alternative to RL. This statement is mainly due to the performance that's reached asymptotically by the algorithm and its incredible ability to be scaled across thousands of CPUs.

Before we look at how this algorithm is able to scale so well while learning good policies on difficult tasks, let's take a more in-depth look at EAs.

The core of EAs

EAs are inspired by biological evolution and implement techniques and mechanisms that simulate biological evolution. This means that EAs go through many trials to create a population of new candidate solutions. These solutions are also called **individuals** (in RL problems, a candidate solution is a policy) that are better than the previous generation, in a similar way to the process within nature wherein only the strongest survive and have the possibility to procreate.

One of the advantages of EAs is that they are derivative-free methods, meaning that they don't use the derivative to find the solution. This allows EAs to work very well with all sorts of differentiable and non-differentiable functions, including deep neural networks. This combination is schematized in the following diagram. Note that each individual is a separate deep neural network, and so we'll have as many neural networks as the number of individuals at any given moment. In the following diagram, the population is composed of five individuals:

Chapter 11

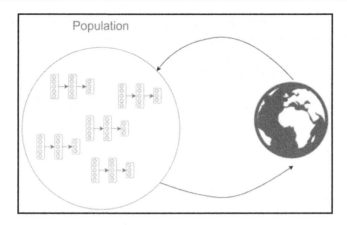

Figure 11.1. Optimization of deep neural networks through evolutionary algorithms

The specificity of each type of evolutionary algorithm differs from the others, but the underlying cycle is common to all the EAs and works as follows:

1. A population of individuals (also called **candidate solutions** or **phenotypes**) is created so that each of them has a set of different properties (called **chromosomes** or **genotypes**). The initial population is initialized randomly.
2. Each candidate solution is evaluated independently by a fitness function that determines its quality. The fitness function is usually related to the objective function and, using the terminology we've used so far, the fitness function could be the total reward accumulated by the agent (that is, the candidate solution) throughout its life.
3. Then, the fitter individuals of the population are selected, and their genome is modified in order to produce the new generation. In some cases, the less fit candidate solution can be used as a negative example to generate the next generation. This whole step varies largely, depending on the algorithm. Some algorithms, such as genetic algorithms, breed new individuals through two processes called **crossover** and **mutation**, which give birth to new individuals (called **offspring**). Others, such as evolution strategies, breed new individuals through mutation only. We'll explain crossover and mutation in more depth later in this chapter, but generally speaking, crossover is the process that combines genetic information from two parents, while mutation only alters some gene values in the offspring.
4. Repeat the whole process, going through steps 1-3 until a terminal condition is met. On each iteration, the population that's created is also called a **generation**.

Understanding Black-Box Optimization Algorithms

This iterative process, as shown in the following diagram, terminates when a given fitness level has been reached or a maximum number of generations have been produced. As we can see, the population is created by crossover and mutation, but as we habe already explained, these processes may vary, depending on the specific algorithm:

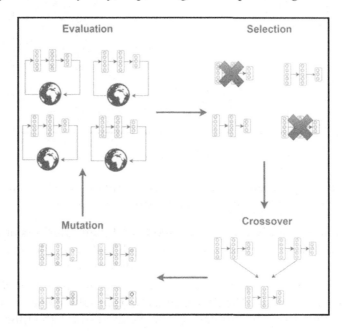

Figure 11.2. The main cycle of evolutionary algorithms

The main body of a general EA is very simple and can be written in just a few lines of code, as shown here. To summarize this code, on each iteration, and until a fitted generation has been produced, new candidates are generated and evaluated. The candidates are created from the best-fitted individuals of the previous generation:

```
solver = EvolutionaryAlgortihm()

while best_fitness < required_fitness:
    candidates = solver.generate_candidates() # for example from crossover and mutation

    fitness_values = []
    for candidate in candidates:
        fitness_values.append(evaluate(candidate))

    solver.set_fitness_values(fitness_values)

    best_fitness = solver.evaluate_best_candidate()
```

Note that the implementation details of the solver are dependent on the algorithm that's used.

The applications of EAs are actually spread across many fields and problems, from economy to biology, and from computer program optimization to ant colony optimization.

Since we are mostly interested in the application of evolutionary algorithms for solving sequential decision-making tasks, we will explain the two most common EAs that are used to solve these kinds of jobs. They are known as **genetic algorithms** (**GAs**) and **evolution strategies** (**ESes**). Later, we'll take a step further with ES by developing a highly scalable version of it.

Genetic algorithms

The idea of GAs is very straightforward—evaluate the current generations, use only the top-performing individuals to generate the next candidate solutions, and discard the other individuals. This is shown in the preceding diagram. The survivors will generate the next population by crossover and mutation. These two processes are represented in the following diagram. Crossover is done by selecting two solutions among the survivors and combining their parameters. Mutation, on the other hand, involves changing a few random parameters on the offspring's genotype:

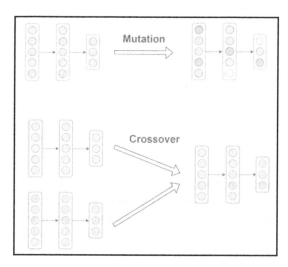

Figure 11.3. Visual illustration of mutation and crossover

Crossover and mutation can be approached in many different ways. In the simpler version, crossover is done by choosing parts from the two parents randomly, and mutation is done by mutating the solution that's obtained by adding Gaussian noise with a fixed standard deviation. By only keeping the best individuals and injecting their genes into the newly born individuals, the solutions will improve over time until a condition is met. However, on complex problems, this simple solution is prone to be stuck in a local optimum (meaning that the solution is only within a small set of candidate solutions). In this case, a more advanced genetic algorithm such as **NeroEvolution of Augmenting Topologies** (NEAT) is preferred. NEAT not only alters the weights of the network but also its structure.

Evolution strategies

Evolution strategies (**ESes**) are even easier than GAs as they are primarily based on mutation to create a new population.

Mutation is performed by adding values that have been sampled from a normal distribution to the genotype. A very simple version of ES is obtained by just selecting the most performant individual across the whole population and sampling the next generation from a normal distribution with a fixed standard deviation and a mean equal to that of the best-performing individual.

Outside of the sphere of small problems, using this algorithm is not recommended. This is because following only a single leader and using a fixed standard deviation could prevent potential solutions from exploring a more diverse search space. As a consequence, the solution to this method would probably end in a narrow local minimum. An immediate and better strategy would be to generate the offspring by combining the N top performing candidate solutions and weighing them by their fitness rank. Ranking the individuals according to their fitness values is called fitness ranking. This strategy is preferred to using the actual fitness values as it is invariant to the transformation of the objective function and it prevents the new generation from moving too much toward a possible outlier.

CMA-ES

The **Covariance Matrix Adaptation Evolution Strategy**, or **CMA-ES** for short, is an evolutionary strategy algorithm. Unlike the simpler version of the evolution strategy, it samples the new candidate solution according to a multivariate normal distribution. The name CMA comes from the fact that the dependencies between the variables are kept in a covariance matrix that has been adapted to increase or decrease the search space on the next generation.

Put simply, CMA-ES shrinks the search space by incrementally decreasing the covariance matrix in a given direction when it's confident of the space around it. Instead, CMA-ES increases the covariance matrix and thus enlarges the possible search space when it's less confident.

ES versus RL

ESes are an interesting alternative to RL. Nonetheless, the pros and cons must be evaluated so that we can pick the correct approach. Let's briefly look at the main advantages of ES:

- **Derivative-free methods**: There's no need for backpropagation. Only the forward pass is performed for estimating the fitness function (or equivalently, the cumulative reward). This opens the door to all the non-differentiable functions, for example; hard attention mechanisms. Moreover, by avoiding backpropagation, the code gains efficiency and speed.
- **Very general**: The generality of ES is mainly due to its property of being a black-box optimization method. Because we don't care about the agent, the actions that it performs, or the states visited, we can abstract these and concentrate only on its evaluation. Furthermore, ES allows learning without explicit targets and also with extremely sparse feedback. Additionally, ESes are more general in the sense that they can optimize a much larger set of functions.
- **Highly parallelizable and robust**: As we'll soon see, ES is much easier to parallelize than RL, and the computations can be spread across thousands of workers. The robustness of evolution strategies is due to the few hyperparameters that are required to make the algorithms work. For example, in comparison to RL, there's no need to specify the length of the trajectories, the lambda value, the discount factor, the number of frames to skip, and so on. Also, the ES is very attractive for tasks with a very long horizon.

On the other hand, reinforcement learning is preferred for the following key aspects:

- **Sample efficiency**: RL algorithms make better use of the information that's acquired from the environment and as a consequence, they require less data and fewer steps to learn the tasks.
- **Excellent performance**: Overall, reinforcement learning algorithms outperform performance evolution strategies.

Scalable evolution strategies

Now that we've introduced black-box evolutionary algorithms and evolution strategies in particular, we are ready to put what we have just learned into practice. The paper called *Evolution Strategies as a Scalable Alternative to Reinforcement Learning* by OpenAI made a major contribution to the adoption of evolution strategies as an alternative to reinforcement learning algorithms.

The main contribution of this paper is in the approach that scales ES extremely well with a number of CPUs. In particular, the new approach uses a novel communication strategy across CPUs that involves only scalars, and so it is able to scale across thousands of parallel workers.

Generally, ES requires more experience and thus is less efficient than RL. However, by spreading the computation across so many workers (thanks to the adoption of this new strategy), the task can be solved in less wall clock time. As an example, in the paper, the authors solve the 3D Humanoid Walking pattern in just 10 minutes with 1,440 CPUs, with a linear speedup in the number of CPU cores. Because usual RL algorithms cannot reach this level of scalability, they take hours to solve the same task.

Let's look at how they are able to scale so well.

The core

In the paper, a version of ES is used that maximizes the average objective value, as follows:

$$E_{\theta \sim p_\mu} F(\theta)$$

It does this by searching over a population, p_μ, that's parameterized by μ with stochastic gradient ascent. F is the objective function (or fitness function) while θ is the parameters of the actor. In our problems, $F(\theta)$ is simply the stochastic return that's obtained by the agent with θ in the environment.

The population distribution, p_μ, is a multivariate Gaussian with a mean, μ, and fixed standard deviation, σ, as follows:

$$E_{\theta \sim p_\mu} F(\theta) = E_{\epsilon \sim N(0,I)} F(\theta + \sigma \epsilon) \qquad (11.1)$$

From here, we can define the step update by using the stochastic gradient estimate, as follows:

$$\theta \leftarrow \theta + \alpha \frac{1}{n\sigma} \sum_{i=1}^{n} F(\theta + \sigma\epsilon_i)\epsilon_i \quad (11.2)$$

With this update, we can estimate the stochastic gradient (without performing backpropagation) using the results of the episodes from the population. We can update the parameters using one of the well-known update methods, such as Adam or RMSProp as well.

Parallelizing ES

It's easy to see how ES can be scaled across multiple CPUs: each worker is assigned to a separate candidate solution of the population. The evaluation can be done in complete autonomy, and as described in the paper, optimization can be done in parallel on each worker, with only a few scalars shared between each CPU unit.

Specifically, the only information that's shared between workers is the scalar return, $F(\theta + \sigma\epsilon_i)$, of an episode and the random seed that has been used to sample ϵ_i. The amount of data can be further shrunk by sending only the return, but in this case, the random seed of each worker has to be synchronized with all the others. We decided to adopt the first technique, while the paper used the second one. In our simple implementation, the difference is negligible and both techniques require extremely low bandwidth.

Other tricks

Two more techniques are used to improve the performance of the algorithm:

- **Fitness shaping – objective ranking**: We discussed this technique previously. It's very simple. Instead of using the raw returns to compute the update, a rank transformation is used. The rank is invariant to the transformation of the objective function and thus performs better with spread returns. Additionally, it removes the noise of the outliers.
- **Mirror noise**: This trick reduces the variance and involves the evaluation of the network with both noise ϵ and $-\epsilon$; that is, for each individual, we'll have two mutations: $\theta_+ = \mu + \sigma\epsilon$ and $\theta_- = \mu - \sigma\epsilon$.

Pseudocode

The parallelized evolution strategy that combines all of these features is summarized in the following pseudocode:

```
---------------------------------------------------------------------------
------
Parallelized Evolution Strategy
---------------------------------------------------------------------------
------

Initialize parameters θ_0 on each worker
Initialize random seed on each worker

for iteration = 1..M do:
    for worker = 1..N do:
        Sample ε ~ N(0, I)
        Evaluate individuals F(θ_t + σε) and F(θ_t − σε)

    Spread returns to each other worker

    for worker = 1..N do:
        Compute normalized rank K from the returns
        Reconstruct ε_i from the random seeds of the other workers
        θ_{t+1} ← θ_t + α (1/(nσ)) Σ_{i=1}^{n} K_i ε_i      (maybe using Adam)
```

Now, all that remains is to implement this algorithm.

Scalable implementation

To simplify the implementation and to make the parallelized version of ES work well with a limited number of workers (and CPUs), we will develop a structure similar to the one that's shown in the following diagram. The main process creates one worker for each CPU core and executes the main cycle. On each iteration, it waits until a given number of new candidates are evaluated by the workers. Different from the implementation provided in the paper, each worker evaluates more than one agent on each iteration. So, if we have four CPUs, four workers will be created. Then, if we want a total batch size bigger than the number of workers on each iteration of the main process, let's say, 40, each worker will create and evaluate 10 individuals each time. The return values and seeds are returned to the main application, which waits for results from all 40 individuals, before continuing with the following lines of code.

Then, these results are propagated in a batch to all the workers, which optimize the neural network seperately, following the update provided in the formula (11.2):

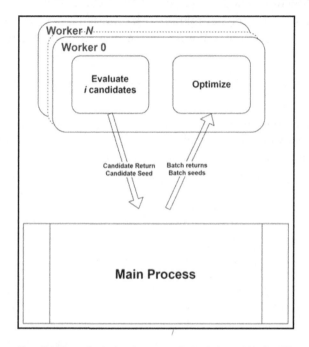

Figure 11.4. Diagram showing the main components involved in the parallel version of ES

Following what we just described, the code is divided into three main buckets:

- The main process that creates and manages the queues and the workers.
- A function that defines the task of the workers.
- Additionally, there are some functions that perform simple tasks, such as ranking the returns and evaluating the agent.

Let's explain the code of the main process so that you have a broad view of the algorithm before going into detail about the workers.

The main function

This is defined in a function called ES that has the following arguments: the name of the Gym environment, the size of the neural network's hidden layers, the total number of generations, the number of workers, the Adam learning rate, the batch size, and the standard deviation noise:

```
def ES(env_name, hidden_sizes=[8,8], number_iter=1000, num_workers=4,
    lr=0.01, batch_size=50, std_noise=0.01):
```

Then, we set an initial seed that is shared among the workers to initialize the parameters with the same weights. Moreover, we calculate the number of individuals that a worker has to generate and evaluate on each iteration and create two multiprocessing.Queue queues. These queues are the entry and exit points for the variables that are passed to and from the workers:

```
    initial_seed = np.random.randint(1e7)
indiv_per_worker = int(batch_size / num_workers)
    output_queue = mp.Queue(maxsize=num_workers*indiv_per_worker)
    params_queue = mp.Queue(maxsize=num_workers)
```

Next, the multiprocessing processes, multiprocessing.Process, are instantiated. These will run the worker function, which is given as the first argument to the Process constructor in an asynchronous way. All the other variables that are passed to the worker function are assigned to args and are pretty much the same as the parameters taken by ES, with the addition of the two queues. The processes start running when the start() method is called:

```
    processes = []

    for widx in range(num_workers):
        p = mp.Process(target=worker, args=(env_name, initial_seed,
hidden_sizes, lr, std_noise, indiv_per_worker, str(widx), params_queue,
output_queue))
        p.start()
        processes.append(p)
```

Once the parallel workers have started, we can iterate across the generations and wait until all the individuals have been generated and evaluated separately in each worker. Remember that the total number of individuals that are created on every generation is the number of workers, `num_workers`, multiplied by the individuals generated on each worker, `indiv_per_worker`. This architecture is unique to our implementation as we have only four CPU cores available, compared to the implementation in the paper, which benefits from thousands of CPUs. Generally, the population that's created on every generation is usually between 20 and 1,000:

```
for n_iter in range(number_iter):
    batch_seed = []
    batch_return = []

    for _ in range(num_workers*indiv_per_worker):
        p_rews, p_seed = output_queue.get()
        batch_seed.append(p_seed)
        batch_return.extend(p_rews)
```

In the previous snippet, `output_queue.get()` gets an element from `output_queue`, which is populated by the workers. In our implementation, `output_queue.get()` returns two elements. The first element, `p_rews`, is the fitness value (the return value) of the agent that's generated using `p_seed`, which is given as the second element.

When the `for` cycle terminates, we rank the returns and put the batch returns and seeds on the `params_queue` queue, which will be read by all the workers to optimize the agent. The code for this is as follows:

```
batch_return = normalized_rank(batch_return)

for _ in range(num_workers):
    params_queue.put([batch_return, batch_seed])
```

Finally, when all the training iterations have been executed, we can terminate the workers:

```
for p in processes:
    p.terminate()
```

This concludes the main function. Now, all we need to do is implement the workers.

Workers

The workers' functionalities are defined in the `worker` function, which was previously passed as an argument to `mp.Process`. We cannot go through all the code because it'd take too much time and space to explain, but we'll explain the core components here. As always, the full implementation is available in this book's repository on GitHub. So, if you are interested in looking at it in more depth, take the time to examine the code on GitHub.

In the first few lines of `worker`, the computational graph is created to run the policy and optimize it. Specifically, the policy is a multi-layer perceptron with `tanh` nonlinearities as the activation function. In this case, Adam is used to apply the expected gradient that's computed following the second term of (11.2).

Then, `agent_op(o)` and `evaluation_on_noise(noise)` are defined. The former runs the policy (or candidate solution) to obtain the action for a given state or observation, `o`, and the latter evaluates the new candidate solution that is obtained by adding the perturbation `noise` (that has the same shape as the policy) to the current policy's parameters.

Jumping directly to the most interesting part, we create a new session by specifying that it can rely on, at most, 4 CPUs and initialize the global variables. Don't worry if you don't have 4 CPUs available. Setting `allow_soft_placement` to `True` tells TensorFlow to use only the supported devices:

```
sess = tf.Session(config=tf.ConfigProto(device_count={'CPU': 4}, allow_soft_placement=True))
sess.run(tf.global_variables_initializer())
```

Despite using all 4 CPUs, we allocate only one to each worker. In the definition of the computational graph, we set the device on which the computation will be performed. For example, to specify that the worker has to use only CPU 0, you can put the graph inside a `with` statement, which defines the device to use:

```
with tf.device("/cpu:0"):
    # graph to compute on the CPUs 0
```

Going back to our implementation, we can loop forever, or at least until the worker has something to do. This condition is checked later, inside the `while` cycle.

An important thing to note is that because we perform many calculations on the weights of the neural network, it is much easier to deal with flattened weights. So, for example, instead of dealing with a list of the form [8,32,32,4], we'll perform computations on a one-dimensional array of length 8*32*32*4. The functions that perform the conversion from the former to the latter, and vice versa, are defined in TensorFlow (take a look at the full implementation on GitHub if you are interested in knowing how this is done).

Also, before starting the `while` loop, we retrieve the shape of the flattened agent:

```
agent_flatten_shape = sess.run(agent_variables_flatten).shape

while True:
```

In the first part of the `while` loop, the candidates are generated and evaluated. The candidate solutions are built by adding a normal perturbation to the weights; that is, $\theta + \sigma\epsilon$. This is done by choosing a new random seed every time, which will uniquely sample the perturbation (or noise), σ, from a normal distribution. This is a key part of the algorithm because, later, the other workers will have to regenerate the same perturbation from the same seed. After that, the two new offspring (there are two because we are using mirror sampling) are evaluated and the results are put in the `output_queue` queue:

```
        for _ in range(indiv_per_worker):
            seed = np.random.randint(1e7)

            with temp_seed(seed):
                sampled_noise = np.random.normal(size=agent_flatten_shape)

            pos_rew= evaluation_on_noise(sampled_noise)
            neg_rew = evaluation_on_noise(-sampled_noise)

            output_queue.put([[pos_rew, neg_rew], seed])
```

Note that the following snippet (which we used previously), is just a way to set the NumPy random seed, `seed`, locally:

```
with temp_seed(seed):
    ..
```

Outside the `with` statement, the seed that's used to generate random values will not be `seed` anymore.

The second part of the `while` loop involves the acquisition of all the returns and seeds, the reconstruction of the perturbations from those seeds, the computation of the stochastic gradient estimate following the formula (11.2), and the policy's optimization. The `params_queue` queue is populated by the main process, which we saw earlier. It does this by sending the normalized ranks and seeds of the population that were generated by the workers in the first phase. The code is as follows:

```
batch_return, batch_seed = params_queue.get()
batch_noise = []

# reconstruction of the perturbations used to generate the individuals
for seed in batch_seed:
    with temp_seed(seed):
        sampled_noise = np.random.normal(size=agent_flatten_shape)

    batch_noise.append(sampled_noise)
    batch_noise.append(-sampled_noise)

# Computation of the gradient estimate following the formula (11.2)
vars_grads = np.zeros(agent_flatten_shape)
for n, r in zip(batch_noise, batch_return):
    vars_grads += n * r

vars_grads /= len(batch_noise) * std_noise

sess.run(apply_g, feed_dict={new_weights_ph:-vars_grads})
```

The last few lines in the preceding code compute the gradient estimate; that is, they calculate the second term of formula (11.2):

$$\frac{1}{n\sigma} \sum_{i=1}^{n} F_i \epsilon_i \qquad (11.3)$$

Here, F_i is the normalized rank of i and ϵ_i candidates their perturbation.

`apply_g` is the operation that applies the `vars_grads` gradient (11.3) using Adam. Note that we pass `-var_grads` as we want to perform gradient ascent and not gradient descent.

That's all for the implementation. Now, we have to apply it to an environment and test it to see how it performs.

Applying scalable ES to LunarLander

How well will the scalable version of evolution strategies perform in the LunarLander environment? Let's find out!

As you may recall, we already used LunarLander against A2C and REINFORCE in Chapter 6, *Learning Stochastic and PG optimization*. This task consists of landing a lander on the moon through continuous actions. We decided to use this environment for its medium difficulty and to compare the ES results to those that were obtained with A2C.

The hyperparameters that performed the best in this environment are as follows:

Hyperparameter	Variable name	Value
Neural network size	`hidden_sizes`	[32, 32]
Training iterations (or generations)	`number_iter`	200
Worker's number	`num_workers`	4
Adam learning rate	`lr`	0.02
Individuals per worker	`indiv_per_worker`	12
Standard deviation	`std_noise`	0.05

The results are shown in the following graph. What immediately catches your eye is that the curve is very stable and smooth. Furthermore, notice that it reaches an average score of about 200 after 2.5-3 million steps. Comparing the results with those obtained with A2C (in Figure 6.7), you can see that the evolution strategy took almost 2-3 times more steps than A2C and REINFORCE.

As demonstrated in the paper, by using massive parallelization (using at least hundreds of CPUs), you should be able to obtain very good policies in just minutes. Unfortunately, we don't have such computational power. However, if you do, you may want to try it for yourself:

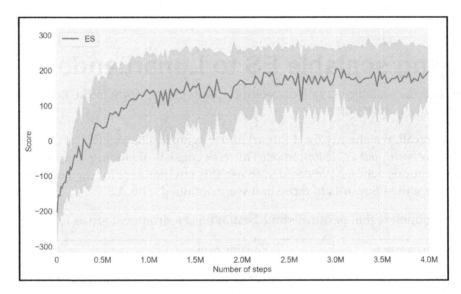

Figure 11.5 The performance of scalable evolution strategies

Overall, the results are great and show that ES is a viable solution for very long horizon problems and tasks with very sparse rewards.

Summary

In this chapter, you learned about EAs, a new class of black-box algorithms inspired by biological evolution that can be applied to RL tasks. EAs solve these problems from a different perspective compared to reinforcement learning. You saw that many characteristics that we have to deal with when we design RL algorithms are not valid in evolutionary methods. The differences are in both the intrinsic optimization method and the underlying assumptions. For example, because EAs are black-box algorithms, we can optimize whatever function we want as we are no longer constrained to using differentiable functions, like we were with RL. EAs have many other advantages, as we saw throughout this chapter, but they also have numerous downsides.

Next, we looked at two evolutionary algorithms: genetic algorithms and evolution strategies. Genetic algorithms are more complex as they create offspring from two parents through crossover and mutation. Evolution strategies select the best-performing individuals from a population that has been created only by mutation from the previous generation. The simplicity of ES is one of the key elements that enables the immense scalability of the algorithm across thousands of parallel workers. This scalability has been demonstrated in the paper by OpenAI, showing the ability of ES to perform at the levels of RL algorithms in complex environments.

To get hands-on with evolutionary algorithms, we implemented the scalable evolution strategy from the paper we cited throughout this chapter. Furthermore, we tested it on LunarLander and saw that ES is able to solve the environment with high performance. Though the results are great, ES used two to three times more steps than AC and REINFORCE to learn the task. This is the main drawback of ESes: they need a lot of experience. Despite this, thanks to their capacity to scale linearly to the number of workers, with enough computational power, you might be able to solve this task in a fraction of the time compared to reinforcement learning algorithms.

In the next chapter, we'll go back to reinforcement learning and talk about a problem known as the exploration-exploitation dilemma. We'll see what it is and why it's crucial in online settings. Then, we'll use a potential solution to the problem to develop a meta-algorithm called ESBAS, which chooses the most appropriate algorithm for each situation.

Questions

1. What are two alternative algorithms to reinforcement learning for solving sequential decision-making problems?
2. What are the processes that give birth to new individuals in evolutionary algorithms?
3. What is the source of inspiration for evolutionary algorithms such as genetic algorithms?
4. How does CMA-ES evolve evolution strategies?
5. What's one advantage and one disadvantage of evolution strategies?
6. What's the trick that's used in the *Evolution Strategies as a Scalable Alternative to Reinforcement Learning* paper to reduce the variance?

Further reading

- To read the original paper of OpenAI that proposed the scalable version of ES, that is, the *Evolution Strategies as a Scalable Alternative to Reinforcement Learning* paper, go to https://arxiv.org/pdf/1703.03864.pdf.
- To read the paper that presented NEAT, that is, *Evolving Neural Networks through Augmenting Topologies*, go to http://nn.cs.utexas.edu/downloads/papers/stanley.ec02.pdf.

12
Developing the ESBAS Algorithm

By now, you are capable of approaching RL problems in a systematic and concise way. You are able to design and develop RL algorithms specifically for the problem at hand and get the most from the environment. Moreover, in the previous two chapters, you learned about algorithms that go beyond RL, but that can be used to solve the same set of tasks.

At the beginning of this chapter, we'll present a dilemma that we have already encountered in many of the previous chapters; namely, the exploration-exploitation dilemma. We have already presented potential solutions for the dilemma throughout the book (such as the ϵ-greedy strategy), but we want to give you a more comprehensive outlook on the problem, and a more concise view of the algorithms that solve it. Many of them, such as the **upper confidence bound** (**UCB**) algorithm, are more sophisticated and better than the simple heuristics that we have used so far, such as the ϵ-greedy strategy. We'll illustrate these strategies on a classic problem, known as multi-armed bandit. Despite being a simple tabular game, we'll use it as a starting point to then illustrate how these strategies can also be employed on non-tabular and more complex tasks.

This introduction to the exploration-exploitation dilemma offers a general overview of the main methods that many recent RL algorithms employ in order to solve very hard exploration environments. We'll also provide a broader view of the applicability of this dilemma when solving other kinds of problems. As proof of that, we'll develop a meta-algorithm called **epochal stochastic bandit algorithm selection**, or **ESBAS**, which tackles the problem of online algorithm selection in the context of RL. ESBAS does this by using the ideas and strategies that emerged from the multi-armed bandit problem to select the best RL algorithm that maximizes the expected return on each episode.

The following topics will be covered in this chapter:

- Exploration versus exploitation
- Approaches to exploration
- Epochal stochastic bandit algorithm selection

Exploration versus exploitation

The exploration-exploitation trade-off dilemma, or exploration-exploitation problem, affects many important domains. Indeed, it's not only restricted to the RL context, but applies to everyday life. The idea behind this dilemma is to establish whether it is better to take the optimal solution that is known so far, or if it's worth trying something new. Let's say you are buying a new book. You could either choose a title from your favorite author, or buy a book of the same genre that Amazon is suggesting to you. In the first case, you are confident about what you're getting, but by selecting the second option, you don't know what to expect. However, in the latter case, you could be incredibly pleased, and end up reading a very good book that is indeed better than the one written by your favorite author.

This conflict between exploiting what you have already learned and taking advantage of it or exploring new options and taking some risks, is very common in reinforcement learning as well. The agent may have to sacrifice a short-term reward, and explore a new space, in order to achieve a higher long-term reward in the future.

All this may not sound new to you. In fact, we started dealing with this problem when we developed the first RL algorithm. Up until now, we have primarily adopted simple heuristics, such as the ϵ-greedy strategy, or followed a stochastic policy to decide whether to explore or exploit. Empirically, these strategies work very well, but there are some other techniques that can achieve theoretical optimal performance.

In this chapter, we'll start with an explanation of the exploration-exploitation dilemma from the ground up, and introduce some exploration algorithms that achieve nearly-optimal performance on tabular problems. We'll also show how the same strategies can be adapted to non-tabular and more complex tasks.

Chapter 12

For an RL algorithm, one of the most challenging Atari games to solve is Montezuma's Revenge, rendered in the following screenshot. The objective of the game is to score points by gathering jewels and killing enemies. The main character has to find all the keys in order to navigate the rooms in the labyrinth, and gather the tools that are needed to move around, while avoiding obstacles. The sparse reward, the long-term horizon, and the partial rewards, which are not correlated with the end goal, make the game very challenging for every RL algorithm. Indeed, these four characteristics make Montezuma's Revenge one of the best environments for testing exploration algorithms:

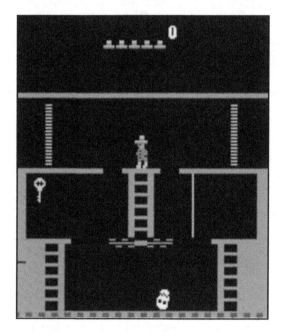

Screenshot of Montezuma's Revenge

Let's start from the ground up, in order to give a complete overview of this area.

Multi-armed bandit

The multi-armed bandit problem is the classic RL problem that is used to illustrate the exploration-exploitation trade-off dilemma. In the dilemma, an agent has to choose from a fixed set of resources, in order to maximize the expected reward. The name multi-armed bandit comes from a gambler that is playing multiple slot machines, each with a stochastic reward from a different probability distribution. The gambler has to learn the best strategy in order to achieve the highest long-term reward.

Developing the ESBAS Algorithm

This situation is illustrated in the following diagram. In this particular example, the gambler (the ghost) has to choose one of the five slot machines, all with different and unknown reward probabilities, in order to win the highest amount of money:

Example of a five-armed bandit problem

If you are questioning how the multi-armed bandit problem relates to more interesting tasks such as Montezuma's Revenge, the answer is that they are all about deciding whether, in the long run, the highest reward is yielded when new behaviors are attempted (pulling a new arm), or when continuing to do the best thing done so far (pulling the best-known arm). However, the main difference between the multi-armed bandit and Montezuma's Revenge is that, in the latter, the state of the agent changes every time. In the multi-armed bandit problem, there's only one state, and there's no sequential structure, meaning that past actions will not influence the future.

So, how can we find the right balance between exploration and exploitation in the multi-armed bandit problem?

Approaches to exploration

Put simply, the multi-armed bandit problem, and in general every exploration problem, can be solved either through random strategies, or through smarter techniques. The most notorious algorithm that belongs to the first category, is called ϵ-greedy; whereas optimistic exploration, such as UCB, and posterior exploration, such as Thompson sampling, belong to the second category. In this section, we'll take a look particularly at the ϵ-greedy and UCB strategies.

It's all about balancing the risk and the reward. But, how can we measure the quality of an exploration algorithm? Through *regret*. Regret is defined as the opportunity lost in one step that is, the regret, L, at time, t, is as follows:

$$L_t = V^* - Q(a_t)$$

Here, V^* denotes the optimal value, and $Q(a_t)$ the action-value of a_t.

Thus, the goal is to find a trade-off between exploration and exploitation, by minimizing the total regret over all the actions:

$$L = \sum_i (V^* - Q(a_i))$$

Note that the minimization of the total regret is equivalent to the maximization of the cumulative reward. We'll use this idea of regret to show how exploration algorithms perform.

The ϵ-greedy strategy

We have already expanded the ideas behind the ϵ-greedy strategy and implemented it to help our exploration in algorithms such as Q-learning and DQN. It is a very simple approach, and yet it achieves very high performance in non-trivial jobs as well. This is the main reason behind its widespread use in many deep learning algorithms.

To refresh your memory, ϵ-greedy takes the best action most of the time, but from time to time, it selects a random action. The probability of choosing a random action is dictated by the ϵ value, which ranges from 0 to 1. That is, with ϵ probability, the algorithm will exploit the best action, and with $(1 - \epsilon)$ probability, it will explore the alternatives with a random selection.

In the multi-armed bandit problem, the action values are estimated based on past experiences, by averaging the reward obtained by taking those actions:

$$Q_t(a) = \frac{1}{N_t(a)} \sum_t r_t 1[a_t = a]$$

In the preceding equation, $N_t(a)$ is the number of times that the a action has been picked, and 1 is a Boolean that indicates whether at time t, action a has been chosen. The bandit will then act according to the ϵ-greedy algorithm, and explore by choosing a random action, or exploit by picking the a action with the higher Q value.

A drawback of ϵ-greedy, is that it has an expected linear regret. But, for the law of large numbers, the optimal expected total regret should be logarithmic to the number of timesteps. This means that the ϵ-greedy strategy isn't optimal.

A simple way to reach optimality involves the use of an ϵ value that decays as time goes by. By doing this, the overall weight of the exploration will vanish, until only greedy actions will be chosen. Indeed, in deep RL algorithms ϵ-greedy is almost always combined with a linear, or exponential decay of ϵ.

That being said, ϵ and its decay rate is difficult to choose, and there are other strategies that solve the multi-armed bandit problem optimally.

The UCB algorithm

The UCB algorithm is related to a principle known as optimism in the face of uncertainty, a statistics-based principle based on the law of large numbers. UCB constructs an optimistic guess, based on the sample mean of the rewards, and on the estimation of the upper confidence bound of the reward. The optimistic guess determines the expected pay-off of each action, also taking into consideration the uncertainty of the actions. Thus, UCB is always able to pick the action with the higher potential reward, by balancing the risk and the reward. Then, the algorithm switches to another one when the optimistic estimate of the current action is lower than the others.

Specifically, UCB keeps track of the average reward of each action with $Q_t(a)$, and the U UCB (hence the name) for each action. Then, the algorithm picks the arm which maximizes the following:

$$a_t = argmax_{a \in A} \; Q_t(a) + U_t(a) \quad (12.1)$$

In this formula, the role of U is to provide an additional argument to the average reward that accounts for the uncertainty of the action.

UCB1

UCB1 belongs to the UCB family, and its contribution is in the selection of U.

In UCB1, the $U_t(a)$ UCB is computed by keeping track of the number of times an action, (a), has been selected, along with $N_t(a)$, and the total number of actions that are selected with T, as represented in the following formula:

$$U_t(a) = c\sqrt{\frac{\ln T}{N_t(a)}} \quad (12.2)$$

The uncertainty of an action, is thus related to the number of times it has been selected. If you think about it, this makes sense as, according to the law of large numbers, with an infinite number of trials, you'd be sure about the expected value. On the contrary, if you tried an action only a few times, you'd be uncertain about the expected reward, and only with more experience, would you be able to say whether it is a good or a bad action. Therefore, we'll incentivize the exploration of actions that have been chosen only few times, and that therefore have a high uncertainty. The main takeaway is that if $N_t(a)$ is small, meaning that the action has been experienced only occasionally, then $U_t(a)$ will be large, with an overall high uncertain estimate. However, if $N_t(a)$ is large, then $U_t(a)$ will be small, and the estimate will be accurate. We'll then follow a only if it has a high mean reward.

The main advantage of UCB compared to ϵ-greedy, is actually due to the counting of the actions. Indeed, the multi-armed bandit problem can be easily solved with this method, by keeping a counter for each action that is taken, and its average reward. These two pieces of information can be integrated into formula (12.1) and formula (12.2), in order to get the best action to take at time (t); that is:

$$a_t = argmax_{a \in A}\, Q_t(a) + c\sqrt{\frac{\ln T}{N_t(a)}} \quad (12.3)$$

UCB is a very powerful method for exploration, and it achieves a logarithmic expected total regret on the multi-armed bandit problem, therefore reaching an optimal trend. It is worth noting that ϵ-greedy exploration could also obtain a logarithmic regret, but it would require careful design, together with a finely-tuned exponential decay, and thus it would be harder to balance.

There are additional variations of UCB, such as UCB2, UCB-Tuned, and KL-UCB.

Exploration complexity

We saw how UCB, and in particular UCB1, can reduce the overall regret and accomplish an optimal convergence on the multi-armed bandit problem with a relatively easy algorithm. However, this is a simple stateless task.

So, how will UCB perform on more complex tasks? To answer this question, we can oversimplify the division and group all of the problems in these three main categories:

- **Stateless problems**: An instance of these problems is the multi-armed bandit. The exploration in such cases can be handled with a more sophisticated algorithm, such as UCB1.
- **Small-to-medium tabular problems**: As a basic rule, exploration can still be approached with more advanced mechanisms, but in some cases, the overall benefit is small, and is not worth the additional complexity.
- **Large non-tabular problems**: We are now in more complex environments. In these settings, the outlook isn't yet well defined, and researchers are still actively working to find the best exploration strategy. The reason for this is that as the complexity increases, optimal methods such as UCB are intractable. For example, UCB cannot deal with problems with continuous states. However, we don't have to throw everything away, and we can use the exploration algorithms that were studied in the multi-armed bandit context as inspiration. That said, there are many approaches that approximate optimal exploration methods, and that work well in continuous environments, as well. For example, counting-based approaches, such as UCB, have been adapted with infinite state problems, by providing similar counts for similar states. An algorithm of these has also been capable of achieving significant improvement in very difficult environments, such as Montezuma's Revenge. Still, in the majority of RL contexts, the additional complexity that these more complex approaches involve is not worth it, and simpler random strategies such as ϵ-greedy work just fine.

It's also worth noting that, despite the fact that we outlined only a count-based approach to exploration such as UCB1, there are two other sophisticated ways in which to deal with exploration, which achieve optimal value in regret. The first is called posterior sampling (an example of this is Thompson sampling), and is based on a posterior distribution, and the second is called information gain, and relies upon an internal measurement of the uncertainty through the estimation of entropy.

Epochal stochastic bandit algorithm selection

The main use of exploration strategies in reinforcement learning is to help the agent in the exploration of the environment. We saw this use case in DQN with ϵ-greedy, and in other algorithms with the injection of additional noise into the policy. However, there are other ways of using exploration strategies. So, to better grasp the exploration concepts that have been presented so far, and to introduce an alternative use case of these algorithms, we will present and develop an algorithm called ESBAS. This algorithm was introduced in the paper, *Reinforcement Learning Algorithm Selection*.

ESBAS is a meta-algorithm for online **algorithm selection (AS)** in the context of reinforcement learning. It uses exploration methods in order to choose the best algorithm to employ during a trajectory, so as to maximize the expected reward.

In order to better explain ESBAS, we'll first explain what algorithm selection is and how it can be used in machine learning and reinforcement learning. Then, we'll focus on ESBAS, and give a detailed description of its inner workings, while also providing its pseudocode. Finally, we'll implement ESBAS and test it on an environment called Acrobot.

Unboxing algorithm selection

To better understand what ESBAS does, let's first focus on what algorithm selection (AS) is. In normal settings, a specific and fixed algorithm is developed and trained for a given task. The problem is that if the dataset changes over time, the dataset overfits, or another algorithm works better in some restricted contexts, there's no way of changing it. The chosen algorithm will remain the same forever. The task of algorithm selection overcomes this problem.

Developing the ESBAS Algorithm

AS is an open problem in machine learning. It is about designing an algorithm called a meta-algorithm that always chooses the best algorithm from a pool of different options, called a portfolio, which is based on current needs. A representation of this is shown in the following diagram. AS is based on the assumption that different algorithms in the portfolio will outperform the others in different parts of the problem space. Thus, it is important to have algorithms with complementary capabilities.

For example, in the following diagram, the meta-algorithm chooses which algorithm (or agent) among those available in the portfolio (such as PPO and TD3) will act on the environment at a given moment. These algorithms are not complementary to each other, but each one provides different strengths that the meta-algorithm can choose in order to better perform in a specific situation:

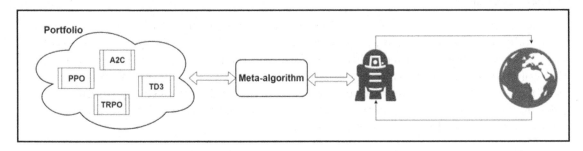

Representation of an algorithm selection method for RL

For example, if the task involves designing a self-driving car that drives on all kinds of terrains, then it may be useful to train one algorithm that is capable of amazing performance on the road, in the desert, and on ice. Then, AS could intelligently choose which one of these three versions to employ in each situation. For instance, AS may find that on rainy days, the policy that has been trained on ice works better than the others.

In RL, the policy changes with a very high frequency, and the dataset increases continuously over time. This means that there can be big differences in the optimal neural network size and the learning rate between the starting point, when the agent is in an embryonic state, compared to the agent in an advanced state. For example, an agent may start learning with a high learning rate, and decrease it as more experience is accumulated. This highlights how RL is a very interesting playground for algorithm selection. For this reason, that's exactly where we'll test our AS.

Under the hood of ESBAS

The paper that proposes ESBAS, tests the algorithm on batch and online settings. However, in the remainder of the chapter, we'll focus primarily on the former. The two algorithms are very similar, and if you are interested in the pure online version, you can find a further explanation of it in the paper. The AS in true online settings is renamed as **sliding stochastic bandit AS (SSBAS)**, as it learns from a sliding window of the most recent selections. But let's start from the foundations.

The first thing to say about ESBAS, is that it is based on the UCB1 strategy, and that it uses this bandit-style selection for choosing an off-policy algorithm from the fixed portfolio. In particular, ESBAS can be broken down into three main parts that work as follows:

1. It cycles across many epochs of exponential size. Inside each epoch, the first thing that it does is update all of the off-policy algorithms that are available in the portfolio. It does this using the data that has been collected until that point in time (at the first epoch the dataset will be empty). The other thing that it does, is reset the meta-algorithm.
2. Then, during the epoch, the meta-algorithm computes the optimistic guess, following the formula (12.3), in order to choose the off-policy algorithm (among those in the portfolio) that will control the next trajectory, so as to minimize the total regret. The trajectory is then run with that algorithm. Meanwhile, all the transitions of the trajectory are collected and added to the dataset that will be later used by the off-policy algorithms to train the policies.
3. When a trajectory has come to an end, the meta-algorithm updates the mean reward of that particular off-policy algorithm with the RL return that is obtained from the environment, and increases the number of occurrences. The average reward, and the number of occurrences, will be used by UCB1 to compute the UCB, as from formula (12.2). These values are used to choose the next off-policy algorithm that will roll out the next trajectory.

To give you a better view of the algorithm, we also provided the pseudocode of ESBAS in the code block, here:

```
------------------------------------------------------------
------
ESBAS
------------------------------------------------------------
------

Initialize policy $\pi^a$ for every algorithm $a$ in the portfolio $P$
Initialize empty dataset $D$
```

Developing the ESBAS Algorithm

```
for β = 1..M do
    for a in P do
        Learn policy π^a on D with algortihm a
        Initialize AS variables: n ← 0 and for every a ∈ P: n^a ← 0, x^a ← 0
        for t = 2^β..2^(β+1) - 1 do
            ▷ Select the best algorithm according to UCB1
```
$$a^{max} = argmax_{a \in P} \left(x^a + \sqrt{\frac{\xi \ln(n)}{n^a}} \right)$$

Generate trajectory τ with policy π^{max} and add transitions to D
▷ Update the average return and the counter of a^{max}

$$x^{max} \leftarrow \frac{n^{max} x^{max} + R(\tau)}{n^{max} + 1} \quad (12.4)$$

$$n^{max} \leftarrow n^{max} + 1$$
$$n \leftarrow n + 1$$

Here, ξ is a hyperparameter, $R(\tau)$ is the RL return obtained during the τ trajectory, n^a is the counter of algorithm a, and x^a is its mean return.

As explained in the paper, online AS addresses four practical problems that are inherited from RL algorithms:

1. **Sample efficiency**: The diversification of the policies provides an additional source of information that makes ESBAS sample efficient. Moreover, it combines properties from curriculum learning and ensemble learning.
2. **Robustness**: The diversification of the portfolio provides robustness against bad algorithms.
3. **Convergence**: ESBAS guarantees the minimization of the regret.
4. **Curriculum learning**: AS is able to provide a sort of curriculum strategy, for example, by choosing easier, shallow models at the beginning, and deep models toward the end.

Implementation

The implementation of ESBAS is easy, as it involves the addition of only a few components. The most substantial part is in the definition and the optimization of the off-policy algorithms of the portfolio. Regarding these, ESBAS does not bind the choice of the algorithms. In the paper, both Q-learning and DQN are used. We have decided to use DQN, so as to provide an algorithm that is capable of dealing with more complex tasks that can be used with environments with the RGB state space. We went through DQN in great detail in Chapter 5, *Deep Q-Network*, and for ESBAS, we'll use the same implementation.

The last thing that we need to specify before going through the implementation is the portfolio's composition. We created a diversified portfolio, as regards the neural network architecture, but you can try with other combinations. For example, you could compose the portfolio with DQN algorithms of different learning rates.

The implementation is divided as follows:

- The `DQN_optimization` class builds the computational graph, and optimizes a policy with DQN.
- The `UCB1` class defines the UCB1 algorithm.
- The `ESBAS` function implements the main pipeline for ESBAS.

We'll provide the implementation of the last two bullet points, but you can find the full implementation on the GitHub repository of the book: https://github.com/PacktPublishing/Reinforcement-Learning-Algorithms-with-Python.

Let's start by going through `ESBAS(..)`. Besides the hyperparameters of DQN, there's only an additional `xi` argument that represents the ξ hyperparameter. The main outline of the `ESBAS` function is the same as the pseudocode that was given previously, so we can quickly go through it.

After having defined the function with all the arguments, we can reset the default graph of TensorFlow, and create two Gym environments (one for training, and one for testing). We can then create the portfolio, by instantiating a `DQN_optimization` object for each of the neural network sizes, and appending them on a list:

```
def ESBAS(env_name, hidden_sizes=[32], lr=1e-2, num_epochs=2000,
buffer_size=100000, discount=0.99, render_cycle=100,
update_target_net=1000, batch_size=64, update_freq=4, min_buffer_size=5000,
test_frequency=20, start_explor=1, end_explor=0.1, explor_steps=100000,
xi=16000):
    tf.reset_default_graph()

    env = gym.make(env_name)
    env_test = gym.wrappers.Monitor(gym.make(env_name),
"VIDEOS/TEST_VIDEOS"+env_name+str(current_milli_time()),force=True,
video_callable=lambda x: x%20==0)
    dqns = []
    for l in hidden_sizes:
        dqns.append(DQN_optimization(env.observation_space.shape,
env.action_space.n, l, lr, discount))
```

Developing the ESBAS Algorithm

Now, we define an inner function, `DQNs_update`, that trains the policies in the portfolio in a DQN way. Take into consideration that all the algortihms in the portfolio are DQN, and that the only difference is in their neural network size. The optimization is done by the `optimize` and `update_target_network` methods of the `DQN_optimization` class:

```
def DQNs_update(step_counter):
    if len(buffer) > min_buffer_size and (step_counter % update_freq == 0):
        mb_obs, mb_rew, mb_act, mb_obs2, mb_done = buffer.sample_minibatch(batch_size)
        for dqn in dqns:
            dqn.optimize(mb_obs, mb_rew, mb_act, mb_obs2, mb_done)
    if len(buffer) > min_buffer_size and (step_counter % update_target_net == 0):
        for dqn in dqns:
            dqn.update_target_network()
```

As always, we need to initialize some (self-explanatory) variables: resetting the environment, instantiating an object of `ExperienceBuffer` (using the same classes that we used in others chapters), and setting up the exploration decay:

```
step_count = 0
batch_rew = []
episode = 0
beta = 1
buffer = ExperienceBuffer(buffer_size)
obs = env.reset()
eps = start_explor
eps_decay = (start_explor - end_explor) / explor_steps
```

We can finally start the loop that iterates across the epochs. As for the preceding pseudocode, during each epoch, the following things occur:

1. The policies are trained on the experience buffer
2. The trajectories are run by the policy that is chosen by UCB1

The first step is done by invoking `DQNs_update`, which we defined earlier, for the entire length of the epoch (which has an exponential length):

```
for ep in range(num_epochs):
    # policies training
    for i in range(2**(beta-1), 2**beta):
        DQNs_update(i)
```

With regard to the second step, just before the trajectories are run, a new object of the UCB1 class is instantiated and initialized. Then, a `while` loop iterates over the episodes of exponential size, inside of which, the UCB1 object chooses which algorithm will run the next trajectory. During the trajectory, the actions are selected by dqns[best_dqn]:

```
ucb1 = UCB1(dqns, xi)
list_bests = []
beta += 1
ep_rew = []

while step_count < 2**beta:
    best_dqn = ucb1.choose_algorithm()
    list_bests.append(best_dqn)

    g_rew = 0
    done = False

    while not done:
        # Epsilon decay
        if eps > end_explor:
            eps -= eps_decay

        act = eps_greedy(np.squeeze(dqns[best_dqn].act(obs)), eps=eps)

        obs2, rew, done, _ = env.step(act)
        buffer.add(obs, rew, act, obs2, done)

        obs = obs2
        g_rew += rew
        step_count += 1
```

After each rollout, `ucb1` is updated with the RL return that was obtained in the last trajectory. Moreover, the environment is reset, and the reward of the current trajectory is appended to a list in order to keep track of all the rewards:

```
ucb1.update(best_dqn, g_rew)

obs = env.reset()
ep_rew.append(g_rew)
g_rew = 0
episode += 1
```

That's all for the ESBAS function.

Developing the ESBAS Algorithm

`UCB1` is made up of a constructor that initializes the attributes that are needed for computing (12.3); a `choose_algorithm()` method that returns the current best algorithm among the ones in the portfolio, as in (12.3); and `update(idx_algo, traj_return)`, which updates the average reward of the `idx_algo` algorithm with the last reward that was obtained, as understood from (12.4). The code is as follows:

```
class UCB1:
    def __init__(self, algos, epsilon):
        self.n = 0
        self.epsilon = epsilon
        self.algos = algos
        self.nk = np.zeros(len(algos))
        self.xk = np.zeros(len(algos))

    def choose_algorithm(self):
        return np.argmax([self.xk[i] + np.sqrt(self.epsilon * np.log(self.n) / self.nk[i]) for i in range(len(self.algos))])

    def update(self, idx_algo, traj_return):
        self.xk[idx_algo] = (self.nk[idx_algo] * self.xk[idx_algo] + traj_return) / (self.nk[idx_algo] + 1)
        self.nk[idx_algo] += 1
        self.n += 1
```

With the code at hand, we can now test it on an environment and see how it performs.

Solving Acrobot

We'll test ESBAS on yet another Gym environment—`Acrobot-v1`. As described in the OpenAI Gym documentation, *the Acrobot system includes two joints and two links, where the joint between the two links is actuated. Initially, the links are hanging downward, and the goal is to swing the end of the lower link up to a given height.* The following diagram shows the movement of the acrobot in a brief sequence of timesteps, from the start to an end position:

Sequence of the acrobot's movement

The portfolio comprises three deep neural networks of different sizes. One small neural network with only one hidden layer of size 64, one medium neural network with two hidden layers of size 16, and a large neural network with two hidden layers of size 64. Furthermore, we set the hyperparameter of $\xi = 0.25$ (the same value that is used in the paper).

Results

The following diagram shows the results. This plot presents both the learning curve of ESBAS: the complete portfolio (comprising the three neural networks that were listed previously) in the darker shade; and the learning curve of ESBAS, with only one best performing neural network (a deep neural network with two hidden layers of size 64) in *orange*. We know that ESBAS with only one algorithm in the portfolio will not really leverage the potential of the meta-algorithm, but we introduced it in order to have a baseline with which to compare the results. The plot speaks for itself, showing the *blue* line always above the *orange*, thus proving that ESBAS actually chooses the best available option. The unusual shape is due to the fact that we are training the DQN algorithms offline:

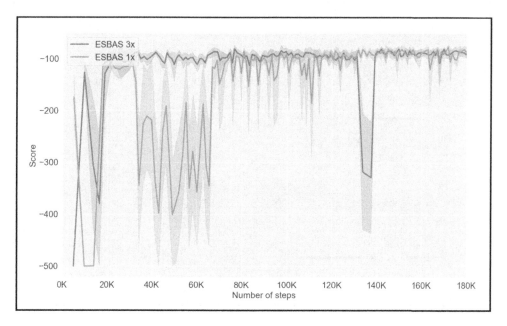

The performance of ESBAS with a portfolio of three algorithms in a dark shade, and with only one algorithm in a lighter shade

Developing the ESBAS Algorithm

 For all the color references mentioned in the chapter, please refer to the color images bundle at http://www.packtpub.com/sites/default/files/downloads/9781789131116_ColorImages.pdf.

Also, the spikes that you see at the start of the training, and then at around steps, 20K, 65K, and, 131K, are the points at which the policies are trained, and the meta-algorithm is reset.

We can now ask ourselves at which point in time ESBAS prefers one algorithm, compared to the others. The answer is shown in the plot of the following diagram. In this plot, the small neural network is characterized by the value 0, the medium one by the value 1, and the large by the value 2. The dots show the algorithms that are chosen on each trajectory. We can see that, right at the beginning, the larger neural network is preferred, but that this immediately changes toward the medium, and then to the smaller one. After about 64K steps, the meta-algorithm switches back to the larger neural network:

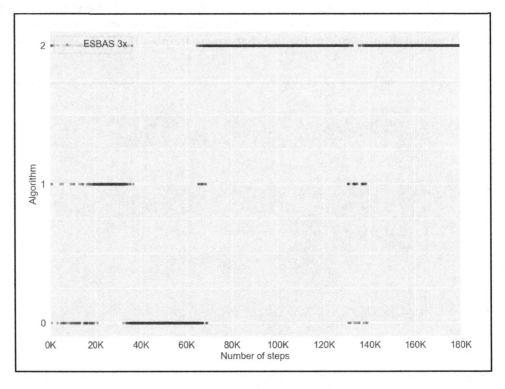

The plot shows the preferences of the meta-algorithm

From the preceding plot, we can also see that both of the ESBAS versions converge to the same values, but with very different speeds. Indeed, the version of ESBAS that leverages the true potential of AS (that is, the one with three algorithms in the portfolio) converges much faster. Both converge to the same values because, in the long run, the best neural network is the one that is used in the ESBAS version with the single option (the deep neural network with two hidden layers of size 64).

Summary

In this chapter, we addressed the exploration-exploitation dilemma. This problem has already been tackled in previous chapters, but only in a light way, by employing simple strategies. In this chapter, we studied this dilemma in more depth, starting from the notorious multi-armed bandit problem. We saw how more sophisticated counter-based algorithms, such as UCB, can actually reach optimal performance, and with the expected logarithmic regret.

We then used exploration algorithms for AS. AS is an interesting application of exploratory algorithms, because the meta-algorithm has to choose the algorithm that best performs the task at hand. AS also has an outlet in reinforcement learning. For example, AS can be used to pick the best policy that has been trained with different algorithms from the portfolio, in order to run the next trajectory. That's also what ESBAS does. It tackles the problem of the online selection of off-policy RL algorithms by adopting UCB1. We studied and implemented ESBAS in depth.

Now, you know everything that is needed to design and develop highly performant RL algorithms that are capable of balancing between exploration and exploitation. Moreover, in the previous chapters, you have acquired the skills that are needed in order to understand which algorithm to employ in many different landscapes. However, until now, we have overlooked some more advanced RL topics and issues. In the next and final chapter, we'll fill these gaps, and talk about unsupervised learning, intrinsic motivation, RL challenges, and how to improve the robustness of algorithms. We will also see how it's possible to use transfer learning to switch from simulations to reality. Furthermore, we'll give some additional tips and best practices for training and debugging deep reinforcement learning algorithms.

Questions

1. What's the exploration-exploitation dilemma?
2. What are two exploration strategies that we have already used in previous RL algorithms?
3. What's UCB?
4. Which problem is more difficult to solve: Montezuma's Revenge or the multi-armed bandit problem?
5. How does ESBAS tackle the problem of online RL algorithm selection?

Further reading

- For a more comprehensive survey about the multi-armed bandit problem, read *A Survey of Online Experiment Design with Stochastic Multi-Armed Bandit*: https://arxiv.org/pdf/1510.00757.pdf.
- For reading the paper that leverages intrinsic motivation for playing Montezuma's Revenge, refer to *Unifying Count-Based Exploration and Intrinsic Motivation*: https://arxiv.org/pdf/1606.01868.pdf.
- For the original ESBAS paper, follow this link: https://arxiv.org/pdf/1701.08810.pdf.

13
Practical Implementation for Resolving RL Challenges

In this chapter, we will wrap up some of the concepts behind **deep reinforcement learning** (**deep RL**) algorithms that we explained in the previous chapters to give you a broad view of their use and establish a general rule for choosing the most suitable one for a given problem. Moreover, we will propose some guidelines so that you can start the development of your own deep RL algorithm. This guideline shows the steps you need to take from the start of development so that you can easily experiment without losing too much time on debugging. In the same section, we also list the most important hyperparameters to tune and additional normalization processes to take care of.

Then, we'll address the main challenges of this field by addressing issues such as stability, efficiency, and generalization. We'll use these three main problems as a pivotal point to transition to more advanced reinforcement learning techniques such as unsupervised RL and transfer learning. Unsupervised RL and transfer learning are of fundamental importance for deploying and solving demanding RL tasks. This is because they are techniques that address the three challenges we mentioned previously.

We will also look into how we can apply RL to real-world problems and how RL algorithms can be used for bridging the gap between simulation and the real world.

To conclude this chapter and this book as a whole, we'll discuss the future of reinforcement learning from both a technical and social perspective.

The following topics will be covered in this chapter:

- Best practices of deep RL
- Challenges in deep RL
- Advanced techniques
- RL in the real world
- Future of RL and its impact on society

Best practices of deep RL

Throughout this book, we covered plenty of reinforcement learning algorithms, some of which are only upgrades (for example TD3, A2C, and so on), while others were fundamentally different from the others (such as TRPO and DPG) and propose an alternative way to reach the same objective. Moreover, we addressed non-RL optimization algorithms such as imitation learning and evolution strategies to solve sequential decision-making tasks. All of these alternatives may have created confusion and you may not know exactly which algorithm is best for a particular problem. If that is the case, don't worry, as we'll now go through some rules that you can use in order to decide which is the best algorithm to use for a given task.

Also, if you implemented some of the algorithms we went through in this book, you might find it hard to put all the pieces together to make the algorithm work properly. Deep RL algorithms are notoriously difficult to debug and train, and the training time is very long. As a result, the whole training process is very slow and arduous. Luckily, there are a few strategies that you can adopt that will prevent some terrible headaches while developing deep RL algorithms. But before looking at what these strategies are, let's deal with choosing the appropriate algorithm.

Choosing the appropriate algorithm

The main driving force that differentiates the various types of RL algorithms is sample efficiency and training time.

We consider sample efficiency as the number of interactions with the environment that an agent has to make in order to learn the task. The numbers that we'll provide are an indication of the efficiency of the algorithm and are measured with respect to other algorithms on typical environments.

Clearly, there are other parameters that influence this choice, but usually, they have a minor impact and are of less importance. Just to give you an idea, the other parameters to be evaluated are the availability of CPUs and GPUs, the type of reward function, the scalability, and the complexity of the algorithm, as well as that of the environment.

For this comparison, we will take into consideration gradient-free black-box algorithms such as evolution strategies, model-based RL such as DAgger, and model-free RL. Of the latter, we will differentiate between policy gradient algorithms such as DDPG and TRPO and value-based algorithms such as DQN.

The following diagram shows the data efficiency of these four categories of algorithms (note that the leftmost methods are less sample efficient than the rightmost methods). In particular, the efficiency of the algorithm increases as you move to the right of the diagram. So, you can see that gradient-free methods are those that require more data points from the environment, followed by policy gradient methods, value-based methods, and finally model-based RL, which are the most sample efficient:

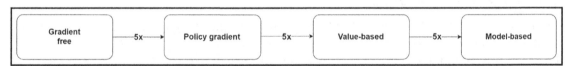

Figure 13.1. Sample efficiency comparison between model-based RL methods, policy gradient algorithms, value-based algorithms, and gradient-free algorithms (the leftmost methods are less efficient than the rightmost methods)

Conversely, the training time of these algorithms is inversed related to their sample efficiency. This relationship is summarized in the following diagram (note that the leftmost methods are slower to train than the rightmost methods). We can see that **Model-based** algorithms are way slower to train than **Value-based** algorithms, almost by a factor of 5, which in turn almost quintuples the time of policy gradient algorithms, which are about **5x** slower to train than gradient-free methods.

Practical Implementation for Resolving RL Challenges

Be aware that these numbers are just to highlight the average case, and the training time is only related to the speed at which the algorithm is trained, and not to the time needed to acquire new transitions from the environment:

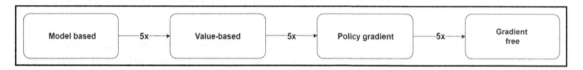

Figure 13.2. Training time efficiency comparison between model-based RL methods, policy gradient algorithms, value-based algorithms, and gradient-free algorithms (the leftmost methods are slower to train than the rightmost methods)

We can see that the sample efficiency of an algorithm is complementary to its training time, meaning that an algorithm that is data efficient is slow to train and vice versa. Thus, because the overall learning time of an agent takes into account both the training time and the speed of the environment, you have to find a trade-off between sample efficiency and training time that meet your needs. In fact, the main purpose of model-based and more efficient model-free algorithms is to reduce the number of steps with the environment so that these algorithms are easier to deploy and train in the real world, where the interactions are slower than in simulators.

From zero to one

Once you have defined the algorithm that best fits your needs, whether that's one of the well-known algorithms or a new one, you have to develop it. As you saw throughout this book, reinforcement learning algorithms don't have much in common with supervised learning algorithms. For this reason, there are different aspects that are worth pointing out in order to facilitate the debugging, experimentation, and tuning of the algorithm:

- **Start with easy problems**: Initially, you would want to experiment with a workable version of the code as fast as possible. However, it would be advisable to gradually proceed with increasingly complex environments. This will greatly help to reduce the overall training and debugging time. Let me present an example. You can start with CartPole-v1 or RoboschoolInvertedPendulum-v1 if you need a discrete or continuous environment, respectively. Then, you can move to a medium-complexity environment such as RoboschoolHopper-v1, LunarLander-v2, or a related environment with RGB images. At this point, you should have a bug-free code that you can finally train and tune on your final task. Moreover, you should be as familiar as possible with the easier tasks so that you know what to look for if something is not working.

- **Training is slow**: Training deep reinforcement learning algorithms takes time and the learning curve can follow any kind of shape. As we saw in the previous chapters, the learning curves (that is, the cumulative reward of the trajectories with respect to the number of steps) can resemble a logarithm function, a hyperbolic tangent function, as shown in the following diagram, or a more complex function. The possible shapes depend on the reward function, its sparsity, and the complexity of the environment. If you are working on a new environment and you don't know what to expect, the suggestion here is to be patient and leave it running until you are sure that the progress has stopped. Also, don't get too involved with the plots while training.

- **Develop some baselines**: For new tasks, the suggestion is to develop at least two baselines so that you can compare your algorithm with them. One baseline could simply be a random agent, with the other being an algorithm such as REINFORCE or A2C. These baselines can then be used as a lower bound for performance and efficiency.

- **Plots and histograms**: To monitor the progress of the algorithm and to help during the debugging phase, an important factor is to plot and display histograms of key parameters such as the loss function, the cumulative reward, the actions (if possible), the length of the trajectories, the KL penalty, the entropy, and the value function. In addition to plotting the means, you can add the minimum and maximum values and the standard deviation. In this book, we primarily used TensorBoard to visualize this information, but you can use any tool you want.

- **Use multiple seeds**: Deep reinforcement learning embeds stochasticity both in the neural networks and in the environments, which often makes the results incoherent between different runs. So, to ensure consistency and stability, it's better to use multiple random seeds.

- **Normalization:** Depending on the design of the environment, it could be helpful to normalize the rewards, the advantage, and the observations. The advantage values (for example, in TRPO and PPO) can be normalized in a batch to have a mean of 0 and a standard deviation of 1. Additionally, the observations can be normalized using a set of initial random steps. Instead, the rewards can be normalized by a running estimate of the mean and standard deviation of the discounted or undiscounted reward.

- **Hyperparameter tuning**: Hyperparameters change a lot based on the class and type of algorithm. For example, value-based methods have multiple distinct hyperparameters compared to policy gradients, but also instances of these classes such as TRPO and PPO have many unique hyperparameters. That being said, for each algorithm that was introduced throughout this book, we specified the hyperparameters that were used and the most important ones to tune. Among them, there are at least two hyperparameters that are used by all the RL algorithms: learning rate and discount factor. The former is slightly less important than in supervised learning, but nevertheless, it remains one of the first hyperparameters to tune so that we have a working algorithm. The discount factor is unique to RL algorithms. The introduction of a discount factor may introduce bias as it modifies the objective function. However, in practice, it produces a better policy. Thus, to a certain degree, the shorter the horizon, the better it is, as it reduces instability:

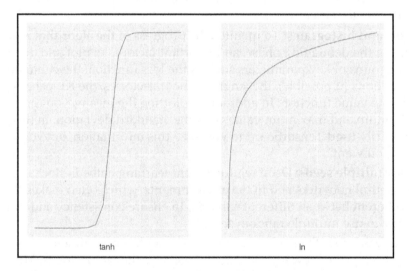

Figure 13.3. Example of a logarithmic and hyperbolic tangent function

 For all the color references mentioned in the chapter, please refer to the color images bundle at `http://www.packtpub.com/sites/default/files/downloads/9781789131116_ColorImages.pdf`.

Adopt these techniques and you'll be able to train, develop, and deploy your algorithms much more easily. Furthermore, you'll have algorithms that are more stable and robust.

Having a critical view and understanding of the drawbacks of deep reinforcement learning is a key factor when it comes to actually pushing the boundaries on what RL algorithms can do to design better state-of-the-art algorithms. In the following section, we'll present the main challenges of deep RL in a more concise view.

Challenges in deep RL

The efforts that have been put into the research of reinforcement learning algorithms in recent years has been huge. Especially since the introduction of the deep neural network as a function approximation, the advancement and results have been outstanding. Yet some major issues remain unsolved. These limit the applicability of RL algorithms to more extensive and interesting tasks. We are talking about the issues of stability, reproducibility, efficiency, and generalization, although scalability and the exploration problem could be added to this list.

Stability and reproducibility

Stability and reproducibility are somehow interconnected with each other as the goal is to design an algorithm that is capable of consistency across multiple runs and that is not too invariant to small tweaks. For example, the algorithm shouldn't be too sensitive to changes in the values of the hyperparameters.

The main factor that makes deep RL algorithms difficult to replicate is intrinsic to the nature of deep neural networks. This is mainly due to random initialization of the deep neural networks and the stochasticity of optimization. Moreover, this situation is exacerbated in RL, considering that the environments are stochastic. Combined, these factors are also to the detriment of the interpretability of results.

Stability is also put to the test by the high instability of RL algorithms, as we saw in Q-learning and REINFORCE. For example, in value-based algorithms, there isn't any guarantee of convergence and the algorithms suffer from high bias and instability. DQN uses many tricks to stabilize the learning process, such as an experienced replay and a delay in the update of the target network. Though these strategies can alleviate the instability problems, they don't go away.

Practical Implementation for Resolving RL Challenges

To overcome any constraints that are intrinsic to the algorithm in terms of stability and reproducibility, we need to intervene outside of it. To this end, many different benchmarks and some rules of thumb can be employed to ensure a good level of reproducibility and consistency of results. These are as follows:

- Whenever possible, test the algorithms on multiple but similar environments. For example, test it on a suite of environments such as Roboschool or Atari Gym where the tasks are comparable to each other in terms of action and state spaces but have different goals.

- Run many trials across different random seeds. The results may vary significantly by changing the seeds. As an example of this, the following diagram shows two runs of the exact same algorithm with the same hyperparameters, but with a different seed. You can see that the differences are large. So, depending on your goal, it could be helpful to use multiple random seeds, generally between three and five. For example, in academic papers, it is good practice to average all the results across five runs and take the standard deviation into account as well.

- If the results are unsteady, consider using a more stable algorithm or employing some further strategies. Also, keep in mind that the effects in the changes of the hyperparameters can vary significantly across algorithms and environments:

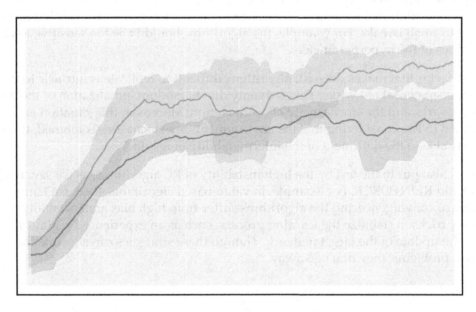

Figure 13.4. Performance of two trials of the same algorithm with different random seeds

Efficiency

In the previous section, *Choosing the appropriate algorithm*, we saw that the sample efficiency between the algorithms is highly variable. Moreover, from the previous chapters, we saw that more efficient methods, such as value-based learning, still require a substantial number of interactions with the environment to learn. Maybe only model-based RL can save itself from the hunger of data. Unfortunately, model-based methods have other downsides, such as a lower performance bound.

For this reason, hybrid model-based and model-free approaches have been built. However, these are difficult to engineer and are impractical for use in real-world problems. As you can see, the efficiency-related problem is very hard to solve but at the same time very important to address so that we can deploy RL methods in the real world.

There are two alternative ways to deal with very slow environments such as the physical world. One is to use a lower-fidelity simulator in the first place and then fine-tune the agent in the final environment. The other is to train the agent directly in the final environment, but transferring some prior related knowledge so as to avoid learning the task from scratch. It's like learning to drive when you've already trained your sensory system. In both cases, because we are transferring knowledge from one environment to another, we talk about a methodology called transfer learning. We'll elaborate on this methodology very soon in the *Advanced techniques* section.

Generalization

The concept of generalization refers to two aspects that are different, but somehow related. In general terms, the concept of generalization in reinforcement learning refers to the capability of an algorithm to obtain good performance in a related environment. For example, if an agent has been trained to walk on dirty roads, we might expect that the same agent will perform well on paved roads. The better the generalization capabilities, the better the agent will perform in different environments. The second and lesser-used means of generalization refers to the property of the algorithm to achieve good performance in an environment where only limited data can be gathered.

In RL, the agent can choose the states to visit by itself and do so for as long as it wants so that it can also overfit on a certain problem space. However, if good generalization capabilities are required, a trade-off has to be found. This is only partially true if the agent is allowed to gather potentially infinite data for the environment as it will act as a sort of self-regularization method.

Nonetheless, to help with generalization across other environments, an agent must be capable of abstract reasoning to discern from the mere state-action mapping and interpret the task using multiple factors. Examples of abstract reasoning can be found in model-based reinforcement learning, transfer learning, and in the use of auxiliary tasks. We'll cover the latter topic later, but in brief, it is a technique that's used to improve generalization and sample efficiency by augmenting an RL agent with auxiliary tasks that were learned jointly with the main task.

Advanced techniques

The challenges we listed previously have no simple solutions. However, there has been an effort in trying to overcome them and to come up with novel strategies to improve efficiency, generalization, and stability. Two of the most widespread and promising techniques that focus on efficiency and generalization are unsupervised reinforcement learning and transfer learning. In most cases, these strategies work in symbiosis with the deep reinforcement learning algorithms that we developed in the previous chapters.

Unsupervised RL

Unsupervised RL is related to the usual unsupervised learning in how both methods don't use any source of supervision. While in unsupervised learning the data isn't labeled, in the reinforced counterpart, the reward is not given. That is, given an action, the environment returns only the next state. Both the reward and the **done** status are removed.

Unsupervised RL can be helpful in many occurrences, for example, when the annotation of the environment with hand-designed rewards is not scalable, or when an environment can serve multiple tasks. In the latter case, unsupervised learning can be employed so that we can learn about the dynamics of the environment. Methods that are able to learn from unsupervised sources can also be used as an additional source of information in environments with very sparse rewards.

How can we design an algorithm that can learn about the environment without any source of supervision? Can't we just employ model-based learning? Well, model-based RL still needs the reward signal to plan or infer the next actions. Therefore, a different solution is required.

Intrinsic reward

A potential fair alternative is to develop a reward function that is intrinsic to the agent, meaning that it's controlled exclusively by the belief of the agent. This method comes close to the approach that's used by newborns to learn. In fact, they employ a pure explorative paradigm to navigate the world without an immediate benefit. Nonetheless, the knowledge that's acquired may be useful later in life.

The intrinsic reward is a sort of exploration bonus based on the estimation of the novelty of a state. The more unfamiliar a state is, the higher the intrinsic reward. Thus, with it, the agent is incentivized to explore new spaces of the environment. It may have become clear by now that the intrinsic reward can be used as an alternative exploration strategy. In fact, many algorithms use it in combination with the extrinsic reward (that is the usual reward that's returned by the environment) to boost the exploration in very sparse environments such as Montezuma's revenge. However, though the methods to estimate the intrinsic reward are very similar to those we studied in `Chapter 12`, *Developing ESBAS Algorithm*, to incentivize policy exploration (these exploration strategies were still related to the extrinsic reward), here, we are only concentrating on pure unsupervised exploration methods.

Two primary curiosity-driven strategies that provide rewards on unfamiliar states and explore the environment efficiently are count-based and dynamics-based:

- Count-based strategies (also known as **visitation counts** strategies) aim to count or estimate the visitation count of each state and encourage the exploration of those states with low visitation, assigning a high intrinsic reward to them.
- Dynamics-based strategies train a dynamic model of the environment, along with the agent's policy, and compute the intrinsic reward either on the prediction error, on the prediction uncertainty, or on the prediction improvement. The underlying idea is that by fitting a model on the states visited, the new and unfamiliar states will have a higher uncertainty or estimation error. These values are then used to compute the intrinsic reward and incentivize the exploration of unknown states.

What happens if we apply only curiosity-driven approaches to the usual environments? The paper *Large-scale study of curiosity-driven learning* addressed this question and found that, on Atari games, pure curiosity-driven agents can learn and master the tasks without any external reward. Furthermore, they noted that, on Roboschool, walking behavior emerged purely out of these unsupervised algorithms based on intrinsic reward. The authors of the paper also suggested that these findings were due to the way in which the environments have been designed. Indeed, in human-designed environments (such as games), the extrinsic reward is often aligned with the objective of seeking novelty. Nonetheless, in environments that are not gamified, pure curiosity-driven unsupervised approaches are able to explore and learn about the environment exclusively by themselves without any need for supervision whatsoever. Alternatively, RL algorithms can also benefit from a huge boost in exploration and consequently in performance by combining the intrinsic with the extrinsic reward.

Transfer learning

Transferring knowledge between two environments, especially if these environments are similar to each other, is a hard task. Transfer learning strategies propose to bridge the knowledge gap so that the transition from an initial environment to a new one is as easy and smooth as possible. Specifically, transfer learning is the task of efficiently transferring knowledge from a source environment (or multiple environments) to a target environment. Thus, the more experience that has been acquired from a set of source tasks and transferred to a new target task, the faster the agent will learn and the better it will perform on the target task.

Generally speaking, when you think about an agent that hasn't been trained yet, you have to imagine a system that does not have any kind of information in it. Instead, when you play a game, you use a lot of prior knowledge. For example, you may guess the meaning of the enemies from their shapes and colors, as well as their dynamics. This implies that you are able to recognize the enemies when they shoot you, like in the Space Invaders game that's shown in the following diagram. Also, you can easily guess the general dynamics of the game. Instead, at the start of the training, an RL agent won't know anything. This comparison is important because it provides valuable insight into the importance of transferring knowledge between multiple environments. An agent that has the ability to use the experience that was acquired from a source task can learn exponentially faster on the target environment. For example, if the source environment is Pong and the target environment is Breakout, then many of the visual components could be reused, saving a lot of time for computation. To have an accurate understanding of its overall importance, imagine the efficiency that's gained in much more complex environments:

Chapter 13

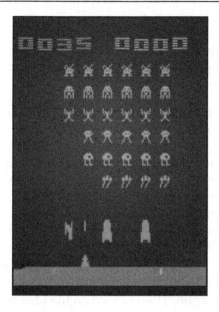

Figure 13.5. A screenshot of Space Invaders. Are you able to infer the role of the sprites?

When speaking about transfer learning, we refer to 0-shot learning, 1-shot learning, and so on, as the number of attempts required in the target domain. For example, 0-shot learning means that the policy that has been trained on a source domain is directly employed on the target domain without further training. In this case, the agent must develop strong generalization capabilities to adjust itself to the new task.

Types of transfer learning

Many types of transfer learning exist, and their usage depends on the specific case and needs. One of the distinctions is related to the number of source environments. Obviously, the more source environments you are training the agent on, the more diversity it has, and the more experience can be used in the target domain. Transfer learning from multiple source domains is called multi-task learning.

1-task learning

1-task learning or simply transfer learning is the task of training the policy on one domain and transferring it onto a new one. Three major techniques can be employed to do that. These are as follows:

- **Fine-tuning**: This involves the refinement of the learned model on the target task. If you get involved in machine learning, and especially in computer vision or natural language processing, you have probably used this technique already. Unfortunately, in reinforcement learning, fine-tuning is not as easy as it is in the aforementioned fields, as it requires more careful engineering and generally has lower benefits. The reason for this is that, in general, the gap between the two RL tasks is bigger than the gap between two different image domains. For example, the differences between the classification of a cat and a dog are minor compared to the differences between Pong and Breakout. Nonetheless, fine-tuning can also be used in RL and tuning just the last few layers (or substituting them if the action space is totally different) could give better generalization properties.
- **Domain randomization**: This is based on the idea that the diversification of the dynamics on a source domain increases the robustness of the policy on a new environment. Domain randomization works by manipulating the source domain, for example, by varying the physics of the simulator, so that the policy that has been trained on multiple randomly modified source domains is robust enough to perform well on a target domain. This strategy is more effective for training agents that need to be employed in the real world. In such circumstances, the policy is more robust and the simulation doesn't have to be exactly the same as the physical world to provide the required levels of performance.

- **Domain Adaptation**: This is another process that's used, especially to map a policy from a simulation-based source domain to a target physical world. Domain adaptation consists of changing the data distribution of the source domain to match that of the target. It is mainly used in image-based tasks, and the models usually make use of **generative adversarial networks (GANs)** to turn synthetic images into realistic ones.

Multi-task learning

In multi-task learning, the higher the number of environments the agent has been trained on, the more diversity and the better performance the agent will achieve on the target environment. The multiple source tasks can either be learned by one or multiple agents. If only one agent has been trained, then its deployment on the target task is easy. Otherwise, if multiple agents learned separate tasks, then the resulting policies can either be used as an ensemble, and the predictions on the target task averaged, or an intermediate step called distillation is employed to merge the policies into one. Specifically, the process of distillation compresses the knowledge of an ensemble of models into a single one that is easier to deploy and that infers faster.

RL in the real world

So far, in this chapter, we went through the best practices when developing deep RL algorithms and the challenges behind RL. We also saw how unsupervised RL and meta-learning can alleviate the problem of low efficiency and bad generalization. Now, we want to show you the problems that need to be addressed when employing an RL agent in the real world, and how the gap within a simulated environment can be bridged.

Designing an agent that is capable of performing actions in the real world is demanding. But most reinforcement learning applications need to be deployed in the world. Thus, we have to understand the main challenges that we face when dealing with the complexity of the physical world and consider some useful techniques.

Facing real-world challenges

Besides the big problems of sample-efficiency and generalization, when dealing with the real world, we need to face problems such as safety and domain constraints. In fact, the agent is often not free to interact with the world due to safety and cost constraints. A solution may come from the use of constraint algorithms such as TRPO and PPO, which are embedded into the system mechanisms to limit the change of actions while training. This could prevent the agent from a drastic change in its behavior. Unfortunately, in highly sensitive domains, this is not enough. For example, nowadays, you cannot start training a self-driving car on the road straight away. The policy may take hundreds or thousands of cycles to understand that falling off a cliff leads to a bad conclusion and learn to avoid it. The alternative option of training the policy in a simulation first is a viable option. Nevertheless, when employed in cities, more safety-related decisions have to be made.

As we just hinted at, a simulation-first solution is a feasible approach and depending on the complexity of the real task, it may lead to good performance. However, the simulator has to mimic the real-world environment as closely as possible. For example, the simulator on the left-hand side of the following image cannot be used if the world resembles the right-hand side of the same image. This gap between the real and the simulated world is known as the reality gap:

Figure 13.6. Comparison between an artificial world and the physical world

On the other hand, using a highly accurate and realistic environment may not be feasible either. The bottleneck is now the computation power that's required by the simulator. This limitation can be partially overcome by starting with a faster and less accurate simulator, and then progressively increasing the fidelity so as to decrease the reality gap. Eventually, this is to the detriment of the speed, but at this point, the agent should have already learned most of the tasks and may need only a few iterations to fine-tune itself. However, it is very difficult to develop highly accurate simulators that mimic the physical world. Thus, in practice, the reality gap will remain and techniques that improve generalization will have the responsibility to handle the situation.

Bridging the gap between simulation and the real world

To seamlessly transition from the simulation to the real world and thus overtake the reality gap, some generalization techniques that we presented earlier, such as domain adaptation and domain randomization, could be used. For example, in the paper *Learning Dexterous In-Hand Manipulation*, the authors trained a human-like robot to manipulate physical objects with incredible dexterity using domain randomization. The policy learned from many different parallel simulations that were designed to provide a variety of experiences with random physical and visual attributes. This mechanism that prefers generalization over realism overall has been key, considering that the system, when deployed, showed a rich set of in-hand dexterous manipulation strategies, many of which are used by humans as well.

Creating your own environment

For educational purposes, in this book, we have predominantly used fast and small-scale tasks that could best fit our needs. However, there are plenty of simulators in existence for locomotion tasks (such as Gazebo, Roboschool, and Mujoco), mechanical engineering, transportation, self-driving cars, security, and many more. These existing environments are diverse, but there isn't one for every possible application. Thus, in some situations, you may find yourself in charge of creating your own.

The reward function by itself is difficult to design, but it is a key part of RL. With the wrong reward function, the environment can be impossible to solve and the agent may learn the wrong behaviors. In `Chapter 1`, *The Landscape of Reinforcement Learning*, we gave the example of the boat-racing game, in which the boat maximized the reward by driving in a circle to capture repopulating targets instead of running toward the end of the trajectory as fast as possible. These are the kinds of behaviors to avoid while designing the reward function.

The general advice for designing the reward function (that can be applied in any environment) is to use positive rewards to incentive exploration and discourage the terminal states or negative rewards if the goal is to reach a terminal state as quickly as possible. The shape of the reward function is important to consider. Throughout this book, we have warned against sparse rewards. An optimal reward function should offer a smooth and dense function.

If, for some reason, the reward function is very difficult to put into formulas, there are two additional ways in which a supervision signal can be provided:

- Give a demonstration of the task using imitation learning or inverse reinforcement learning.
- Use human preferences to provide feedback about the agent's behavior.

The latter point is still a novel approach and if you are interested in it, you may find the paper *Deep Reinforcement Learning from Policy-Dependent Human Feedback* an interesting read (https://arxiv.org/abs/1902.04257).

Future of RL and its impact on society

The first foundations of AI were built more than 50 years ago, but only in the last few years has the innovation brought by AI spread through the world as a mainstream technology. This new wave of innovation is mainly due to the evolution of deep neural networks in supervised learning systems. However, the most recent breakthrough in artificial intelligence involves reinforcement learning, and most notably, deep reinforcement learning. Results like the ones that were obtained in the game of Go and Dota highlight the impressive quality of RL algorithms that are able to show long-term planning, ability in teamwork, and discover new game strategies that are difficult to comprehend even for humans.

The remarkable results that were obtained in the simulated environments started a new wave of applications of reinforcement learning in the physical world. We are only at the beginning, but many areas are and will be impacted, bringing with it profound transformations. RL agents that are embedded in our everyday life can enhance the quality of life by automating tedious work, addressing world-level challenges, and discovering new drugs – just to name a few possibilities. However, these systems, which will populate both our world and our lives, need to be safe and reliable. We aren't at this point yet, but we are on the right track.

The ethical use of AI has become a broad concern, such as in the employment of autonomous weapons. With this rapid technological progress, it is hard for the policymakers and the population to be at the forefront of creating open discussions about these issues. Many influential and reputable people also suggest that AI is a potential threat to humanity. But the future is impossible to predict, and the technology has a long way to go before developing agents that can actually show abilities that are comparable to those of humans. We have creativity, emotions, and adaptability that, for now, cannot be emulated by RL.

With careful attention, the near-term benefits brought by RL can dramatically outweigh the negative side. But to embed sophisticated RL agents in the physical environment, we need to work on the RL challenges we outlined previously. These are solvable and, once addressed, reinforcement learning has the potential to decrease social inequalities, improve the quality of our life, and the quality of our planet.

Summary

Throughout this book, we learned and implemented many reinforcement learning algorithms, but all this variety can be quite confusing when it comes to choosing one. For this reason, in this final chapter, we provided a rule of thumb that can be used to pick the class of RL algorithms that best fits your problem. It mainly considers the computational time and the sample efficiency of the algorithm. Furthermore, we provided some tips and tricks so that you can train and debug deep reinforcement learning algorithms better so as to make the process easier.

We also discussed the hidden challenges of reinforcement learning: stability and reproducibility, efficiency, and generalization. These are the main issues that have to be overcome in order to employ RL agents in the physical world. In fact, we detailed unsupervised reinforcement learning and transfer learning, two strategies that can be used to greatly improve generalization and sample efficiency.

Additionally, we detailed the most critical open problems and the cultural and technological impacts that reinforcement learning may have on our lives.

We hope that this book has provided you with a comprehensive understanding of reinforcement learning and piqued your interest in this fascinating field.

Questions

1. How would you rank DQN, A2C, and ES based on their sample efficiency?
2. What would their rank be if they were rated on the training time and 100 CPUs were available?
3. Would you start debugging an RL algorithm on CartPole or MontezumaRevenge?
4. Why is it better to use multiple seeds when comparing multiple deep RL algorithms?

5. Does the intrinsic reward help with the exploration of an environment?
6. What's transfer learning?

Further reading

- For an approach that uses a pure curiosity-driven approach in the Atari games, read the paper *Large-scale study of curiosity-driven learning* (https://arxiv.org/pdf/1808.04355.pdf).
- For practical use of domain randomization for learning dexterous in-hand manipulation, read the paper *Learning Dexterous In-Hand Manipulation* (https://arxiv.org/pdf/1808.00177.pdf).
- For some work that shows how human feedback can be applied as an alternative to the reward function, read the paper *Deep Reinforcement Learning from Policy-Dependent Human Feedback* (https://arxiv.org/pdf/1902.04257.pdf).

Assessments

Chapter 3

- What's a stochastic policy?
    - It's a policy defined in terms of a probability distribution
- How can a return be defined in terms of the return at the next time step?
    - $G_t = r_t + \lambda G_{t+1}$
- Why is the Bellman equation so important?
    - Because it provides a general formula to compute the value of a state using the current reward and the value of the subsequent state.
- Which are the limiting factors of DP algorithms?
    - Due to a complexity explosion with the number of states, they have to be limited. The other constraint is that the dynamics of the system have to be fully known.
- What's policy evaluation?
    - Is an iterative method to compute the value function for a given policy using the Bellman equations.
- How does policy iteration and value iteration differs?
    - Policy iteration alternate between policy evaluation and policy improvement, value iteration instead, combine the two in a single update using the max function.

Chapter 4

- What's the main property of the MC method used in RL?
    - The estimation of the value function as the average return from a state.
- Why are MC methods offline?
    - Because they update the state value only when the complete trajectory is available. Thus they have to wait until the end of the episode.
- What are the two main ideas of TD learning?
    - They combine the ideas of sampling and bootstrapping

- What are the differences between MC and TD?
    - MC learn from the full trajectory, whereas TD learn at every step acquiring knowledge also from an incomplete trajectory.
- Why is exploration important in TD learning?
    - Because the TD update is done only on the action-state visited, so if some of them has not been discovered, in the absence of an exploration strategy they will never be visited. Thus, some good policy may not be discovered.
- Why Q-learning is off-policy?
    - Because the Q-learning update is done independently of the behavior policy. It uses the greedy policy of the max operation.

Chapter 5

- What arise of the deadly triad problem?
    - When off-policy learning are combined with function approximation and boostrapping.
- How DQN overcome the instabilities?
    - Using a replay buffer and a separate online and target network.
- What's the moving target problem?
    - It's a problem that arises when the target values aren't fixed and they change as the network is optimized.
- How the moving target problem is mitigated in DQN?
    - Introducing a target network that is updated less frequently than the online network.
- What's the optimization procedure used in DQN?
    - A mean square error loss function is optimized through stochastic gradient descent, an iterative method that performs gradient descent on a batch.
- What's the definition of a state-action advantage value function?
    - $A(s,a) = Q(s,a) - V(s)$

Chapter 6

- How PG algorithms maximize the objective function?
    - They do it by taking a step in the opposite direction of the objective function's derivative. The step is proportional to the return.

- What's the main intuition behind PG algorithms?
    - Encourage good actions and dissuade the agent from the bad ones.
- Why introducing a baseline in REINFORCE it remains unbiased?
    - Because in expectation $E[\nabla_\theta log\pi_\theta(\tau)\, b] = 0$
- To which broader class of algorithms belong to REINFORCE?
    - It is a Monte Carlo method as it relies on full trajectories like MC methods do.
- How the critic in AC methods differs from a value function used as a baseline in REINFORCE?
    - Besides the learned function is the same, the critic uses the approximated value function for bootstrap the action-state value instead in REINFORCE (but also in AC) it is used as a baseline to reduce the variance.
- If you had to develop an algorithm for an agent that has to learn to move, would you prefer REINFORCE or AC?
    - You should first try an actor-critic algorithm as the agent has to learn a continuous task.
- Could you use an n-step Actor-Critic algorithm as a REINFORCE algorithm?
    - Yes, you could as far as n is greater than the maximum possible number of steps in the environment.

Chapter 7

- How can a policy neural network control a continuous agent?
    - One way to do it is to predict the mean and the standard deviation that describe a Gaussian distribution. The standard deviation could either be conditioned on a state (the input of the neural network) or be a standalone parameter.
- What's the KL divergence?
    - Is a measure of proximity of two probability distributions.
- What's the main idea behind TRPO?
    - To optimize the new objective function in a region near the old probability distribution.
- How is the KL divergence used in TRPO?
    - It is used as a hard constraint to limit the digression between an old and a new policy.

Assessments

- What's the main benefit of PPO?
    - It uses only a first-order optimization that increase the simplicity of the algorithm and has a better sample efficiency and performance.
- How does PPO achieve good sample efficiency?
    - It run minibatch updates several times exploiting better the data.

Chapter 8

- Which is the primary limitation of Q-learning algorithms?
    - Ther action space has to be discrete and small in order to compute the global maximum.
- Why are stochastic gradient algorithms sample inefficient?
    - Because the are on-policy and need new data every time the policy changes.
- How does deterministic policy gradient overcome the maximization problem?
    - DPG model the policy as a deterministic function predicting only a deterministic action and the deterministic policy gradient theorem gives a way to compute the gradient used to update the policy.
- How does DPG guarantee enough exploration?
    - By adding noise into the deterministic policy or by learning a different behavior policy.
- What DDPG stands for? And what is its main contribution?
    - DDPG stands for Deep Deterministic Policy Gradient and is an algorithm that adapts the deterministic policy gradient to work with deep neural networks. They use new strategies to stabilize and speed up learning.
- Which problems does TD3 propose to minimize?
    - Overestimation bias common in Q-learning and high variance estimates.
- What new mechanisms does TD3 employ?
    - To reduce the overestimation bias, they use a Clipped Double Q-learning while they address the variance problem with a delayed policy update and a smoothing regularization technique.

Chapter 9

- Would you use a model-based or a model-free algorithm if you had only 10 games to train your agent to play checkers?
    - I would use a model-based algorithm. The model of checkers is known and plan on is a feasible task.
- What are the disadvantages of model-based algorithms?
    - Overall, they require more computational power and achieve lower asymptotical performance with respect to model-free algorithms.
- If a model of the environment is unknown, how can it be learned?
    - Once a dataset is collected through interactions with the real environment, the dynamics model can be learned in a usual supervised way.
- Why data-aggregation methods are used?
    - Because usually the first interactions with the environment are done with a naive policy that doesn't explore all of it. Further interactions with a more defined policy are required to affine the model of the environment.
- How does ME-TRPO stabilize training?
    - ME-TRPO employs two main features: an ensemble of models and early stopping techniques.
- Why an ensemble of models improve policy learning?
    - Because predictions that are done by an ensemble of models take into account any uncertainty of the single model.

Chapter 10

- Is imitation learning considered a reinforcement learning technique?
    - No, because the underlying frameworks are different. The objective of IL isn't to maximize the reward as in RL.
- Would you use imitation learning to build a unbitable agent in Go?
    - Probably not, because it requires an expert from which to learn. And if the agent has to be the best player in the world means that there's no worthy expert.
- What's the full name of DAgger?
    - Dataset aggregations

Assessments

- What's the main strength of DAgger?
    - It overcomes the problem of distribution mismatch by employing the expert to teach actively the learner to recover from errors.
- Where would you use IRL instead of IL?
    - In problems where the reward function is easier to learn and where there's the necessity to learn a policy better than that of the expert.

Chapter 11

- What are two alternative algorithms to reinforcement learning for solving sequential decision problems?
    - evolution strategies and genetic algorithms
- What are the processes that give birth to new individuals in evolutionary algorithms?
    - The mutation that mutates the gene of a parent and crossover that combines genetic information from two parents.
- What is the source of inspiration of evolutionary algorithms like genetic algorithms?
    - Evolutionary algorithms are principally inspired by biological evolution.
- How does CMA-ES evolve evolution strategies?
    - CMA-ES samples new candidate from a multivariate normal distribution with the covariance matrix that is adapted to the population.
- What's one advantage and one disadvantage of evolution strategies?
    - One advantage is that they are derivative-free methods while a disadvantage is that of being sample inefficient.
- What's the trick used in the "Evolution Strategies as Scalable Alternative to Reinforcement Learning" paper to reduce the variance?
    - They propose to use mirroring noise and generate an additional mutation with a perturbation with the opposite sign.

Chapter 12

- What's the exploration-exploitation dilemma?
  - Is a decision problem of whether it's better to explore in order to make better decisions in the future or exploit the best current option.
- What are two exploration strategies that we already used in previous RL algorithms?
  - ϵ-greedy and a strategy that introduces some additional noise into the policy.
- What's UCB?
  - Upper Confidence Bound is an optimistic exploration algorithm that estimates an upper confidence bound for each value and selects the action that maximizes (12.3)
- Is Montezuma's Revenge or Multi-armed bandit problem more difficult to solve?
  - Montezuma's Revenge is much more difficult than the multi-armed bandit problem just for the fact that the latter is stateless while the former has an astronomical number of possible states. Montezuma's Revenge has also more complexity intrinsic in the game.
- How ESBAS tackle the problem of online RL algorithm selection?
  - By employing a meta-algorithm that learns which algorithm among a fixed portfolio performs better in a given circumstance.

Chapter 13

- How would you rank DQN, A2C, and ES based on their sample efficiency?
  - DQN is the most sample-efficiency followed by A2C and ES.
- What would their rank be if rated on the training time and 100 CPUs are available?
  - ES probably would be the faster to train, then A2C and DQN.
- Would you start debugging an RL algorithm on CartPole or MontezumaRevenge?
  - CartPole. You should start the debug of an algorithm with an easy task.

Assessments

- Why is it better to use multiple seeds when comparing multiple deep RL algorithms?
    - The results from a single trial can be highly volatile due to the stochasticity of the neural network and environment. By averaging multiple random seeds the results would approximate the average case.
- Does the intrinsic reward help the exploration of an environment?
    - Yes, this's because the intrinsic reward is a sort of exploration bonus that would increase the curiosity of the agent to visit novel states.
- What's transfer learning?
    - Is the task of efficiently transfer knowledge between two environments.

Other Books You May Enjoy

If you enjoyed this book, you may be interested in these other books by Packt:

Hands-On Reinforcement Learning with Python
Sudharsan Ravichandiran

ISBN: 978-1-78883-652-4

- Understand the basics of reinforcement learning methods, algorithms, and elements
- Train an agent to walk using OpenAI Gym and Tensorflow
- Understand the Markov Decision Process, Bellman's optimality, and TD learning
- Solve multi-armed-bandit problems using various algorithms
- Master deep learning algorithms, such as RNN, LSTM, and CNN with applications
- Build intelligent agents using the DRQN algorithm to play the Doom game
- Teach agents to play the Lunar Lander game using DDPG
- Train an agent to win a car racing game using dueling DQN

Python Reinforcement Learning Projects
Rajalingappaa Shanmugamani, Sean Saito, Et al

ISBN: 978-1-78899-161-2

- Train and evaluate neural networks built using TensorFlow for RL
- Use RL algorithms in Python and TensorFlow to solve CartPole balancing
- Create deep reinforcement learning algorithms to play Atari games
- Deploy RL algorithms using OpenAI Universe
- Develop an agent to chat with humans
- Implement basic actor-critic algorithms for continuous control
- Apply advanced deep RL algorithms to games such as Minecraft
- Autogenerate an image classifier using RL

Leave a review - let other readers know what you think

Please share your thoughts on this book with others by leaving a review on the site that you bought it from. If you purchased the book from Amazon, please leave us an honest review on this book's Amazon page. This is vital so that other potential readers can see and use your unbiased opinion to make purchasing decisions, we can understand what our customers think about our products, and our authors can see your feedback on the title that they have worked with Packt to create. It will only take a few minutes of your time, but is valuable to other potential customers, our authors, and Packt. Thank you!

Index

A

Action 10
action-value function 19, 58
action-value method (value-function methods) 20
active imitation
  versus passive imitation 258
Actor-Critic (AC) algorithms
  about 62, 159
  advancements 166
  implementation 161, 162, 163
  tips 166
  tricks 166
  used, for helping actor 159
  used, for landing spacecraft 164, 165
actor-critic methods 20
Advantage Actor-Critic (A2C) 166
Agent 10
algorithm selection (AS) 301
applications, RL
  economics and finance 24
  energy optimization 24
  games 22, 23
  healthcare 24
  industrial robotics 23
  Industry 4.0 23
  intelligent transportation systems 24
  machine learning 23
  smart grid 24
approaches, exploration
  about 297
  element of-greedy strategy 297
  UCB algorithm 298
Arcade Learning Environment (ALE) 112, 258
Asynchronous Advantage Actor-Critic (A3C) 166
Atari games 112, 113

B

behavior policy 18
Bellman equation 58
BipedalWalker-v2
  DDPG, applying to 214, 215
BipedalWalker
  TD3, applying to 221, 222
bootstrapping 64, 82

C

candidate solutions 275
chromosomes 275
CoinRun
  reference link 51
Conjugate Gradient (CG) method 181
continuous system
  controlling 171, 172, 173
convolutional neural network (CNN) 16
core, scalable evolution strategies
  ES, parallelizing 281
  pseudocode 282
  techniques 281
Covariance Matrix Adaptation Evolution Strategy (CMA-ES) 278, 279
crossover 275
curse of dimensionality problem 14

D

Dataset Aggregation (DAgger) algorithm
  about 261, 262
  DAgger loop, creating 265, 266
  expert inference model, loading 263
  implementing 262
  learner's computational graph, creating 264, 265
DDPG algorithm
  about 207, 208

replay buffer 207
target network 207
DDQN
  implementation 129
  implementation, results 130, 131
deep deterministic policy gradient (DDPG)
  about 201, 206
  applying, to BipedalWalker-v2 214, 215
  implementing 209, 210, 211, 212, 213
deep neural networks (DNNs) 102, 103
deep q network (DQN) 15
deep Q-learning
  instabilities 105, 106
deep reinforcement learning (deep RL)
  about 15, 16
  best practices 314
  challenges 17
deep RL algorithms
  creating, tools 28
  drawbacks 316, 319
  selecting 314, 316
deep RL, challenges
  about 319
  efficiency 321
  generalization 321
  reproducibility 319, 320
  stability 319, 320
DeepMind Lab 51
DeepMind PySC2 51
DeepMind
  reference link 230
dense reward 21
deterministic policy 55
deterministic policy gradient (DPG) 203, 204, 205, 206
discount factor 56
domain adaptation 329
domain randomization 329
done variable 32
Double DQN 128, 129
DQN algorithm
  about 107, 108
  loss function 108
  pseudocode 109, 110
DQN code, components

computational graph 119, 120, 122, 124
DNNs 117, 118
experienced buffer 118
training loop 119, 120, 122, 124
DQN variations
  about 127
  Double DQN 128, 129
  dueling DQN 131, 132
  N-step DQN 133
DQN, applying to Pong
  about 112
  Atari games 112, 113
  preprocessing 113, 114, 116
  testing results 124, 126
DQN, solution
  about 106
  replay memory 107
  target network 107
DQN
  about 106
  architecture 111
  implementation 116
Duckietown
  reference link 50
dueling DQN
  about 131, 132
  implementation 132
  test rewards, results 133
dynamic programming (DP)
  about 14, 63, 77
  policy evaluation 64, 66
  policy improvement 64, 66
  policy iteration 66
  value iteration 70

E

element of-greedy strategy 297, 298
elements, RL
  model 21
  policy 17
  reward 20
  value function 19
episodic 57
epochal stochastic bandit algorithm selection
  (ESBAS)

about 293, 303, 304
Acrobot, solving 308, 309
implementation 304, 306, 308
practical problems 304
selection 301
selection, unboxing 301, 302
testing, result 309, 311
epsilon-decay 81
ES function 284
evolution strategies (ES), advantages
derivative-free methods 279
generality 279
highly parallelizable 279
robust 279
evolution strategies (ES)
about 271, 278
parallelizing 281
versus reinforcement learning (RL) 279
evolutionary algorithms (EAs)
about 271, 273, 274
core 274, 275, 276, 277
Covariance Matrix Adaptation Evolution Strategy (CMA-ES) 278, 279
evolution strategies (ES), versus reinforcement learning (RL) 279
evolution strategies (ESes) 278
genetic algorithms (GAs) 277, 278
exploration complexity
large non-tabular problems 300
small-to-medium tabular problem 300
stateless problems 300
exploration problem
about 80
dealing with 81
deterministic policy 81
exploration, versus exploitation
about 294
multi-armed bandit problem 295
exploration
approaches 297
complexity 300
versus exploitation 294

F

features 16
feedforward neural network (FNN) 16
FIFO (First In, First Out) 118
Fisher Information Matrix (FIM) divergence 177, 178
fitness shaping
objective ranking 281
Flappy Bird
environment, using 259, 260
installation link 252
installing 252, 253
playing 258
results, analyzing 267, 268
FrozenLake game
policy iteration, applying 67, 68, 69
value iteration, applying 70, 72
fully observable property 55
function approximation 102, 103

G

Generalized Advantage Estimation (GAE) 193
generation 275
generative adversarial networks (GANs) 326
genetic algorithms (GAs) 277, 278
genotypes 275
gradient
computing 143, 144
Gym Atari
reference link 50
Gym Classic control
reference link 50
Gym interface 258
Gym MuJoCo
reference link 50

H

has distribution 55
hybrid algorithms 62

I

images
model, building from 239
imitation approach

about 253, 254
driving assistant example 254
imitation learning (IL)
  about 21, 251
  active, versus passive imitation 258
  expert 256
  structure 256, 258
  versus reinforcement learning (RL) 254, 256
inaccurate model 235
independent and identically distributed (IID) 105
individuals 274
info 32
inverse RL 21
IRL 268

K

known model 231, 232, 233
Kullback-Leibler (KL) divergence 177, 178

L

learning, without model
  about 78
  exploration problem 80
  policy evaluation 80
  user experience 79, 80
linear regression example 41, 43, 44
LunarLander
  scalable ES, applying 289

M

MalmoEnv
  reference link 50
Markov decision process (MDP)
  about 14, 53, 54, 55
  Bellman equation 58
  policy 55
  return 56
  value functions 57
Markov property 55
mean squared error (MSE) 43, 104
mirror noise 281
ML models
  developing, with TensorFlow 35
model-based learning
  about 231

advantages 235
combining, with model-free learning 236, 237, 238
disadvantages 236
model-based methods 21, 230
model-ensemble trust region policy optimization (ME-TRPO)
  about 229, 240, 241
  applying, to inverted pendulum 240
  implementing 241, 242, 243, 244, 245
model-free (MF) algorithms
  about 60
  hybrid algorithms 62
  policy gradient algorithms 61
  value-based algorithms 61
model
  building, from images 239
  overfitting 235
Monte Carlo methods 80
move 37 15
multi-armed bandit problem 295, 296
mutation 275

N

n-step AC model 160, 161
N-step DQN
  about 133
  implementation 134
  implementation results 134
natural language processing (NLP) 23
Natural Policy Gradient (NPG)
  about 174, 175
  complications 179
  Fisher Information Matrix (FIM) divergence 178
  intuition 176, 177
  issues 174
  Kullback-Leibler (KL) divergence 179
NeroEvolution of Augmenting Topologies (NEAT) 278
neural architecture design (NAD) 24
neural networks
  Q-learning, using with 103, 105

O

observation 31, 32, 55, 102
off-policy algorithm 18
offspring 275
on-policy algorithm 18
on-policy PG 146
OpenAI Gym
  and RL cycles 30
  installing 29
OpenAI
  reference link 230
optimal policy
  about 55
  policy iteration 66
  value iteration 66

P

partially observable system 55
passive target policy 18
phenotypes 275
planning process 231
PLE
  reference link 51
policy 17, 144, 146
policy gradient (PG) theorem 142, 143
policy gradient (PG)
  about 140, 141, 142
  methods 140
policy gradient algorithms
  about 61
  Actor-Critic (AC) algorithms 62
policy gradient optimization
  combining, with Q-learning 202, 203
policy iteration
  about 66
  applying, to FrozenLake game 67
policy-gradient method 19
Pommerman
  reference link 50
Pong
  DQN, applying to 112
PPO algorithm 193
Proximal Policy Optimization (PPO)
  about 192
  application 197
  implementing 193, 194, 196
  overview 192
  versus trust region policy optimization (TRPO) 197
pseudocode 282
PyGame Learning Environment (PLE) 258

Q

Q-function 58
Q-learning 102
  about 93, 102
  algorithm 94, 95
  applying, to Taxi-v2 95, 96, 98
  policy gradient optimization, combining 202, 203
  theory 93
  using, with neural networks 103, 105
  versus SARSA 98, 99

R

recurrent neural network (RNN) 16
REINFORCE, used for landing spacecraft
  about 153
  result, analyzing 154, 155
REINFORCE
  about 147, 148
  implementing 149, 150, 152
  implementing, with baseline 157, 159
  with baseline 155, 157
reinforcement learning (RL), key aspects
  excellent performance 279
  sample efficiency 279
reinforcement learning (RL)
  about 9, 10, 12, 15, 27, 271, 272
  alternative 273
  applications 21
  characteristic 12, 13
  elements 17
  example 12
  exploration 273
  future 330, 331
  history 14, 15
  impact, on society 330, 331
  in real world 327
  overview 272, 273

real-world challenges 327, 328
real-world problems 12
temporal credit assignment 272
versus evolution strategies (ES) 279
versus imitation learning (IL) 254, 256
versus supervised learning 13
reward 20, 32
reward function 329
RL algorithms
  categorizing 59, 60
  diversity 63
  model-based RL 62
  model-free (MF) algorithms 60
RL cycle
  about 30
  developing 30, 31, 32, 34
RL environments, characteristics
  action space 48
  complexity 48
  observation space 48
  reward function 49
RL environments
  need for 48
  open source environments 49, 50
  types 48
Roboschool
  about 170
  installing 29
  reference link 50
  working with 246, 247
RoboSchoolInvertedPendulum
  results 248
rollout 56

S

SARSA
  about 84
  algorithm 85, 86
  applying, to Taxi-v2 86, 88, 92
  versus Q-learning 98, 99
scalable evolution strategies
  about 280
  applying, to LunarLander 289, 290
  core 280, 281
  hyperparameters 289

implementing 282, 283
main function 284, 285
workers 286, 287, 288, 289
self-play 22
sliding stochastic bandit AS (SSBAS) 303
spacecraft
  landing, with AC algorithm 164, 165
  landing, with REINFORCE 153
spaces 34, 35
sparse reward 21
state 31
state-value function 19
stochastic gradient descent (SGD) 272
stochastic policies 55
supervised learning
  versus reinforcement learning (RL) 13

T

tabular methods 14
target policy 18
Taxi-v2
  Q-learning, applying 95, 96, 98
  SARSA, applying to 86, 88, 90, 92
TD target 83
techniques, for 1-task learning
  domain adaptation 326
  domain randomization 326
  fine-tuning 326
temporal difference learning (TD learning)
  about 14, 77, 82
  policy improvement 84
  update 83
tensor
  about 37
  constant 37
  placeholder 38, 39
  variable 39
TensorBoard
  about 44, 45, 46, 47
  reference link 47
TensorFlow
  graph, creating 40, 41
  linear regression example 41
  tensor 37
  used, for developing ML models 35

tools, for creating deep RL algorithms
   deep learning framework 28
   environment 28
   programming language 28
trajectory 56
transfer learning 324, 325
transfer learning, types
   1-task learning 326
   about 325
   multi-task learning 327
TRPO algorithm
   about 180, 181, 182
   implementing 184, 185, 187, 188, 189
trust region policy optimization (TRPO)
   about 180, 240
   application 189, 190, 191, 192
   versus Proximal Policy Optimization (PPO) 197
twin delayed deep deterministic policy gradient (TD3)
   about 201, 216
   applying, to BipedalWalker 221, 222
   delayed policy updates 219
   implementing 217, 218
   overestimation bias, addressing 216
   target regularization 219
   variance reduction, addressing 219

U

Unity ML-Agents
   reference link 51
unknown model 233, 234
unsupervised learning 13
unsupervised RL
   about 13, 322
   intrinsic reward 323, 324
upper confidence bound (UCB) algorithm
   about 293, 298
   UCB1 299, 300

V

V-function 58
value function 17, 19, 20
value iteration
   applying, to FrozenLake game 70, 72
value-based algorithms 61
variable 39
visitation counts strategies 323

Made in United States
North Haven, CT
25 February 2024